JOAN DIDION

Essays & Conversations

Ontario Review Press Critical Series
General Editor, Raymond J. Smith

JOAN DIDION
Essays & Conversations

edited by
Ellen G. Friedman

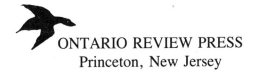

ONTARIO REVIEW PRESS
Princeton, New Jersey

Library of Congress Cataloging in Publication Data

Main entry under title:

Joan Didion : essays & conversations.
    (Ontario Review Press critical series)
    1. Didion, Joan—Criticism and interpretation—
Addresses, essays, lectures.   I. Friedman, Ellen G., 1944–   . II. Title: Joan Didion : essays
and conversations.   III. Series.
PS3554.I33Z72   1984   813'.54   84-5263
ISBN 0-86538-035-X
ISBN 0-86538-036-8 (pbk.)

Distributed by Persea Books, Inc.
225 Lafayette St.
New York, NY 10012

Acknowledgments

Grateful acknowledgment is made to Wallace & Sheil Agency, Inc. and to Joan Didion for permission to quote from the following works of the author: *Run River,* © 1963; *Slouching Towards Bethlehem,* © 1968; *Play It As It Lays,* © 1970; *A Book of Common Prayer,* © 1977; *The White Album,* © 1979; and *Salvador,* © 1983. All copyrights by Joan Didion.

"Why I Write" by Joan Didion originally appeared in *The New York Times Book Review.* Copyright © 1976 by Joan Didion. Reprinted by permission of Wallace & Sheil Agency, Inc.

"A Visit with Joan Didion" by Sara Davidson originally appeared in *The New York Times Book Review* (April 3, 1977), pp. 1, 35–38. Copyright © 1977 The New York Times Company. Reprinted by permission.

"Cautionary Tales," National Public Radio Interview with Joan Didion, April 1977 by Susan Stamberg, was aired on April 4, 1977 on National Public Radio's "All Things Considered" and printed in *Every Night at Five* by Susan Stamberg (New York: Pantheon Press, 1982), pp. 149–56. Copyright © 1982 by National Public Radio. Reprinted by permission.

"Joan Didion: Staking out California" by Michiko Kakutani originally appeared in *The New York Times Magazine* (June 10, 1979), pp. 34–50. Copyright © 1979 The New York Times Company. Reprinted by permission.

"Points West, Then and Now: The Fiction of Joan Didion" by Jennifer Brady first appeared in *Contemporary Literature,* 20, 4 (1979), pp. 452–70. Copyright © 1979 by *Contemporary Literature.* Reprinted with permission of The University of Wisconsin Press.

"The Limits of History in the Novels of Joan Didion" by Thomas Mallon first appeared in *Critique: Studies in Modern Fiction,* 21, 3 (1980), pp. 43–52. Copyright © 1980 by James Dean Young. Reprinted by permission.

"Nothingness and Beyond: Joan Didion's *Play It As It Lays*" by David J. Geherin first appeared in *Critique: Studies in Modern Fiction,* 16, 1 (1974), pp. 64–78. Copyright © 1974 by James Dean Young. Reprinted with permission.

"Joan Didion's *Play It As It Lays* and the Vacuity of the 'Here and Now'" by C. Barry Chabot originally appeared in *Critique: Studies in Modern Fiction,* 21, 3 (1980), pp. 53–60. Copyright © by James Dean Young. Reprinted by permission.

"*Play It As It Lays:* Didion and the New American Heroine" by Cynthia Griffin Wolff will appear in *Contemporary Literature.* Printed with permission of the University of Wisconsin Press.

"A Taut Novel of Disorder" by Joyce Carol Oates originally appeared in *The New York Times Book Review* (April 3, 1977), pp. 1, 34–35. Copyright © 1977 The New York Times Company. Reprinted by permission.

"Joan Didion & Her Characters" by John Romano first appeared in *Commentary,* 64 (July, 1977), pp. 61–63. Copyright © 1977 by the American Jewish Committee. Reprinted by permission.

"Passion and Delusion in *A Book of Common Prayer*" by Victor Strandberg first appeared in *Modern Fiction Studies,* 27, 2 (1981), pp. 225–242. Copyright © 1981 by *Modern Fiction Studies.* Reprinted with permission of the author.

CONTENTS

IN THE SENSE that she records the quality of life in places where civilization and tradition are either memory, twisted to self-serving ends, or simply exhausted, Joan Didion writes about frontiers—whether they be cultural, psychological, political, or geographical. Her first book of essays, *Slouching Towards Bethlehem*, concerns a cultural frontier, California in the sixties, and in the eighties she has moved to another kind of frontier, Central America, with *Salvador*. Her meditations on California continued in the decade after *Slouching Towards Bethlehem* was published and were collected in *The White Album*. In addition, she has covered other cultural frontiers—for instance, *Run River*, which depicts the post-war Sacramento Valley as it shifts from agriculture to aerospace, and *Play It As It Lays*, which depicts Hollywood and Las Vegas. *A Book of Common Prayer* provides the transition from one frontier to another: the narrator, Grace, and the woman, Charlotte, whose story she tells, both come from the West (Colorado and California) to Boca Grande, a fictional Central American country.

Exactly what some of the sources and antecedents of Didion's frontier portraits and dramas are and whether and by what means she offers comfort and redemption to those who populate her frontiers are questions debated here. In choosing the pieces to include in this collection of interviews, reviews, and essays—the first on Joan Didion—I sought to have her major works and the major lines of criticism about them represented. Among critics who write about *Play It As It Lays*, for instance, there is a preoccupation with existentialism as it is reflected in the novel. I reprinted two essays dealing with this issue—by David J. Geherin and C. Barry Chabot. Geherin interprets the novel's central issues in the context of existential nothingness and the void as Sartre and Camus, especially in *The Myth of Sisyphus*, use those terms. Chabot, though agreeing that the novel mirrors an existential view of life, argues that Kierkegaard's ideas of the aesthetic life define the major issues in the novel. While Geherin sees the heroine, Maria, as having achieved illumination, Chabot's view of Maria is more negative—she surrenders meaning and morality for a life of comfort.

The essays by Jennifer Brady, Thomas Mallon, and Leonard Wilcox focus on Didion's use of history, reflecting an obsessive concern in her work. Brady applies Frederick Jackson Turner's thesis about the American frontier to Didion's three novels, concluding that "her novels attempt to recover through an act of imaginative tenacity the mythic truth of worlds now lost to us." Mallon describes how the past puts pressure on the present conditions of the novels' heroines; he is convincing in his assertion that the novels connect personal history with the fate of the American West. Wilcox's interest is in demonstrating how Didion's narrative strategy supports the theme of historical continuity in her novels.

In addition, John Hollowell presents a penetrating analysis of narrative technique in *A Book of Common Prayer*, asserting that although the narrative is filled with the "language of meaning," no meaning for the events is ever discerned. Didion's stance, he argues, is "anti-interpretive" despite the narrator's compulsive efforts to interpret what she concedes are uninterpretable events. Essays that investigate some of Didion's literary and mythic sources include Cynthia Griffin Wolff's on *Play It As It Lays* and Katherine U. Henderson's on *Run River*. In a pioneering essay on *Salvador*, Frederick Kiley compares Didion's narrative art to Picasso's methods in *Guernica* and explores the thematic echoes of Conrad's *Heart of Darkness*.

Other essays—those by Irving Malin and Victor Strandberg—and the reviews by Joyce Carol Oates and John Romano are here by virtue of the acuteness of their perceptions of an individual work. Some of what I learned in gathering this collection is reflected in my own essay that examines Didion's sensibility. In the opening piece of the collection, Didion herself explains why she writes. This explanation includes her confession of feelings of inadequacy in the abstract world of ideas as opposed to the concrete world of images. Standing at the head of this collection, this confession seems a coy and ironic invitation to the pieces—rich with ideas about her work—which follow it. We also hear Didion's voice and feel her presence in the three "conversations" reprinted here, which, I hope, lend an authority to the rest of the volume.

This collection, which contains seven new essays, suggests the rich variety of paths by which Joan Didion's work may be approached. I offer it as an initial effort in the study of a major contemporary writer in the hope that its insights will spur further explorations. There have been a number of attempts to dismiss Didion's work: the frontier as she depicts it is a perilous and unsettling place; anger is a common enough response to such a stimulus. The essays and reviews in this volume argue convincingly that it is one of the places we inhabit and that Didion helps us to know.

ELLEN G. FRIEDMAN

Note: *Slouching Towards Bethlehem* has frequently been abbreviated to *STB* and *The White Album* to *WA* in the text.

I
JOAN DIDION

Why I Write

OF COURSE I stole the title for this talk, from George Orwell. One reason I stole it was that I like the sound of the words: Why I Write. There you have three short unambiguous words that share a sound; and the sound they share is this:

I

I

I

In many ways writing is the act of saying *I*, of imposing oneself upon other people, of saying *listen to me, see it my way, change your mind.* It's an aggressive, even a hostile act. You can disguise its aggressiveness all you want with veils of subordinate clauses and qualifiers and tentative subjunctives, with ellipses and evasions—with the whole manner of intimating rather than claiming, of alluding rather than stating—but there's no getting around the fact that setting words on paper is the tactic of a secret bully, an invasion, an imposition of the writer's sensibility on the reader's most private space.

I stole the title not only because the words sounded right but because they seemed to sum up, in a no-nonsense way, all I have to tell you. Like many writers I have only this one "subject," this one "area": the act of writing. I can bring you no reports from any other front. I may have other interests: I am "interested," for example, in marine biology, but I don't flatter myself that you would come out to hear me talk about it. I am not a scholar. I am not in the least an intellectual, which is not to say that when I hear the word "intellectual" I reach for my gun, but only to say that I do not think in abstracts. During the years when I was an undergraduate at Berkeley I tried, with a kind of hopeless late-adolescent energy, to buy some temporary visa into the world of ideas, to forge for myself a mind that could deal with the abstract.

In short I tried to think. I failed. My attention veered inexorably back to the specific, to the tangible, to what was generally considered, by everyone I knew then and for that matter have known since, the peripheral. I would try to contemplate the Hegelian dialectic and would find myself concentrating instead on a flowering pear tree outside my window and the particular way the petals fell on my floor. I would try to read linguistic theory and would find myself wondering instead if the lights were on in the bevatron up the hill. When I say that I was wondering if the lights were on in the bevatron you might immediately suspect, if you deal in ideas at all, that I was registering the bevatron as a political symbol, thinking in shorthand about the military-in-

---

This essay is adapted from a Regents' Lecture delivered at the University of California at Berkeley.

dustrial complex and its role in the university community, but you would be wrong. I was only wondering if the lights were on in the bevatron, and how they looked. A physical fact.

I had trouble graduating from Berkeley, not because of this inability to deal with ideas—I was majoring in English, and I could locate the house-and-garden imagery in *The Portrait of a Lady* as well as the next person, "imagery" being by definition the kind of specific that got my attention—but simply because I had neglected to take a course in Milton. For reasons which now sound baroque I needed a degree by the end of that summer, and the English department finally agreed, if I would come down from Sacramento every Friday and talk about the cosmology of *Paradise Lost*, to certify me proficient in Milton. I did this. Some Fridays I took the Greyhound bus, other Fridays I caught the Southern Pacific's City of San Francisco on the last leg of its transcontinental trip. I can no longer tell you whether Milton put the sun or the earth at the center of his universe in *Paradise Lost*, the central question of at least one century and a topic about which I wrote ten thousand words that summer, but I can still recall the exact rancidity of the butter in the City of San Francisco's dining car, and the way the tinted windows on the Greyhound bus cast the oil refineries around Carquinez Straits into a grayed and obscurely sinister light. In short my attention was always on the periphery, on what I could see and taste and touch, on the butter, and the Greyhound bus. During those years I was traveling on what I knew to be a very shaky passport, forged papers: I knew that I was no legitimate resident in any world of ideas. I knew I couldn't think. All I knew then was what I couldn't do. All I knew then was what I wasn't, and it took me some years to discover what I was.

Which was a writer.

By which I mean not a "good" writer or a "bad" writer but simply a writer, a person whose most absorbed and passionate hours are spent arranging words on pieces of paper. Had my credentials been in order I would never have become a writer. Had I been blessed with even limited access to my own mind there would have been no reason to write. I write entirely to find out what I'm thinking, what I'm looking at, what I see and what it means. What I want and what I fear. Why did the oil refineries around Carquinez Straits seem sinister to me in the summer of 1956? Why have the night lights in the bevatron burned in my mind for twenty years? *What is going on in these pictures in my mind?*

When I talk about pictures in my mind I am talking, quite specifically, about images that shimmer around the edges. There used to be an illustration in every elementary psychology book showing a cat drawn by a patient in varying stages of schizophrenia. This cat had a shimmer around it. You could see the molecular structure breaking down at the very edges of the cat: the cat became the background and the background the cat, everything interacting, exchanging ions. People on hallucinogens describe the same perception of objects. I'm not a schizophrenic, nor do I take hallucinogens, but certain images do shimmer for me. Look hard enough, and you can't miss the shimmer. It's there. You can't think too much about these pictures that shimmer. You just lie low and let them develop. You stay quiet. You don't talk to many people and you keep your nervous system from shorting out and you try to locate the cat in the shimmer, the grammar in the picture.

Just as I meant "shimmer" literally I mean "grammar" literally. Grammar is a piano I play by ear, since I seem to have been out of school the year the rules were mentioned. All I know about grammar is its infinite power. To shift the structure of a sentence alters the meaning of that sentence, as definitely and inflexibly as the position of a camera alters the meaning of the object photographed. Many people know about camera angles now, but not so many know about sentences. The arrangement of the words matters, and the arrangement you want can be found in the picture in your mind. The picture dictates the arrangement. The picture dictates whether this will be a sentence with or without clauses, a sentence that ends hard or a dying-fall sentence, long or short, active or passive. The picture tells you how to arrange the words and the arrangement of the words tells you, or tells me, what's going on in the picture. *Nota bene*:

It tells you.

You don't tell it.

Let me show you what I mean by pictures in the mind. I began *Play It As It Lays* just as I have begun each of my novels, with no notion of "character" or "plot" or even "incident." I had only two pictures in my mind, more about which later, and a technical intention, which was to write a novel so elliptical and fast that it would be over before you noticed it, a novel so fast that it would scarcely exist on the page at all. About the pictures: the first was of white space. Empty space. This was clearly the picture that dictated the narrative intention of the book—a book in which anything that happened would happen off the page, a "white" book to which the reader would have to bring his or her own bad dreams—and yet this picture told me no "story," suggested no situation. The second picture did. This second picture was of something actually witnessed. A young woman with long hair and a short white halter dress walks through the casino at the Riviera in Las Vegas at one in the morning. She crosses the casino alone and picks up a house telephone. I watch her because I have heard her paged, and recognize her name: she is a minor actress I see around Los Angeles from time to time, in places like Jax and once in a gynecologist's office in the Beverly Hills Clinic, but have never met. I know nothing about her. Who is paging her? Why is she here to be paged? How exactly did she come to this? It was precisely this moment in Las Vegas that made *Play It As It Lays* begin to tell itself to me, but the moment appears in the novel only obliquely, in a chapter which begins: "Maria made a list of things she would never do. She would never: walk through the Sands or Caesar's alone after midnight. She would never: ball at a party, do S-M unless she wanted to, borrow furs from Abe Lipsey, deal. She would never: carry a Yorkshire in Beverly Hills."

That is the beginning of the chapter and that is also the end of the chapter, which may suggest what I meant by "white space."

I recall having a number of pictures in my mind when I began the novel I just finished, *A Book of Common Prayer*. As a matter of fact one of these pictures was of that bevatron I mentioned, although I would be hard put to tell you a story in which nuclear energy figures. Another was a newspaper photograph of a hijacked 707 burning on the desert in the Middle East. Another was the night view from a room in which I once spent a week with paratyphoid, a hotel room on the Colombian coast. My husband and I seemed to be on the Colombian coast representing the United States of America at a film festival (I recall invoking the name "Jack Valenti" a lot, as if its reiteration could make me well), and it was a bad place to have fever, not only because my indisposition offended our hosts but because every night in this hotel the generator failed. The lights went out. The elevator stopped. My husband would go to the event of the evening and make excuses for me and I would stay alone in this hotel room, in the dark. I remember standing at the window trying to call Bogotá (the telephone seemed to work on the same principle as the generator) and watching the night wind come up and wondering what I was doing eleven degrees off the equator with a fever of 103. The view from that window definitely figures in *A Book of Common Prayer*, as does the burning 707, and yet none of these pictures told me the story I needed.

The picture that did, the picture that shimmered and made these other images coalesce, was the Panama airport at 6 A.M. I was in this airport only once, on a plane to Bogotá that stopped for an hour to refuel, but the way it looked that morning remained superimposed on everything I saw until the day I finished *A Book of Common Prayer*. I lived in that airport for several years. I can still feel the hot air when I step off the plane, can see the heat already rising off the tarmac at 6 A.M. I can feel my skirt damp and wrinkled on my legs. I can feel the asphalt stick to my sandals. I remember the big tail of a Pan American plane floating motionless down at the end of the tarmac. I remember the sound of a slot machine in the waiting room. I could tell you that I remember a particular woman in the airport, an American woman, a *norteamericana*, a thin *norteamericana* about forty who wore a big square emerald in lieu of a wedding ring, but there was no such woman there.

I put this woman in the airport later. I made this woman up, just as I later made up a country to put the airport in, and a family to run the country. This woman in the airport is neither catching a plane nor meeting one. She is ordering tea in the airport coffee shop. In fact she is not simply "ordering" tea but insisting that the water be boiled, in front of her, for twenty minutes. Why is this woman in this airport? Why is she going nowhere, where has she been? Where did she get that big emerald? What derangement, or disassociation, makes her believe that her will to see the water boiled can possibly prevail?

> She had been going to one airport or another for four months, one could see it, looking at the visas on her passport. All those airports where Charlotte Douglas's passport had been stamped would have looked alike. Sometimes the sign on the tower would say "Bienvenidos" and sometimes the sign on the tower would say "Bienvenue," some places were wet and hot and others dry and hot, but at each of these airports the pastel concrete walls would rust and stain and the swamp off the runway would be littered with the fuselages of cannibalized Fairchild F-227's and the water would need boiling.
> I knew why Charlotte went to the airport even if Victor did not.
> I knew about airports.

These lines appear about halfway through *A Book of Common Prayer*, but I wrote them during the second week I worked on the book, long before I had any idea where Charlotte Douglas had been or why she went to airports. Until I wrote these lines I had no character called "Victor" in mind: the necessity for mentioning a name, and the name "Victor," occurred to me as I wrote the sentence: *I knew why Charlotte went to the airport* sounded incomplete. *I knew why Charlotte went to the airport even if Victor did not* carried a little more narrative drive. Most important of all, until I wrote these lines I did not know who "I" was, who was telling the story. I had intended until that that the "I" be no more than the voice of the author, a nineteenth-century omniscient narrator. But there it was:

> I knew why Charlotte went to the airport even if Victor did not.
> I knew about airports.

This "I" was the voice of no author in my house. This "I" was someone who not only knew why Charlotte went to the airport but also knew someone called "Victor." Who was Victor? Who was this narrator? Why was this narrator telling me this story? Let me tell you one thing about why writers write: had I known the answer to any of these questions I would never have needed to write a novel.

II

CONVERSATIONS

A Visit with Joan Didion
Sara Davidson

◆───────────────────────────────────

HER OFFICE IS a chamber in which to dream waking dreams. There are props and cue cards. While she worked on *A Book of Common Prayer* a map of Central America hung on the wall. Set out on a table were postcards from Colombia, a newspaper photo of a janitor mopping up blood in a Caribbean hotel, books on tropical foliage and tropical medicine and a Viasa Airlines schedule with "Maracaibo-Paris" circled in blue. "Maracaibo-Paris—I thought those were probably the perimeters of the book," Joan Didion said.

I have been making the drive for six years and it never seems shorter: forty miles up the Pacific Coast Highway to Trancas, where Joan lives with her husband, John Gregory Dunne, and their daughter Quintana. Once past Malibu the landscape changes. Wild mustard and cactus grow on the hills and the ocean front is no longer a protected bay, it is a seacoast.

I associate Joan Didion with the house in Trancas. The living room has a floor of large, square terra-cotta tiles, white brick walls, a redwood ceiling and a wall of glass doors looking out on the Pacific.

The props in the office have changed recently, as Joan prepares to start two new books, *Fairytales*, a non-fiction work about California, and *Angel Visits*, a novel set in Hawaii. "Joan never writes about a place that's not hot," John said. "The day she writes about a Boston winter will be a day it's all over."

On the Saturday in February when I drove out to interview Joan it was with some apprehension. She is not what one would call a virtuoso conversationalist. We taped four hours, of which Joan said later "two hours were pauses." As I set up the machine, John Dunne wandered into the living room wearing a blue bathrobe. "I got the Saturday jits," he said. "I got anxiety crawling over me."

He asked Joan, "Do you have any Coke? Then I'll disappear, so I don't answer all your questions for you."

She brought him a Coca-Cola. He said, "Did you tell Sara the first line of *Angel Visits*?" She shook her head, no. He said the line from memory: "*I have never seen Madame Bovary in the flesh but imagine my mother dancing.*"

"Fantastic," I said. "Is there a comma after 'flesh'?"

Joan: "Yes."

John: "The first line, if you get it right, immediately sets the tone of the book."

Joan said, "It might change." After a pause, "I may take the comma out." (The next morning she indeed decided. "There shouldn't be a comma.")

When John had returned to his study, we settled on the couch. Joan was wearing a light-blue sweatshirt and faded, straight-leg jeans. Her reddish-blond hair was parted in the center and brushed behind her ears. She smoked Pall Malls or twisted a blue rubber band around her fingers, and at times her sentences trailed into a soft, rapid laughter.

Question. Could you talk about the origins of *A Book of Common Prayer*?

Answer. In the spring of '73, John and I went to Cartagena, Colombia, and the entire trip was like a hallucination, partly because I had a fever. It seemed to me extraordinary that North America had gone one way and South America had gone another, and I couldn't understand why. I kept reading that they had more resources than we had, they had more of everything and yet they had gone another way.

Question. How would you define the other way?

Answer. In North America, social tensions that arise tend to be undercut and co-opted quite soon, but in Latin America there does not seem to be any political machinery for delaying the revolution. Everything is thrown into bold relief. There is a collapsing of time. Everything is both older than you could ever know, and it started this morning.

Question. Did you read Garcia Márquez's *One Hundred Years of Solitude*?

Answer. Yes, it's so wonderful. I was overcome by the book when I read it, but, when I went down there, I realized the book was far more social realism than it was fantasy. The element which had seemed to me fantastic was quite reportorial.

Question. Did you have a technical intention for this book?

Answer. Yes, I wrote it down on the map of Central America. "Surface like rainbow slick, shifting, fall, thrown away, iridescent." I wanted to do a deceptive surface that appeared to be one thing and turned color as you looked through it.

Question. What about the repetitions of phrases?

Answer. It seemed constantly necessary to remind the reader to make certain connections. Technically it's almost a chant. You could read it as an attempt to cast a spell or come to terms with certain contemporary demons. I can't think what those demons are at the moment, but there's a range: flash politics, sexual adventurism.

Question. What has been your experience with politics?

Answer. I never had faith that the answers to human problems lay in anything that could be called political. I thought the answers, if there were answers, lay someplace in man's soul. I have an aversion to social action because it usually meant social regulation. It meant interference, rules, doing what other people wanted me to do. The ethic I was raised in was specifically a Western frontier ethic. That means being left alone and leaving others alone. It is regarded by members of my family as the highest form of human endeavor.

Question. Do you vote?

Answer. Once in a while, I'm hardly ever conscious of issues. I mean they seem to me like ripples on an ocean. In the life of the body politic the actual movement is going on underneath, and I am interested in what's going on underneath. The politics I personally want are anarchic. Throw out the laws. Tear it down. Start all over. That is very romantic because it presumes that, left to their own devices, people would do good things for one another. I doubt that that's true. But I would like to believe it.

Question. Do you feel identified with Charlotte and Grace in this book?

Answer. I think you identify with all your characters. They become your family, closer to you than anybody you know. They kind of move into the house and take over the furniture. It's one of the difficult things about writing a book and leading a normal, social, domestic life.

Question. What is the effect of seeing people and getting a lot of stimulation?

Answer. It's quite destructive. Either you sit there and just close off or, if you do become engaged in what is going on with other people, then you have lost the thread. You've turned off the computer, and it is not for that period of time making the connections it ought to be making. I really started thinking of my mind mechanically. I almost heard a steady humming if it was working all right, but if it stopped for a couple of days then it would take a while to get it back.

Question. In "Why I Write," there's a confidence expressed about the process of writing that I know you don't always feel.

Answer. I didn't express confidence so much as blind faith that if you go in and work every day it will get better. Three days will go by and you will be in that office and you will think every day is terrible. But on the fourth day, if you do go in, if you don't go into town or out in the garden, something usually will break through.

Question. How do you feel when you wake up?

Answer. Oh, I don't want to go in there at all. It's low dread, every morning. That dread goes away after you've been in there an hour. I keep saying "in there" as if it's some kind of chamber, a different atmosphere. It is, in a way. There's almost a psychic wall. The air changes. I mean you don't want to go through that door. But once you're in there, you're there, and it's hard to go out.

Question. I'd always assumed that, after you'd been writing for a number of years, that fear would disappear.

Answer. No, it doesn't. It's a fear you're not going to get it right. You're going to ruin it. You're going to fail. The touchy part on a book—when there's not the dread in the morning, when there's the dread all day long—is before it takes. Once it takes, there's just the morning dread and the occasional three days of terrible stuff; but before it takes, there's nothing to guarantee that it's going to take. There's a point in a novel where it shifts or the narrative won't carry. That point has to come before a third of the way through. It goes into overdrive. There are some novels you pick up and start reading and they're wonderful. Maybe you have to go to lunch or something and you get to page 70 and never pick them up again. You're not moved to keep turning pages. That's the narrative curve you've got to allow, around page 70 or 80, to give it enough thrust to send it out. Imagine a rocket taking off. There's a point at which it drops its glitter or glamor and starts floating free.

Question. How do you feel about a book while you're writing it?

Answer. I try to hold my opinion in suspension. I hate the book when I'm working on it. But if I give way to that thought I would never finish the book, and then I would feel depressed and useless and have nothing to do all day.

Question. Have you ever not finished a book?

Answer. I've put things aside at forty pages.

Question. Did you get depressed?

Answer. Yes. There's a certain euphoric mania at first, when you think you've made the right decision and are really taking charge, but it sort of lies there as something you haven't finished. And you always wonder if maybe you had pushed a little harder it might have broken through. I mean it's a failure. So, starting anything, there's a great chance for psychic loss.

Question. How did you feel after finishing *A Book of Common Prayer?*

Answer. I was tired, so tired. I didn't want to read it. I haven't read it. I like it though, in an abstract way. It's like a dream again.

Question. I take it success and failure are important issues for you?

Answer. Yes, I suppose they are. I don't want to do anything that I don't do well. I don't want to ski. (*She laughs.*)

Question. What about tennis?

Answer. I do play tennis, not well, but I've moved into thinking of it as a way of getting color on my face and mild exercise, not as playing tennis. I haven't learned to serve yet. Every once in a while my teacher brings it up, but it takes too much coordination. He brought it up again last week, and I was on the verge of tears. I was furious, because I was really hitting the ball across the net pretty well.

Question. Could you talk about your writing method?

Answer. When I started this book, I wrote the first paragraph and continued for about three pages. Then I got scared and started skipping around and writing odd things.

Question. What did you get scared of?

Answer. Scared I couldn't sustain it. So I started writing odd bits here and there, and then I stopped being so scared when I had a pile of little things that appeared to be in the same tone as the beginning of the book. I just went back and started writing straight through until about page 40. By then the book was taking a slightly different direction. It was clear there was a narrator, for example. I had not intended there to be a narrator. I was going to be the female author's voice. I the author was going to tell you the reader the story. But the "I" became so strong that it became a character, so I went back and rewrote those forty pages with that narrator. As the story developed, things kept changing; and you can push ahead for a little while knowing that those things are wrong back there, but you can't push too far or you lose precision. It doesn't matter to you as much, if you know it's wrong back there, so I started over again. I started over about twelve times. I wanted to start over when I went to Sacramento to finish it, but I didn't have time.

Question. You always go to Sacramento to finish your books. Is that a ritual?

Answer. It's very easy for me to work there. My concentration can be total because nobody calls me. I'm not required to lead a real life. I'm like a child, in my parents' house.

Question. Do you have a room there?

Answer. Yes. It's sort of a carnation-pink, and the vines and trees have grown up over the windows. It's exactly like a cave. It's a very safe place. It's a good room to work in; it's a finishing room. I once tried working in John's office here, and I was beside myself. There were too many books. I mean there was this weight of other people's opinions around me. I worked in the faculty club in Berkeley for a month, and it was very hard to work there because I didn't have the map of Central America. Not that Boca Grande is on the map, but the map took on a real life in my mind. I mean that very narrow isthmus. One of the things that worried me about this book was that there were several kinds of weather. It took place in San Francisco, the American South, and Central America. This sounds silly, but I was afraid that the narrative wouldn't carry if the weather changed. You wouldn't walk away from the book remembering one thing. The thing I wanted you to walk away remembering was the Central American weather. So all the things I had around my office had to do with Central America.

Question. Where did you get the title?

Answer. It just seemed right. *A Book of Common Prayer* was very important to this book. Why, I had no idea. At one point, my editor, Henry Robbins, asked what the title meant. I made up some specious thing and told him. I don't remember what I told him, something to the effect that the whole thing was a prayer. You could say that this was Grace's prayer for Charlotte's soul.

If you have a narrator, which suddenly I was stuck with, the narrator can't just be telling you a story, something that happened, to entertain you. The narrator has got to be telling you the story for a reason. I think the title probably helped me with that.

Question. Are you as skeptical about religion as you are about politics?

Answer. I am quite religious in a certain way. I was brought up Episcopalian, and I stopped going to church because I hated the stories. You know the story about the prodigal son? I have never understood that story. I have never understood why the prodigal son should be treated any better than the other son. I have missed the point of a lot of parables. But I like the words of the Episcopal service, and I say them over and over in my mind. There's one particular phrase which is part of every service: "As it was in the beginning, is now, and ever shall be, world without end. Amen." It's a very comforting phrase to a child. And to an adult. I have a very rigid sense of right and wrong. What I mean is, I use the words all the time. Even the smallest things. A table can be right or wrong.

Question. What about behavior?

Answer. Behavior is right or wrong. I was once having dinner with a psychiatrist who told me that I had monocular vision, and there was no need for everything to be right or wrong. Well, that way lies madness. In order to maintain a semblance of purposeful behavior on this earth you have to believe that things are right or wrong.

Question. What authors have influenced you?

Answer. As far as influence on a style goes, I don't think you're influenced by anybody you read after age 20. That all happens before you start working yourself. You would never know it from reading me, but I was very influenced by Hemingway when I was 13, 14, 15. I learned a lot about how sentences worked. How a short sentence worked in a paragraph, how a long sentence worked. Where the commas worked. How every word had to matter. It made me excited about words. Conrad, for the same reasons. The sentences sounded wonderful. I remember being so excited once, when I discovered that the key lines in *Heart of Darkness* were in parentheses. James, whom I didn't read until I was in college, was important to me in trying to come to terms with the impossibility of getting it right. James's sentences, with all those clauses, had to do with keeping the options open, letting the sentence cover as much as it could. That impressed me a great deal.

Question. What determines what you read now?

Answer. When I'm working I don't read much. If it's a good book it will depress me because mine isn't as good. If it's a bad book it will depress me because mine's just as bad. I don't want anybody else's speech rhythms in my dream. I never read *Ragtime*. I opened the first page and saw it had a very strong rhythm, so I just put it away like a snake.

Question. There's a certain esthetic to the way you live. You once talked about using good silver every day.

Answer. Well every day is all there is.

Question. Do you admire elegance?

Answer. Yes, because it makes you feel better. It's a form. I'm very attached to certain forms, little compulsive rituals. I like to cook; I like to sew. They're peaceful things, and they're an expression of caring.

Question. Could you talk about what you refer to as your shyness?

Answer. I like a lot of people, and I'm glad to see them, but I don't give the impression of being there. Part of it is that I'm terribly inarticulate. A sentence doesn't occur to me as a whole thing unless I'm working.

Question. Isn't it a surprise to people who read you and expect the same fluency in your conversation?

Answer. I don't know what they expect, but they certainly don't get it. (*Laughs.*) I don't know why, and I don't know what I can do about it, and it is easier for me to just write it off and try to do better at what I do well.

Question. Is John your editor?

Answer. Yes, we edit each other. A lot of people wonder how we can edit each other and live together, but it works out very well. We trust each other. Sometimes we don't agree. Obviously you never want to agree when somebody tells you something doesn't work. I don't mean that kind of not agreeing. That's just when you're tired and it's midnight. I mean, sometimes, even on reflection, we don't agree, and there is a tacit understanding that neither of us will push too far. Each of us is aware that it would be easy to impose our sensibility, particularly our own style, on each other. And so there is a tacit agreement not to push beyond saying, "It doesn't work. This is how to fix it." If there is still a substantive disagreement it's never mentioned again.

Question. Are you more interested in writing fiction these days than non-fiction?

Answer. I'm trying to do a non-fiction book now. I have always sort of wanted to write a book about California water. I'm interested in water—the pipes that water goes through, the mechanics of getting the water from place to place. I could look at a flume all day. I love dams, the way they are almost makes me weak, it's so beautiful.

Question. Are you intrigued with the movie community?

Answer. It interests me as an industry; you can watch it working. I like following the moves of the particular game. I like movie people. If I lived in Detroit, I would want to see automotive people. I would want to know what the moves were.

Question. Why do you write for movies?

Answer. One reason, obviously, is for the money. It's specious to say you could make the same amount of money writing a book. You can't write a book every year, but you have to keep on living every year. A lot of writers support themselves by teaching and lecturing. I don't like to do that. It uses up far more energy.

Question. What about the frustrations—deals falling through?

Answer. If your whole conception of yourself depended on whether or not you got a movie going, you might as well go up to San Francisco and get sad and jump. But ours doesn't. Our real life is someplace else. It's sort of a game. Also, it's very gratifying; it's fun, at least a first draft is fun. It's not like writing, it's like doing something else.

Question. Do you think it's proper or feasible to write about sex in an explicit way?

Answer. I don't think anything is improper in fiction, that there's any area that can't be dealt with. I don't in point of fact know very many people who deal with sex well. The only person who deals with sex in an explicit way whom I can read without being made profoundly uncomfortable is Norman Mailer. I know that's not an opinion shared by many. Mailer deals with sex in a very clean, direct way. There's no sentimentality around it. He takes it seriously. I tend to deal with sex obliquely. There is a lot of sexual content in *Common Prayer*, there was quite a lot in *Play It As It Lays* too, but it was underneath. I'm just more comfortable dealing with it as an undertone.

Question. Some people complain that your female characters are passive drifters who lead purposeless lives. Do you see Charlotte Douglas that way?

Answer. No, I don't see that about any women I've written about. I think there is a confusion between passive and successful. Passive simply means passive, and active means active. Active doesn't necessarily imply success. Charlotte is very much in control there in Boca Grande when everyone else is running out.

Question. She doesn't seem to have a center, something in herself for which she's living.

Answer. Obviously the book finds her at a crisis. I don't know too many people who have what you could call clearly functioning centers.

Question. You have your work, that sustains you no matter what. And devotion to your family.

Answer. They could all fall apart tomorrow. This is not a problem peculiar to women, it is a problem for all of us to find something at the center. Charlotte finds her center in Boca Grande. She finds her life by leaving it. I think most of us build elaborate structures to fend off spending much time in our own center.

Question. Do you think of yourself as sad or depressed?

Answer. No, I think of myself as really happy. Cheerful. I'm always amazed at what simple things can make me happy. I'm really happy every night when I walk past the windows and the evening star comes out. A star of course is not a simple thing, but it makes me happy. I look at it for a long time. I'm always happy, really.

Question. How do you feel about getting older?

Answer. I'm a very slow writer and I could count, if I wanted to—which I don't—the number of books I will have time to write. I work more. I work harder. There is a sense of urgency now.

Cautionary Tales
Susan Stamberg

This interview with Joan Didion by Susan Stamberg was aired on April 4, 1977 on National Public Radio's "All Things Considered."

STAMBERG: You've said there are no terrific stories. There are only terrific ways of writing them down. Is that really true? Aren't there some terrific stories that are terribly written but still fascinate the reader?

DIDION: Well, yes, there are. But most stories are banal stories. *Anna Karenina* is a banal story. It could be called a soap opera. *Madame Bovary* is a banal story. It is the way they are written down.

STAMBERG: But what about mystery stories, where the story—the twists of the plot—become much more important than the language the author uses?

DIDION: I don't know. Do you ever read Ross MacDonald? The film *Harper* was based on one of his mystery novels. For years he's been writing the same book. The detective, Lew Archer, goes out on a case and always finds that the solution lies several generations back. But Ross MacDonald has been writing closer and closer and closer until his books are all plot, almost like geometric exercises. They're very exciting. If he wrote that story down any other way I'm not sure it would have such tension. His books are very, very peculiar and frightening.

STAMBERG: I find *your* books very frightening, especially *Play It As It Lays* and *A Book of Common Prayer*. The tension is distasteful.

DIDION: *A Book of Common Prayer* is not as ugly as *Play It As It Lays,* though. It's not a great deal more *cheerful,* but I think it's not as ugly.

Writing *A Book of Common Prayer* aged me a great deal. I don't mean physically. I mean that in adopting Grace's (the narrator's) point of view, I felt much sharper, harsher. I adopted a lot of the mannerisms and attitudes of an impatient, sixty-year-old dying woman. I would cut people off in the middle of conversations. I fell into Grace because I was having to maintain her tone.

It's a very odd thing with novels. You don't know where they come from. They don't exactly come from you, and while you're writing them they seem to influence your mood more than your mood influences them. You begin by trying quite consciously to maintain the mood simply because you don't want to break the tone of the novel.

STAMBERG: John Gardner says that, when he reads, he gets inside the dream of the book and doesn't wake up until the book ends. Is that what happens to you in the course of the actual *writing*? Does the world you are writing about become more real than reality?

DIDION: Yes. More real. And I really resent any intrusion. I didn't answer mail for a long time while I was writing this book, and I didn't talk on the telephone very much, and if I had a certain amount of business that had to be conducted during the morning before I started work I resented it, because it was easiest to move from being asleep directly into this dream without waking up entirely.

STAMBERG: But in your fiction you are in the middle of a dream that is consistently a nightmare. It's on the edge of horror all of the time. You write about people who are not connecting, who have no real relationships and very little happiness or fulfillment in their lives.

DIDION: I've always thought of my novels as stories I tell to myself. They are cautionary tales. Stories I don't want to happen to me. *A Book of Common Prayer* to some extent has to do with my own daughter's growing up. My child is not anywhere near the age of Marin, the girl in the novel, but she's no longer a baby. I think that part of this book came out of the apprehension that we are going to both be adults pretty soon.

STAMBERG: Marin is the daughter of a very wealthy family who turns her back on all of those family connections.

DIDION: And has been misperceived by her mother most of her life.

STAMBERG: "Cautionary tales" you don't want to happen to yourself, you said. Do you really mean it that personally? Or do you mean it as cautionary to all of us, to every one of your readers—

DIDION: (*Interrupting*) No, no, no. They are just cautionary tales for me.

STAMBERG: Why do you jump to say that?

DIDION: What I work out in a book isn't what the book is about. I mean, this book isn't about mothers and daughters. That's part of what it was for me, but I don't think it's what it is for a reader.

STAMBERG: Alfred Kazin called you a "professional moralist." I thought maybe that's what you were getting at here. Cautioning us to pay attention to certain grim possibilities.

DIDION: I am a moralist, but I grew up in such a strong West Coast ethic that

I tend not to impose my own sense of what is wrong and what is right on other people. If I do impose it, I feel very guilty about it, because it is entirely against the ethic in which I was brought up, which was strictly *laissez-faire*. But I myself tend to perceive things as right or wrong, in a very rigid way. And I don't necessarily perceive the same things as wrong that large numbers of people perceive as wrong.

STAMBERG: I think I want you to be telling me, through all of these books, that these women and their life styles are wrong. I want you to tell me that, because I find them so distasteful. I find them to be people I must read about (because you're that good a writer), but people I would never want to know or be near. It's okay for me to enter their nightmare for a while as a reader, but I want to be very sure that you know—sitting there with your pen or your typewriter—that it's wrong.

DIDION: You see, there I can't make a judgment because they are other people. They are not me. I just want to tell you the story. I can't make a judgment on it.

STAMBERG: What about the judgments in your essays about Haight-Ashbury, in *Slouching Towards Bethlehem*? When did you do those?

DIDION: Spring of '67. Just before the "summer of love."

STAMBERG: You went to that section of San Francisco, tooled around, made connections with people who were living there, and gave us bare snapshots— quick glimpses—of some of their lives.

DIDION: That was an extremely frustrating piece to do research on, simply because you couldn't make appointments. To begin with, nobody was up before noon or one o'clock, so you lost the morning. Then, it was a very suspect thing to make appointments.

STAMBERG: You might have been a Fed, or you were too old—over thirty—and they didn't want to talk to you?

DIDION: Right. You just had to hang around.

STAMBERG: Your tone is as cool in these sketches as it is in the pieces of fiction, until you get to the end. It's been sheer description, a catalogue of what you saw, who said what, until the end. There, it seemed to me, the moralist came out, the right-and-wrong lady. At the end you told about the three-year-old child.

DIDION: Yes. I had spent a lot of time hanging around a place called the

Warehouse, a place where a lot of people lived. It wasn't actually a warehouse; it was the basement of an abandoned hotel, and there were a great many people living there on a fluid basis. One of the long-term people living there had a child who was three. It was very dark in this place. There were no windows, or the windows were walled up. It was a very theatrical place with colored spotlights all over. The child was rocking, always, on a rocking horse in a blue spotlight. That was where its rocking horse was. But one day I was over there and the child had somehow started a fire and burned his arm. I was terribly worried, because my child was almost that age. His mother was yelling at him in a kind of desultory way. There had been a floorboard damaged in the fire, and some hash had dropped down through it, and everybody else was trying to fish around and get this hash back. I wanted to take the child out, but I had no business doing that.

STAMBERG: That's where you lost your coolness. The child was badly burned. Nobody had grabbed him in time, or knew that he had to be rushed to the hospital. That's where it all broke down for you. You could be a reporter just that far, and then you really had to make a judgment. And, in making a moral judgment, you gave a context to the whole experience.

The essay "Slouching Towards Bethlehem" became the definitive portrait of Haight-Ashbury in the 1960's and the title piece of that collection of your journalism. In the introduction you write: "My only advantage as a reporter is that I am so physically small, so temperamentally unobtrusive and so neurotically inarticulate that people tend to forget that my presence runs counter to their best interests. And it always does. That is one last thing to remember: *Writers are always selling somebody out.*" This past November I went to a journalism convention in New York, and at three separate sessions that same passage was quoted. Incidentally, none of the people who read it aloud was in any way unobtrusive or inarticulate!

DIDION: It's very odd to have written things that people quote (*laughs*). Especially that introduction. I had written it late one night and hadn't thought much about it. Usually I spend a great deal of time finding a tone that is not my own, and then adopting the tone and getting it right. But with this, I just typed it out, very fast, and rather in my own voice. Normally I have difficulty "expressing myself" in any natural way. I'm not that open. Anyway, I had just written it out as a rough draft. John read it in the morning—

STAMBERG: This is your husband, John Gregory Dunne.

DIDION: Yes. And he said, "This is fine, don't change it."
But to get back to that passage, the statement "writers are always selling

somebody out" means that it is impossible to describe anybody—a friend or somebody you know very well—and *please* them, because your image of them, no matter how flattering, never corresponds with their self-image. [. . .] I can never ask people even simple questions that all reporters know how to ask—like, "How much money do you make?" I don't like sitting in all those Best Western motel rooms trying to make the first telephone call to the district attorney. Many reporters have mentioned to me that they feel the same way. David Halberstam, who seems to me a very aggressive reporter, very confident, said that he hates to make that first phone call, and just sits on the edge of the bed for a while first.

Maybe that's why we chose this work of writing. So we could disappear, in a way. I'm not sure that people who write had much sense of themselves as the center of the room when they were children. I think the way people work often comes out of their weaknesses, out of their failings. In my case, I wasn't a very good reporter. If I got into a town where a story was and I found a *Life* team there, I'd go home. So I had somehow to come out of every story having *interpreted* it, because I wasn't going to get it from anybody else.

STAMBERG: You found a way around something that other people can do straight on?

DIDION: Right. If you can't talk to the mayor, then maybe if you sit around the gas station long enough you can figure out what it's all about. In a lot of situations—particularly when you're dealing with people who are interviewed frequently, like politicians or anybody who is in the middle of a breaking story—they tend pretty much to have an answer to every question you're going to ask them. I mostly use interviews, when I do them in that kind of a situation, as just a way of insinuating myself into the person's day. The actual answers aren't ever very significant.

I'm never happier than if I go on a story and I find myself with the person and they are doing whatever they do—say it's a movie set—and it turns out that they are too busy to give me twenty minutes. Then I am there without having to go through the interview (*laughter*).

STAMBERG: What about all this business of fragility? "Joan Didion is so fragile, so delicate." I notice, talking with you, that you have a thin, almost whispery voice. You speak very softly but with great firmness.

DIDION: I think my physical size is deceptive.

STAMBERG: You are very small.

DIDION: I am not only small, I am too thin, I am pale, I do not look like a California person. It generally makes people think that I must be frail. I'm not actually very frail. I'm very healthy. I eat a lot. I don't cry a lot.

STAMBERG: But do they say that about you because of your physical size, or—getting back to the people and things that you write about—is it because the fragility of your characters and the kind of perceptions you have make people think you must be emotionally fragile? When I read the essays in *Slouching Towards Bethlehem*, I thought of you as someone who was just trembling with antennae that were constantly vibrating, picking up on things that other people simply weren't sensitive to.

That desolate landscape that you create, and those characters who move through it in their parched ways—it seems to me that you'd never get a Nobel Prize for Literature. Not because of any lack of *skill*, mind you, but because that prize is given for optimistic and positive views of life.

DIDION: I think that's probably true. I am more attracted to the underside of the tapestry. I tend to always look for the wrong side, the bleak side. I have since I was a child. I have no idea why. Talk about unexamined lives. . . .

I'm rather a slow study, and I came late to the apprehension that there was a void at the center of experience. A lot of people realize this when they're fifteen or sixteen, but I didn't realize until I was much older that it was possible that the dark night of the soul was . . . it had not occurred to me that it was dryness . . . that it was aridity. I had thought that it was something much riper and more sinful. One of the books that made the strongest impression on me when I was in college was *The Portrait of a Lady*. Henry James's heroine, Isabel Archer, was the prototypic romantic idealist. It trapped her, and she ended up a prisoner of her own ideal. I think a lot of us do. My adult life has been a succession of expectations, misperceptions. I dealt only with an idea I had of the world, not with the world as it was. The reality *does* intervene eventually. I think my early novels were ways of dealing with the revelation that experience is largely meaningless. (*Long pause*)

STAMBERG: You've spoken in the past about the picture that's in your mind before you do a book, and said the act of writing is to find out what's going on in the picture. For *Play It As It Lays*, you imagined a blonde girl in a white halter dress being paged at one o'clock in the morning at a Las Vegas casino. For *A Book of Common Prayer*, the picture was of the Panama City airport, at six A.M., heat steaming up from the tarmac. Do you have a picture in your mind, now, of something else that you're going to have to be working on?

DIDION: Yes. My next novel is going to take place in Hawaii. I can't describe the picture, except that it is very pink and it smells like flowers, and I'm afraid to describe it out loud because if I describe it out loud I won't write it down.

Joan Didion:
Staking out California
Michiko Kakutani

◆—————————————————————————————————

IN HER NEW BOOK, *The White Album*, Joan Didion writes: "Kilimanjaro belongs to Ernest Hemingway. Oxford, Mississippi, belongs to William Faulkner . . . a great deal of Honolulu has always belonged for me to James Jones. . . . A place belongs forever to whoever claims it hardest, remembers it most obsessively, wrenches it from itself, shapes it, renders it, loves it so radically that he remakes it in his image."

California belongs to Joan Didion.

Not the California where everyone wears aviator sunglasses, owns a Jacuzzi and buys his clothes on Rodeo Drive. But California in the sense of the West. The old West where Manifest Destiny was an almost palpable notion that was somehow tied to the land and the climate and one's own family—an unspoken belief that was passed down to children in stories and sayings.

Joan Didion's California is a place defined not so much by what her unwavering eye observes, but by what her memory cannot let go. Although her essays and novels are set amid the effluvia of a new golden state peopled by bored socialites, lost flower children and unsentimental engineers, all is measured against the memory of the old California. And in telling what has happened to California in the past few decades, Didion finds a metaphor for some larger, insidious process at work in American society. The theatrics of James Pike, Episcopal Bishop of California, become a parable of the American penchant for discarding history and starting tabula rasa; the plight of a San Bernardino woman accused of murdering her husband, a lesson in misplaced dreams.

The California Joan Didion lives in, though, is very much the latter-day California. Brentwood Park is one of those sedate residential sections of Los Angeles; her street, one that is lined with Tudor-style homes, white Colonials and pillared mansions.

Didion is sitting in the den. The rooms of her house possess all the soothing order and elegance of a *Vogue* photo spread: sofas covered in floral chintz, lavender love seats the exact color of the potted orchids on the mantelpiece, porcelain elephant end tables, and dozens of framed pictures of family and friends.

Still, this is the kind of day that can give Joan Didion a migraine. In the first place, there is car trouble. Her husband's new pearl-gray Jaguar was dented this morning by a neighbor pulling out of her driveway, and her own 1969 yellow Corvette Sting Ray—a Corvette exactly like the one Maria drove in *Play It As It Lays*—needs a new transmission. Then there are the rats. "The exterminator took one look at the backyard and said we were sure to have rats in the avocado tree," she says. "That's when I started thinking about bubonic plague." Today, though, it isn't so much the rats or the cars that are bothering Didion. It's the dining-room curtains: instead of *gathering* the new curtains, the decorator has *pleated* them. The perfect geometric regularity of those folds triggers migraines, she thinks. She is making a new set of curtains herself.

Wearing a faded blue sweatshirt over brown corduroy levis, Didion at 44 strikes anyone who sees her for the first time as the embodiment of the women in her own novels: like Lily McClellan in *Run River*, she is "strikingly frail" (Didion is 5 feet 2, and weighs 95 pounds); like Maria in *Play It As It Lays*, she used to chain-smoke and wear chiffon scarves over her red hair; and like Charlotte in *A Book of Common Prayer*, she possesses "an extreme and volatile thinness . . . she was a woman . . . with a body that masqueraded as that of a young girl."

There is a certain sadness in the face that indicates a susceptibility to what she calls "early morning dread"; even indoors, she wears oversized sunglasses to protect her light-sensitive eyes. An almost Southern softness lingers in her voice—she identifies it as an Okie accent picked up in Sacramento high schools—and bright laughter punctuates her unfinished sentences. It is a voice so soft, so tentative at times, that one frequently has to strain to hear her.

The "Didion woman" has by now become a recognizable literary figure. Women who have misunderstood the promises of the past, they are habitués of a clearly personal wasteland, wandering along highways or through countries in an effort to blot out the pain of consciousness. They lose their men to suicide, divorce and cancer; their children to abortion, bad genes and history. They are outsiders, but they are also survivors, fatalists who keep on playing the game regardless of the odds.

In her highly praised collection of essays, *Slouching Towards Bethlehem*, Didion meticulously portrayed herself as one also well acquainted with the edge. She wrote of "bad nerves," of drinking "gin and hot water to blunt the pain and . . . [taking] Dexedrine to blunt the gin." Something of a sequel to that first anthology, *The White Album* is a collection of her best work from *Life*, *Esquire*, *The Saturday Evening Post*, *The New York Times* and *The New York Review of Books*.

Novelist and poet James Dickey has called Didion "the finest woman prose stylist writing in English today." And she has created, in her books, one of the most devastating and distinctive portraits of modern America to be found in fiction or non-fiction—a portrait of America where "disorder was its own point." A gifted reporter with an eye for the telling detail—the frayed hem, the shaking hand—she is also a prescient witness, finding in her own experiences parallels of the times. The voice is always precise, the tone unsentimental, the view unabashedly subjective. She takes things personally.

The title of the new book comes, of course, from the Beatles' *White Album*, a record Didion found ominous and disturbing, an album inextricably connected to the Manson murders and the dissonance of the 60's. Didion's own *White Album* contains a number of images from the Manson years: Linda Kasabian awaiting trial in a dress Didion bought for her at I. Magnin; Huey Newton lecturing the press on the "American capitalistic-materialistic system"; students at San Francisco State College breaking the tedium of the academic calendar with a campus revolt.

The White Album, though, is not solely concerned with the 60's. Or, for that matter, with Didion's alienation. Whereas Yeats's poem "The Second Coming" ("Things fall apart; the center cannot hold . . .") served as a perfect epigraph for *Slouching Towards Bethlehem*, no such image exists to sum up *The White Album*. This second volume of essays is not so absolute in its tragic vision of the world, not so unquestioningly bleak about history. As Didion herself puts it, *"The White Album* is more tentative. I don't have as many answers as I did when I wrote *Slouching*."

The White Album includes a brilliant essay on Hollywood as "the last extant stable society"; a tribute to Georgia O'Keeffe, and a charming portrait of one Amado Vazquez, a Mexican gardener who raises orchids in Malibu. The collection, in fact, demonstrates Didion's range as an essayist, her ability not only to portray the extraordinary and apocalyptic, but also to appreciate the ordinary.

"I am alienated," explains Didion, "I would say I *am* a victim. But you don't live every day of your life walking around talking about how alienated you are—you'd start sounding like Woody Allen's *Interiors*."

Both Didion and her husband, John Gregory Dunne, the author of *Vegas*, *True Confessions* and *Quintana & Friends*, have made their lives the subject of their reportage. Their thoughts on divorce, their adoption of their daughter, Quintana, and their nervous breakdowns have all been meticulously chronicled in print. The candor frequently stuns.

"[In person] Joan gives everyone the impression of being very private," observes Ralph Graves, now editorial director of Time Inc. who was editor of *Life* magazine when Didion wrote her column. "Then she'll turn around and write this inside-of-the-stomach stuff that you'd think you'd need to know her five years to find out. This mousy, thin, quiet woman tells you as much about herself as Mailer." For Didion, though, it is merely part of the contract a writer makes with the reader: as she once told her husband, "If you want to write about yourself, you have to give them something."

Why has she chosen this relentless self-scrutiny? One suspects that writing holds for her a kind of talismanic power—the process of putting her life on paper somehow helps to exorcise private demons. Writing, after all, is a means of creating a momentary stay against confusion, of making order out of disorder, understanding out of fear.

In her newest book, Didion does not shirk from exposing herself. "You are getting a woman who somewhere along the line misplaced whatever slight faith she ever had in the social contract, in the meliorative principle . . . I have felt myself a sleepwalker . . . alert only to the stuff of bad dreams, the children burning in the locked car in the supermarket parking lot . . . I have trouble maintaining the basic notion that keeping promises matters in a world where everything I was taught seems beside the point."

She tells us how she went blind for six weeks from a condition diagnosed as multiple sclerosis (the disease has been in remission for the past seven years), and how, in the summer of 1968, she checked into the psychiatric clinic at St. John's Hospital in Santa Monica. She even tells us the doctor's diagnosis: "Patient's thematic productions emphasize her fundamentally pessimistic, fatalistic and depressive view of the world around her. . . ."

Yet this familiar Didion persona masks a writer whose own life is a wealth of contradictions. She is a Westerner who mourns the passing of the frontier ethic, but lives in Los Angeles because the city amuses her. She is a romantic who believes "that salvation [lies] in promises made and somehow kept outside the range of normal social experience," but delights in practical, domestic routines. She is an introvert who says she has always been an outsider, but parties with the biggest names in Hollywood. She is a writer who has dwelled on the atomization of modern society, but maintains what she describes as a "boring, bourgeois" life.

Didion's friends jokingly refer to her as the "Kafka of Brentwood Park," which amuses her husband no end. "Joan's really a rather cheerful person who drives a bright yellow Corvette," says Dunne. "In person, she doesn't have a dark view of life. She just doesn't expect a lot from it or from people."

Dunne, a large, gregarious man, gives the appearance of managing Didion's life. He tends to do most of the talking, frequently answering questions directed at Didion; he always answers the phones and screens the calls. But, according to their friends, it is Didion who handles all their finances and Didion who smooths over situations created by Dunne's volatile temper. "John does not play Leonard Woolf to her Virginia," notes writer Josh Greenfeld, one of the Dunnes' best friends in Los Angeles. "She's more John's Leonard Woolf. John may seem strident and tough, but what you see in John you get in Joan. She is every bit as tough as he is." Another friend describes Didion as "fragile," as in the phrase, "a fragile, little stainless-steel machine."

Didion, too, thinks of herself as an optimist. Hers is an optimism somewhat akin to F. Scott Fitzgerald's definition of a first-rate intelligence: "the ability to hold two opposed ideas in the mind at the same time, and still retain the ability to function." To believe that nothing matters and yet to believe more strongly that it is worth making a record of experience anyway.

Her awareness of "the edge" is, in part, a literary idea that derives from what seized her imagination as a child. The people she read about in the fiction of Conrad, James and Faulkner convinced a young Didion that "salvation lay in extreme and doomed commitments," and later provided models for the characters in her own novels.

"I have a theatrical temperament," explains Didion. "I'm not interested in the middle road—maybe because everyone's on it. Rationality, reasonableness bewilder me. I think it comes out of being a 'daughter of the Golden West.' A lot of the stories I was brought up on had to do with extreme actions—leaving everything behind, crossing the trackless wastes, and in those stories the people who stayed behind and had their settled ways—those people were not the people who got the prize. The prize was California."

We are on a flight from Los Angeles to Sacramento, where Didion's parents live. As the plane circles over the coast toward the valley, Didion turns to look out the window. "It kills me when people talk about California hedonism," she says deliberately. "Anybody who talks about California hedonism has never spent a Christmas in Sacramento."

Didion's family—five generations on her mother's side—come from Sacramento. Although it is the state capital, it remains a valley town where the summers are hot and plagued by drought, and where the winters are cold and menaced by flood. The land here is flat, the rivers and fields stretching clean to the horizon. It is, in short, a landscape of extremes.

In writing of the Sacramento of her childhood, Didion frequently uses the word "Eden," and to the early settlers it probably was—or at least a reasonable facsimile of Paradise. The confluence of the muddy, silt-rich Sacramento and the swiftly flowing American made the region a fertile garden. It is only within the past three decades that the cultivated fields have given way to tract housing, subdivisions and aerospace factories; the dusty roads along the levee to eight-lane freeways.

Even as we drive through town, Didion peruses a map provided by the rent-a-car company. She is unaccustomed to finding her way home via the new highways, for the Sacramento she knows so well is a town of the past. "All that is constant about the California of my childhood is the rate at which it disappears," she wrote in *Slouching Towards Bethlehem*. "California is a place in which a boom mentality and a sense of Chekhovian loss meet in uneasy suspension."

The road leading to the Didions' Tudor house once ran through hop fields; today it is flanked by a thriving industrial park. Inside, their living room is a comfortable assemblage of mementos and assorted knickknacks collected by Eduene Jerrett Didion at local craft fairs. A small forthright woman, she met John Dunne for the first time at her daughter's wedding and told him: "You know those little old ladies in tennis shoes you've heard about? Well, I'm one of them." Her husband is a quiet, shy man. A former Army Air Corps officer who later served on the Sacramento draft board, Frank Didion now dabbles in real estate.

Joan's bedroom is still the faded carnation-pink she painted it when she was a freshman at Berkeley, but bougainvillea and ivy have overgrown the windows, giving the chamber a dark, cavelike effect. Didion returned to this room to finish each of her five books. She wrote the last 150 pages of *A Book of Common Prayer* here in 14 days. After all, there are no distractions in Sacramento: the phones are answered, the meals are prepared, and her parents leave her alone to work.

On a dressing table here, as in her study back in Brentwood, there is a small framed photograph of the Sierras near Donner Pass. The tale of the Donner Party haunts Didion. Traveling from Illinois to California in 1846, the Donner-Reed party was forced by a sudden blizzard to encamp in the Sierras. Faced with starvation, they ate their own dead. Of the eighty-seven who embarked, forty survived. Joan's great-great-great-grandmother, Nancy Hardin Cornwall, was a member of the original Donner party, but she had left the ill-fated group at Humboldt Sink in Nevada to cut north through Oregon.

Nancy Hardin Cornwall's own forebears lived on the frontier, moving from the Carolinas to Georgia to Arkansas to Missouri with the nation's westward migration, and Didion clings to that heritage. "I used to be strongly convinced that the closing of the frontiers was the central event, the turning point in American history," she says. "I am not flatly convinced of that anymore, but I myself feel better the farther west I am." The frontier legacy, she feels, has made her different, has ingrained in her a kind of hard-boiled individualism, an "ineptness at tolerating the complexities of postindustrial life."

And it has made her something of a libertarian, wary of governmental panaceas and distrustful of utopian promises. Like her parents, Didion voted for Goldwater in 1964. Since then, she has voted only twice. "I never had faith that the answers to human problems lay in anything that could be called political," she explained once. "I thought the answers, if there were answers, lay someplace in man's soul."

Joan was a fearful child—scared of ski lifts, of rattlesnakes in the river, even of comic books, filled as they were with violence and monsters. She worried that the funicular at Royal Gorge would crash, that the bridge over the Sacramento River would fall.

During the war years, Frank Didion was transferred from base to base, and the family moved with him. The transience made Joan something of an outsider, and she remained one even when the Didions finally settled again in Sacramento.

If she was ill at ease with people, Joan at least found more congenial company in books. "I tended to perceive the world in terms of things read about it," she says. "I still do." When she was five, Joan wrote her first story: a tale of a woman who dreamed she was freezing to death in the Arctic, only to wake up and find herself in the scorching heat of the Sahara.

By fifteen, she was learning to type and learning how sentences worked by copying over chapters from Ernest Hemingway and Joseph Conrad. Her own stories of that period displayed a somewhat less eclectic taste; they all had one theme—suicide. In some, the hero walked through the streets of San Francisco to jump off the Golden Gate Bridge; in others, he simply walked into the sea.

One summer when she was in the eighth grade and her parents had a beach cottage, Joan determined to find out for herself how it would feel to walk into the ocean. After telling her parents she and her brother, Jimmy, were going to a square dance, she dropped Jimmy off at the Greyhound bus terminal, told him to wait for her and went on to the shore herself. Then, note pad in hand, she gingerly walked into the ocean. The night was dark, and she had no sooner waded in knee-deep than a wave hit her in the face. Sopping wet, her romantic notions of suicide considerably dampened, she made her way back to the terminal, retrieved her brother, and sneaked back into the house.

At Berkeley, Didion majored in English literature, and after graduating in 1956 headed for New York. Her passport there was first prize in the *Vogue* magazine Prix de Paris writing competition, which she received for a piece on the San Francisco architect William Wilson Wurster.

Her editor at *Vogue*, Allene Talmey, was a perfectionist who insisted on the right adjective, the "shock" verb, the well-turned caption. "At first she wrote captions," recalls Talmey. "I would have her write three hundred to four hundred words and then cut it back to fifty. We wrote long and published short and by doing that Joan learned to write." One of her first efforts: "Opposite, above: All through the house, color, verve, improvised treasures in happy but anomalous coexistence. Here, a Frank Stella, an Art Nouveau stained-glass panel, a Roy Lichtenstein. Not shown: A table covered with brilliant oilcloth, a Mexican find at fifteen cents a yard." Joan went on to write stories on furniture, homes and personalities; the exercises honed her unfailing eye for detail and fine-tuned her lean prose.

Homesick for California, Didion began to make notes for a book set in the Sacramento Valley. The book was *Run River*, an earnest first novel about a failed marriage. By the end of the book, there are two suicides, a murder and an abortion; only Lily McClellan survives. Already, many of the obsessional themes of Didion's work are in evidence: a pervasive sense of emotional weariness that surfaces in passionless couplings and the rote acting out of expected roles; a yearning after control and order by those who see their lives falling apart; a fatalistic realization that every particular fate is the fruit born of a particular history.

All of Didion's time in New York, though, was not spent over a typewriter. She liked parties. At twenty-five or so, she says, "I decided it was pathological for a grown woman to be shy, and I began pushing myself to make a contribution. Instead of being shy, I became 'reticent.'" She did not talk a great deal, but maintained a kind of Jamesian distance that insulated her from the rigors of cocktail patter and heightened her reportorial eye.

For several years, Didion attended many of those parties in the company of another writer. After living together for several years, they broke up. "I remember leaving [him] . . . one bad afternoon in New York, packing a suitcase and crying while he watched me," Didion wrote in a *Life* column. "When I asked him finally how he could watch me, he told me that a great many things had happened to him during the ten years before I knew him and nothing much touched him anymore. I remember saying that I never wanted to get the way he was, and he looked at me a long while before he answered. 'Nobody wants to,' he said. 'But you will.'"

A good friend over the years had been an ambitious young writer at *Time* magazine, John Gregory Dunne. The two frequently discussed their work with each other, and Dunne helped her correct the galleys to *Run River*. In 1963 they got an apartment together, and a year later, they were married. "I wonder how the marriage would have worked if we hadn't known each other so many years when we were really close friends," said Dunne once. "People have a hard time believing this, but there is no professional competition between us. I think the reason is the six years of friendship when we were both starting off together." Didion agrees: "Writers are very boring to live with. If I weren't married to a writer, I couldn't be as self-absorbed as I am."

By the time they were married, New York had begun to grate on Didion's nerves—and working at a newsmagazine on Dunne's—and three months later they left for California. In 1966, they adopted a baby girl whom they named Quintana Roo after the Yucatan territory.

Didion says she once believed "that I could live outside history, that the currents of the time in which I lived did not touch or affect me." Then, sometime in 1966, she says, she became "paralyzed by the conviction that the world as I had understood it no longer existed. If I was to work again at all, it would be necessary for me to come to terms with disorder." And disorder was rife in the 60's; Los Angeles, a perfect vantage point from which to watch those years. Her chronicle of that period, *Slouching Towards Bethlehem*, was published in 1968.

At the time Didion was acclaimed for *Slouching*, Dunne had yet to achieve the fame that *True Confessions* would later bring him. In the summer of 1968, suffering from a protracted case of writer's block, Dunne began driving the highways—sometimes to San Bernardino, sometimes to Reno, sometimes to Mexicali. One morning he told Didion he was going out to buy a loaf of bread. He did: 457 miles away at a Safeway in San Francisco. Finally, he moved to a residential motel just off the Strip in Las Vegas, and for 18 months lived there among hookers, card sharks and comedians. Didion bought him three sets of clean sheets and a wastepaper basket; she did not see the apartment until the day he headed home.

After sharing a *Saturday Evening Post* column with her husband and writing another column for *Life*, Didion began her second novel. In 1970, *Play It As It Lays* was published and nominated for a National Book Award. Her editor on the book, Henry Robbins, remembers his first reaction: "It was a brilliant book but cold, almost icy. A devastating book. When I finished it, I wanted to call her up and ask her if she was all right. I *did* see it as the experience of despair."

Arranged in eighty-four staccato-paced takes, the elliptical prose is pared down, perfectly clean. The setting is the desert; the cast, the careless hedonists of Hollywood; the emotional climate, bleak as the surroundings. Having experienced a bad affair, a worse marriage, the birth of a brain-damaged child and the abortion of another, Maria Wyeth suffers that exhaustion of the spirit born of disillusionment and emotional bankruptcy. And yet, she survives. It is Maria, at the end of the book, who can say, "I know what 'nothing' means, and keep on playing. Why, BZ would say. Why not, I say."

Play It As It Lays grew out of a scene Didion once observed at the Sands Hotel in Las Vegas: At midnight, a woman in a white gown walked across the casino floor to answer a phone. Didion began asking herself, "Who is this woman? What had occurred in her past that she should at this very moment be paged in the middle of Las Vegas?"

A Book of Common Prayer, published in 1977, similarly grew out of a single image. In the spring of 1973, Didion and Dunne had gone to South America to attend a film festival. While there, she contracted a case of paratyphoid and her weight dropped to 70 pounds. The entire trip took on a certain hallucinogenic quality, and an image of the Panama airport lodged in Didion's imagination. She became "obsessed with a picture of the airport—its heat, the particular color of the stucco and especially the light which gets absorbed."

The central character in *A Book of Common Prayer*, Charlotte Douglas, is also *de afuera*, an outsider. Imagining she can escape the past, she comes to the imaginary country of Boca Grande, where she is shot in a revolution—a casualty of her own romanticism. A technically difficult novel, the book received mixed reviews. As a number of critics pointed out, the device of a dispassionate, uninvolved narrator results in an oblique narrative that fails to win our complete sympathy for Charlotte's plight.

Given the current visibility of the women's movement, there are those who see Didion's fiction as an example of that nebulous genre—"women's novels." The women in her novels, after all, are haunted by the issues of mothers and daughters, blood and babies. Then, too, they are usually victims of men who have in some way failed them. The men in the novels—Ryder Channing in *Run River*, Ivan Costello in *Play It As It Lays*, and Warren Bogart in *A Book of Common Prayer*—are remarkably similar. All are brash, irreverent skeptics capable of almost cruel belligerence and possessed of a sexual charm that renders the women powerless. They are corrupters of innocence, destroyers of idealism.

The women, for their part, are adept at coping with the immediate, the practical, but have trouble connecting the past with the future. Like Charlotte in *A Book of Common Prayer*, each believes she can remain "a tourist, a traveler with good will and good credentials and no memory."

Didion, however, maintains that her female characters "don't really have specifically women's problems: they have rather more general problems." Indeed, Didion is skeptical of the women's movement. As she writes in *The White Album*: "To those of us who remain committed mainly to the exploration of moral distinctions and ambiguities, the feminist analysis . . . [denies] one's actual apprehension of what it is like to be a woman, the irreconcilable difference of it—that sense of living one's deepest life underwater, that dark involvement with blood and birth and death."

Didion occasionally forces herself to do reporting (which she dislikes) to replenish her image bank, to gather new material for her novels. And in both *Play It As It Lays* and *A Book of Common Prayer*, the reporter's eye is very much in evidence, grounding the melodramatics of the plot in a precision of detail. Didion has carefully observed the manners and mores of the moneyed set that frequents Los Angeles and expertly records those observations with a mordant wit. "Le island. Le weekend. Les monkey-gland injections," babbles a silly socialite in *A Book of Common Prayer*. Asked about her husband at a cocktail party, Charlotte replies: "He runs guns. I wish they had caviar."

Ma Maison is one of those peculiarly Hollywood phenomena. A modest wooden structure on Melrose Avenue that resembles a country hamburger stand, it is probably the most celebrated celebrity hangout since Romanoff's in the days of the Rat Pack. On this particular Wednesday, George Cukor is there, as are Jackie Bisset, Dustin Hoffman and the Jack Lemmons. There are nods and greetings all around as the Dunnes and Carl Bernstein walk in for lunch. "The same old faces," says Bernstein looking around. "This place never changes."

"No," says Didion. "Time stands still here."

The Dunnes and Bernstein talk about writing as writers will: how many pages a day constitutes a good day's work; where the ideal place to write would be. Dunne, who, as his friend Calvin Trillin puts it, is a "creative gossip," regales the others with stories, which Didion occasionally embroiders. The Dunnes' work on screenplays has made them regulars on the local dinner party-screening circuit, and they are frequently mentioned in *The Hollywood Reporter*'s column "The Great Life" along with the likes of Bianca Jagger, Paul Morrissey and Linda Ronstadt.

Collaborators on all their screenplays, the Dunnes regard writing for the movies not so much as a creative effort but as a respite from the solitary rigors of fiction and reportage; and they have worked on a dozen films, including dramatizations of *Play It As It Lays*, *The Panic in Needle Park* and *A Star Is Born*.

They are currently finishing a screenplay of Dunne's best-selling novel *True Confessions*. That project completed, Didion will go back to work on her next novel, *Angel Visits*. The title, she explains, comes from a Victorian expression meaning "pleasant visits of short duration." Although the book started off as an extended dinner party in which the lives of three generations

of a family are revealed, Didion says that the narrative of the book continues
to change as she works on it.

When she is in the midst of a book, Didion works at a typewriter in her
office from 11 in the morning until 4 or 5 in the afternoon. Before cooking
dinner (and she is an excellent cook), she sits down with a drink and her
day's work, penciling in sentences, crossing out others.

"Order and control are terribly important to me," says Didion as she sits on
a couch in her den, fingering a tiny green pillbox. "I would love to just have
control over my own body—to stop the pain, to stop my hand from shaking.
If I were 5 feet 10 and had a clear gaze and a good strong frame, I would
not have such a maniacal desire for control because I would have it."

If control is elusive, order at least is provided by a multitude of domestic
tasks Didion enjoys: making her own pastry; polishing the silver; taking her
orchids to the greenhouse for repotting; preparing dinner parties; helping Q.
with her vocabulary. In Didion's novels, the women, too, practice little rituals—improvised regimens relied upon in lieu of any greater order. Even while
she is wildly driving the highways, Maria "tried always to let the [gas station]
attendant notice her putting the [Coke] bottle in the rack, a show of thoughtful
responsibility."

There is in such gestures a means of warding off what Didion has called
"the unspeakable peril of the everyday." A means of keeping man's frail
civilization roadmarked from the wilderness (the coyotes by the interstate,
the snakes in the playpen, the fires and winds of California) that for Didion
is always lurking just outside the house. "All the time we were living at the
beach [in Trancas] I wanted a house like this," she says of their two-story
Colonial home. "I wanted a house with a center-hall plan with the living room
on your right and the dining hall on your left when you come in. I imagined
if I had this house, a piece of order and peace would fall into my life, but
order and peace did not fall into my life. Living in a two-story house doesn't
take away the risks."

III

ESSAYS

Points West, Then and Now:
The Fiction of Joan Didion
Jennifer Brady

From *Run River* to *A Book of Common Prayer*, the subject of Joan Didion's fiction has been a dilemma she identified more than a decade ago in the novels of John Cheever: that of "tragic obsolescence."[1] Unlike Cheever, however, Didion connects this sense of obsolescence with the closing of the frontier, the termination of America's original dream of new beginnings in that unknown country of the setting sun. In her review of *The Wapshot Scandal*, written the year after *Run River* was published, Didion explores two aspects of Cheever's chronicles of the "twilight world" of the eastern seaboard: their elegiac evocation of a "lost world . . . capable of paralyzing its exiles" and the writer's means of claiming that "imagined territory" of the past for our time. What draws Didion to Cheever's fiction is the fact that its concerns with "then" and "now" and the haunting "countries of the mind" parallel those of her own prose. Both writers confront the effects of cultural loss and change over time. Their works show a continuing preoccupation with the quality of modern life and the need to make connections, cultural and literary, in and for the present. These connections tend nonetheless to be deeply conservative in the sense that they relate to ideals of generational, cultural, and historical continuity.

Didion's writings in particular demand an act of historical imagination on the part of the reader, an understanding of the mythic heritage of "Points West." While she is first and always a writer rather than a social historian of the Far West, her novels and essays return ineluctably to that promise of starting afresh that the American frontier once seemed to offer: the "cutting clean which was to have redeemed them"—and us—"all" (*Run River*). Didion's novels attempt to claim the history of this national dream for the province of fiction. A review of Kazan's *America America* captures the thematic impetus for Didion's own work:

> *America, America, God shed His grace on thee:* it is the idea which has informed all our history, the idea which sent and still sends us West, the failing dream which drives us into easy violence and neurotic resignation and off the Golden Gate bridge; the remembered dream which haunts our uneasy wakening. No people ever expected so much of a country; none ever risked such failure.[2]

The dream of the frontier was crucial to the development of our history because it seemed to reify the promise of providential grace. What Didion traces so eloquently in her novels, then, is the history of paradise lost, betrayed, forfeited—that, and the ultimate obsolescence of the lives of frontier children who have "run out of continent" (*STB*) and purpose.

In 1837, John Peck's *New Guide to the West* could confidently proclaim to emigrants that "the real Eldorado is still farther on."[3] In the watershed paper delivered before the American Historical Association in 1893, Frederick Jackson Turner described the frontier as a "new field of opportunity, a gate of escape from the bondage of the past." His conclusion, however, introduced a new note:

> He would be a rash prophet who should assert that the expansive character of American life has now entirely ceased. Movement has been its dominant fact, and, unless this training has no effect upon a people, the American energy will continually demand a wider field for its exercise. But never again will such gifts of free land offer themselves . . . the frontier has gone, and with its going has closed the first period of American history.[4]

Turner recognized the central predicament of this national dream of destiny and of heroic self-determination. The Western experience was not only the "arbiter" of America's democratic hopes of social regeneration, but the full consciousness of the significance of this opportunity would be recognized only in retrospect (213). The conditions under which the pioneer could start afresh were exceptional and timebound. For both Turner and Didion, the closing of the frontiers signaled the turning point of American history, an event as definitive in its implications as the expulsion from Eden.

Before considering the achievements of *Run River, Play It As It Lays, A Book of Common Prayer*, and the other short fiction, Didion's qualifications as a mythographer of the West Coast ought to be recognized. Didion is very much a child of the frontier promise, being a descendant of the kind of American family Turner spoke of in his influential social history, yet she cannot subscribe to the optimism with which Turner depicts the frontier mentality. He believed that frontier individualism, because it represented a movement away from the influences of European civilization and government, promoted a uniquely American form of democracy. Turner describes the antisocial tendencies engendered by the frontier without much elaboration, but one of his observations is key to Didion's works: he notes that "Complex society is precipitated by the wilderness into a kind of primitive organization based on the family" (30), a theme Didion echoes when she discusses the code of ethics known as "wagon-train morality." The lure of the frontier revolved in many ways around its promise of individual liberty and the absence of social controls; but for this ideal to be realized, for the pioneers to survive, they had to recognize and uphold the primal loyalties due to each other as blood kin.

Didion's ancestors were pioneers destined to pursue the dream of an Edenic Eldorado farther west, moving restlessly from frontier to frontier. The location of that frontier was reinvented as Kentucky, West Virginia, Missouri, and, finally, the Sacramento Valley in California. The 1846-47 overland crossing into California is associated for Didion, through her ancestors' involvement, with the tragic fiasco of the Donner-Reed party. As Kevin Starr observes, "the Donner party was Everyman in a morality play of frontier disintegration."[5] The blizzards encountered in the Sierras, hunger, lost time, the wrong route, and an ill-equipped group of men, women, and children culminated in the deaths of nearly half of the group. The survivors' fates were as unfortunate. They were rescued only to become social outcasts because they had resorted to cannibalism during the mismanaged crossing. Didion's family had separated from the Donner-Reed clan before its final humiliation, but the powerful image of their sufferings haunts her as it haunts all Californians. The experience of these families has become the original antimyth of the golden land in which the promised land becomes the heart of darkness.

The contiguity between Didion's family history and the afflictions of the Donner-Reed party forms an essential context for the recurrent metaphors and thematic preoccupations of her prose. The root of the undeniable fascination of the Donner episode is evidently its paradigmatic notoriety in the Far West. It is, of course, a cautionary tale of the "grief awaiting those who failed in their loyalties to each other" (*STB*), the epitome of the betrayal of human bonds which made a hell of America's finest hour. The extent to which the frontier can exist as a place of exile from human contact, capable of paralyzing its inhabitants in the traumas of the past, connects the fate of the Donner-Reed party with that of the protagonists of both *Play It As It Lays* and *A Book of Common Prayer*. As an ironic counter to these cautionary metaphors, however, the tale can be interpreted as a celebration of California as a type of Eden, for "Did not the Donner-Reed Party, after all, eat its own dead to reach Sacramento?" (*STB*). Didion's novels contain numerous suggestive variations on this haunting story of the frontier past: it becomes the historical frame within which she explores the atomization of a country and its mission, the imaginative link joining the West of then and now.

John Peck's prophetic appeal to the immigrants of 1837 that the "real Eldorado" lay in the Far West forms the epigraph to Didion's first novel, *Run*

River. If Peck's guide captures the optimistic spirit of the new country and its confidence that the difficulties of the American wilderness could be surmounted by the efforts of courageous, self-made men, Didion's novel depicts what became of that dream and what happened to a nation that found Eldorado to be an ever-receding horizon of the mind. The quotation from *The New Guide to the West* is appropriate in a novel whose characters are "afflicted with memory" of a mythic "finest hour" of frontier expansion. In striking contrast to the sanguine optimism of Peck's manual for immigrant travelers, *Run River* charts the history of a lost world, an Eldorado "that in some respects never was."[6] The depth of Didion's early novel and the intelligence and maturity of its statement derive from a complicated counterpointing of the frontier past with the California culture of a century later and from a suggestive use of the landscape of the West Coast.

Peck recognized, as did Turner in the 1890's, that the frontier dream of discovering a new, free place where enterprise and hard work would be rewarded meant that the idea of Eldorado was inextricably tied to the possession and cultivation of land. Eldorado had to be "real" in order for the sacrifices of the Protestant pioneers to be justified and to make manifest that their overland migration exemplified God's national mission. The census report of 1890 announced that the American frontier had closed. With the wilderness receding into the historical past, the dream of paradise found took the only literal form which remained: the rich land the pioneers were to make into a "giant outdoor hothouse with a billion-dollar crop" (*STB*), the California characterized in *Run River* as "God's own orchard." The Sacramento Valley, then, carries the freight of the pioneers' expectations and beliefs concerning the land they settled after the harsh overland crossing. For the characters of Didion's novel, who inherit their ancestors' ideas with the farms they have cultivated for generations, the land is the literal symbol of their destiny, the vital and real sign of the continuity between then and now.

The McClellans and the Knights, the two established California families whose fates interweave throughout *Run River*, are descendants of the original pioneers. "Sometimes I think this whole valley belongs to me," the young Lily (of-the-valley) Knight tells her father, her words echoing the rich rhetorical tradition passed down through the family. Her belief is initially as unexamined as her conviction that Walter Knight will be elected governor of California and that she has inherited the character and opportunity of pioneer ancestors who "wanted things and got them." The Valley was to have been theirs forever. The land had shaped their lives and defined their desires; and in return it contained their dead, the generations of family tombstones marking the blood contributed to the struggle for possession.

The California of the 1940's and 1950's is, however, a society in transition. The Knights and McClellans find themselves exiled from the past by irrevocable changes, both cultural and economic. The Sacramento Valley, envisioned by frontiersmen as the promised land, is rapidly changing in character. The new wealth is in the hands of Eastern industrialists who work for Aerojet General and Douglas Aircraft. The growing of hops is no longer as lucrative a business in the Valley; ranches have become a corporation concern. Didion captures the psychological impact of these changes on the lives of her characters in finely-etched, poignant details: Walter Knight's puzzled recognition that his kind of gentleman grower is politically expendable when he is defeated in the 1938 election for the legislature by an ex-postal worker who campaigns for the Democrats; Everett McClellan's sudden tears when he watches his sister Sarah depart for Philadelphia after their father's funeral "carrying a paper bag full of dried hops to show to her children and to the stranger who was now her husband." It is in this type of disappointment that the reality of the frontier dream of belonging to a place and time is questioned.

By the midpoint of our century the timebound quality of the frontier experiment had become clear, even to those most reluctant to relinquish its disarming promises. *Run River* is set in these crucial decades because Didion understands that period of social and economic change to be the cutting edge of California's destiny as a land made by people who "wanted things and got them." The energies of her characters dissipate into indecision and crippling self-doubts when the mantle of Eldorado slips from their grasp and they have to confront the obsolescence of their old world. Only then, when the continuity which seemed to link past and present is lost, do the Knights and McClellans begin confusedly to glimpse the failure of the frontier dream, the flaw endemic to its origins. With the new perspective born of a harsher reality, Didion's characters discover a different past comprised of "failures of love and faith and honor," and with that discovery, they know a deeper loss than the one which prompted their retrospection: the loss of a world that never existed. To reassess the past with disillusioned eyes is, however, to hazard all sources of hope. The McClellans and Knights are, finally, ordinary people, "with the normal ratio of nobility to venality," whose distinction rests in their persistent adherence to the frontier dream. They inhabit a world blurred with the gratulatory fictions passed down through the generations about their heroic pioneer history, repressing for the most part the chilling truth Lily senses when she recognizes that the frontier past "had been above all a history of accidents: of moving on and of accidents."

From their Protestant forebears the McClellans and Knights inherit the tendency to interpret personal experience through reference to inspiring analogues. Kevin Starr notes the prevalence of this disposition among the early pioneers: "In the transcontinental migrations of the 1840's and 1850's, hundreds of diaries, journals and memoirs attest to the power of scriptural analogue. Lost in the desert, besieged by Indians, hunger, thirst, confusion and despair, Protestant pioneers found in the memory of earlier wilderness wanderings sources of sanity and hope."[7] It is, then, entirely appropriate— though at a temporal remove—for the characters of *Run River* to remember the trials of their own ancestral wilderness wanderers when they are faced with a hostile environment of change. When Everett joins the army, his sister Martha presents him with her family copy of *The McClellan Journal, An Account of an Overland Journey to California in the Year 1848*. Headed for the Pacific front, Everett wants to emulate the courage of his ancestors by becoming a modern pioneer going "Forward into battle with the Cross before." The chosen analogue rings hollow, for Everett never sees action. The promised land where energetic men might, as Turner hoped, "escape the bondage of the past," is a closed frontier. Didion's characters are victims of the past, both of its myth of extraordinary achievements and of the bleak failures of purpose that tainted the original dream, and their grasp of the painful import of change therefore remains partial and baffled. They look back to family scripture, such as *The McClellan Journal*, for solace because the present confronts them with a series of bereavements to which they cannot adapt. What they discover or decide to have been true of the past differs with each character of *Run River*, yet the very fact of their obsessive retrospection signals the death knell of that hope the frontier once fostered: the hope of redemptive beginnings in an Eldorado unshadowed by history, insulated from the burden of original sin by God's grace.

In a world where irrevocable acts have been committed and final borders reached, the Knights and McClellans have recourse only to dramatic gestures, desperate attempts to recreate the reckless courage of their equally flawed ancestors. Lily alone understands that choice, for these descendants of the ill-fated Donner-Reed clan, is no more than the sum "of all the choices gone before." Her fatalistic insight underscores the futility of their attempts to free themselves from repeating the miscalculations of these original families or to forge for themselves lives of comparable significance. Their history is comprised of impotent acts of internecine violence. Waiting for the shot that will announce Everett's suicide, Lily remembers an earlier episode of what it could mean to find the frontiers closed, involving

> a blue-eyed boy who was at sixteen the best shot in the county and who when there was nothing left to shoot rode out one day and shot his brother,

an accident. It had been above all a history of accidents: of moving on and of accidents. What is it you want, she had asked Everett tonight. It was a question she might have asked them all.

For Everett and Martha McClellan, the frontier ideal of heroic self-determination degenerates into its antithesis, the confused striving to step into the same river twice. Martha, like her brother, is obsessed by the violent history of California's early development. Her favorite childhood game is "Donner Party," in which she assumes the role of Tamsen Donner; she despairs that her own ancestors made the overland journey without the sacrifice exemplified by Tamsen's refusal to leave her dying husband. The cautionary story of the pioneers' collapse into mutual betrayal and final descent into cannibalism in the Sierra snows is metamorphosed, in Martha's selective version, into romantic suicide pacts and heroic death wishes. Martha's sense of past glories long outlived paralyzes her in neurotic despondency and madness. When she is jilted by Ryder Channing, an opportunistic newcomer to the West, Martha drowns herself, but her hysterical suicide bears only an ironic analogy to her warped conception of the Donner tragedy. In her obliviousness to the negative implications of the frontier experience she chooses to emulate, Martha dooms herself to a death poignant in its example of misspent energy, its ultimate lack of purpose or meaning.

It is Lily who comes closest to re-enacting the role of Tamsen Donner when she holds her dying husband in her arms at the close of the novel, trying to "imprint her ordinary love upon his memory through all eternity." Once again, the understated historical echoes are ironic. Everett has shot himself after murdering Lily's current lover. The betrayal their history traces is mutual. Neither can handle the strains of a bad marriage; each has failed in his loyalties to the other. The analogy between the experiences of the Donner-Reed party and the Knight and McClellan families is implied with sensitivity in *Run River*, even to the moment when Lily licks "the blood from the arm she held around Everett," and wishes she could tell their children he had been a good man. Unlike Martha's attempt to duplicate Tamsen Donner's pathetic but moving renunciation of life during the original crossing, Lily's gestures are utterly unself-conscious. The characters of *Run River* do repeat the choices of the past, whether their acts are instinctual or deliberate. The crucial drama— that brief period of frontier expansion when it seemed that America might discover a "real" Eldorado free of time and memory—has already been played out, the failure of the dream of its possession determined.

Four years after the publication of *Run River*, a period during which the articles eventually collected as *Slouching Towards Bethlehem* were written,

Didion returned to her concern with cultural atomization with a short story
entitled "When Did Music Come This Way? Children, Dear, Was It Yesterday?"[8] As in her first novel, the structure of this short fiction is based on the
framing of contemporary events by those remembered from the past. The
narrator juxtaposes the years 1945 and 1967 in order to compare an incident
from her early puberty with an analogous experience in her adult life. The
story has much in common with Didion's portrait in *Run River* of acrimonious
betrayals of blood kin and, once again, it is the history of America's frontier
experiment that provides the metaphoric backdrop to the narrator's own memory of dreams bankrupted and honor lost.

The narrator begins her "annotated catalogue" of Christmases past and present
with the wish that we could see the tale "as finished and as self-contained as
a painting on a gallery wall." She ends, however, with a series of bewildered
questions posed to the reader, the most telling of which is the final "How
exactly did we get from there to here?" All of Didion's prose asks such
questions: how does the past shape the present, and what are the consequences
for those who remember that past and those who repress its memory? The
short story depicts the narrator's inability either to return to her past as a
refuge from despair or fully to understand the import of her recollections.
The connections she makes serve only to imprison her further in the conviction
that she might "start over, but never fresh." In the fatalistic world of Didion's
fiction, there is no exit. The narrator of "When Did Music Come This Way?"
is old enough to realize that changes bring sadness and irrevocable loss; but
there is no opportunity for new beginnings among those people who inherit
from their forebears the tendency to abdicate their primal responsibilities.

The narrator, who wants to believe that "refuge was simpler then, to find
and to maintain," recalls a wartime Christmas as bereft of its ideal spirit as
the present holiday. Her aunt Inez' husband, Ward, disrupts the family's
celebration by a deliberate failure to arrive for the Christmas dinner. After
the meal the narrator and her cousin Cary quarrel about marriage, in the
course of which the gift of a perfect music box is shattered. Didion shows
these two adolescents encountering the painful recognition that adults are not
able to call the tune of their lives, nor to achieve what they most want, in a
story that is a sensitive exploration of human sin. Like those in *Run River*,
the characters of "When Did Music Come This Way?" renounce their moral
responsibilities through acts of mutual betrayal. Later in the same evening,
the narrator overhears this exchange between Ward and Inez:

> "Say it out loud. Who would you betray."
> "I can't tonight."

"*Say* it."

There was a silence, and then Aunt Inez said, as if by rote, "I would betray my mother. I would betray my sister. I would betray Cary."

"OK," Ward said softly then, and sat back. "OK."

They said nothing for a long time, and when I woke there was a comforter over me and the lights were off and it was December 26, another Christmas gone, and when Cary came downstairs I could not look at her.

If the central question posed by Didion's fiction is "How exactly did we get from there to here?" the answer the story gives (distinct from the consciousness of its narrator) is that there and here have become the same place. No shelter is available to children who inherit a world already saddened by betrayals, nor is any individual identity. In *Run River*, Martha prays at her niece's baptism that Julie will "choose right every day she lives," but Lily knows her daughter to be without choice from birth, her fate merged from the beginning with the family destiny; and Ryder recognizes years later that Julie McClellan resembles Martha at the same age, sharing both her looks and her desperate recklessness. The submersion of personal identity in a pattern of obsessive, instinctual repetition of past miscalculations is even more pronounced in the history of the nameless narrator of "When Did Music Come This Way?" As a child the narrator cannot bear to look at Cary because she has betrayed her in their loveless quarrel and been a party to the subsequent ritual of betrayal enacted by Ward and Inez. Linking Christmases past and present, she observes,

I cannot now tell you why I turned on Cary, for I loved her.... Had we not spent Christmas together always? How could I have not loved her? In any case what I did was stupid, blunted, vicious only in tone. It is the kind of thing I still do. I did something very like it this morning, when Charlie came in and threw the snow on the bed. As he pointed out before he left, I did not even get her name right. I said everything that was ugly and nothing that hit the mark.

There is a frozen stasis in the repetitious quality of these betrayals. Even the narrator's understanding that these events are connected does not free her to start afresh. The tension between past and present is unresolved in her life, and because it is unresolved no balance is possible. She remains paralyzed in a present as dark as the ghostly past, "trying very hard . . . to hold on."

"When Did Music Come This Way?" embodies the structural balance of Didion's finest writing. The juxtaposition of related incidents, the development of image patterns, and the controlled tone all establish with characteristic precision a coherent and traditional perspective within which the social vacuum of modern life can be explored. Because the characters of this story and of *Run River* are imprisoned in the memory of things past, attempting to elucidate their sense of change and loss through the use of historical frames, their recollections have an allusive quality quite removed from the thinness of the narrative of Didion's next novel, *Play It As It Lays*. Didion's reiterated concern with what she speaks of as society's atomization—the breakdown of values traditionally held by the community and passed down through the generations—is effectively expressed in these early pieces, in which her protagonists' tensions mirror her own. She chooses in *Play It As It Lays* to portray Maria Wyeth from within the confines of a deliberately limited self-consciousness because of her perception that the decision to live in a truncated present causes life to become two-dimensional, or "thin" viewed from an imaginative perspective. Nonetheless, there is a constructive proximity of temperament between Didion and the characters of *Run River* and "When Did Music Come This Way?" and her preoccupation with America's failing dream of redemptive beginnings is more suggestively and intelligently articulated in these two works.

Play It As It Lays introduces another character who has problems with "as it was," but Maria Wyeth differs from the old Californians of *Run River* in her resolve to live exclusively "in the now," a world of cinematic stills and unconnected "facts." Two of the dominant metaphors of the novel's Hollywood landscape are the clean work of its abortionists and the freeways, both of which provide opportunities for escape from past failures. In a recent *Esquire* article, Didion describes the West Coast phenomenon of the freeway experience as the only "secular communion Los Angeles has,"[9] a narcotic surrender of the mind to the present moment. The freeway is the "new free land" designed to satisfy the needs of a people whose training (as Turner suggested) leads them constantly to demand new frontiers in order to release their expansive energies. No choice or act seems irrevocable and no sin finally culpable in the willing abandon of the freeway driver to the "rhythm of the lane change." In *Play It As It Lays*, Maria induces weeks of dreamless sleep through obsessive risk-taking on the Los Angeles freeways. One day she miscalculates, however, and drives as far as Baker, sixty miles from her husband's movie location. The rhythm of motion without destination is broken by this incident, and though Maria decides to return to the city without contacting Carter, she is forced to recognize the failure of her attempt to find a refuge from thought and memory on the freeway. America's new frontier is even more timebound than that which inspired the original migrations westward. Finding her escape closed, Maria avoids the freeways "except as a way of getting somewhere."

Maria dreams of a *tabula rasa* existence in an ideal world innocent of history, a place where no past flaw will touch her. When she discovers that she is pregnant, she passively agrees to her husband's suggestion of an abortion. *Play It As It Lays* traces this abortion back to its origins in betrayals of responsibility; in this novel, as in *Run River*, it is Didion's profound belief in the primacy of "primitive" and instinctual moral obligations and family bonds that forms the basis for our judgment of Maria's act. The abortion symbolizes Maria's effort to order her life by "cutting clean" (to appropriate the image Didion uses in reference to the frontier migration) from the past, both the immediate past of the child's inception and that of her own childhood. Maria abandoned her parents when she went east to New York, and she betrays them again when she aborts the child which would provide a link to a world that was lost with her parents' deaths. Didion's portrait of the psychological effects of this abortion is chilling. Its traumatic impact on Maria derives in part from the fact that her bereavement is never acknowledged on a conscious level, but her irresponsible decision has an even deeper significance. Maria transgresses the code of "wagon-train" ethics, which dictate that blood kin must recognize the value of each other's lives and struggle for mutual survival. As the narrator of "When Did Music Come This Way?" comprehends and voices so clearly, "if we don't have our families, then who do we have—we have no one, no one at all." It was the betrayal of this truth that forfeited the Donner-Reed party's claim to the paradise they sought in the West; and like these unfortunate pioneers, Maria learns its value only in retrospect.

Play It As It Lays ironically supports conservative values by showing their utter absence in the characters' lives. We see a Hollywood society with no sense of history, of the links between then and now, and we watch this world disintegrate into suicides, abortion, sexual promiscuity, divorce, and neurotic lethargy: into *nada*. The cautionary import of Maria's narrative, without the context of Didion's early work, seems obvious. Tradition functions as an unstated positive in *Play It As It Lays*, in contrast to the ambivalent and subtle point of reference it becomes in *Run River* and again in *A Book of Common Prayer*. Maria and the other characters are cut loose from the bonds and values associated with the family and, by extension, from any sense of continuity with the past. While this vision of life "in the now" conveys Didion's alarm at the progressive fragmentation of American society since World War II, the white spaces of its moral judgments communicate a nostalgia at odds with the complexity of her exposition of the imagined past over the two-decade span of her career. The Hollywood novel is a dramatic cautionary tale, a condemnation of our tendency to shed the "old ways" in favor of a "*tabula rasa* cosmopolitanism."[10] If we fail to remember, however, that for Didion the idealization of a "lost world" imbued with traditional norms is itself suspect since our remembered past is a mythic construction, *Play It As It Lays* offers an illusory refuge from its own bleak portrait of contemporary life.

Didion's fictions conclude thus far with *A Book of Common Prayer*, a novel that extends and further clarifies the implications of her concern with America's failing dream of redemptive beginnings. The elegiac voice of Grace Strasser-Mendana returns us to the discriminating acumen which characterized Didion's early prose. In keeping with its status as a sequel to *Run River* and "When Did Music Come This Way?" this study of grief and loss reflects the culmination of years of absorption with our frontier heritage. Whereas *Play It As It Lays* examined what it can mean to abandon the past and *Run River* the impact of obsessive memory, *A Book of Common Prayer* explores and interrelates both of these possibilities through its use of two protagonists, Americans whose lives crucially intersect in Boca Grande, a fictional country located in Central America.

Frederick Jackson Turner's words illuminate the predictive significance Didion ascribes to the sectional history of the Far West and further explain the rationale for her decision to expand the geographical canvas of *Common Prayer* beyond the confines of California. Turner suggested in 1896 that "the problem of the West is nothing less than the problem of American development. . . . What is the West? What has it been in American life? To have the answers to these questions, is to understand the most significant features of the United States of to-day . . ." (205). The perception of the relationship between the closing of the frontiers and the dilemma of America's national destiny originated with the Turner thesis, and the assumption of their profound connectedness, both then and throughout our century, is key to Didion's work. In *A Book of Common Prayer*, the question of how exactly we reached here from there is, as the title insists, restated in bold universals. As Didion's frontier landscapes transcend regional borders and her exiled characters begin to perceive themselves as the representatives of a "common" American culture, the symbolic link between the West and the larger problem of the country's mission emerges in high relief. The belief that the course of American history— and arguably of universal history—is revealed in the frontier experience informs all of Didion's work, but only in *A Book of Common Prayer* is it given such prominence and such an eloquent voice. *Common Prayer* redefines our conception of Didion's regionalism, for it is through her portrayal of the experiences of Westerners abroad that we are convinced of the synecdochic truth of her partisan claims.

Boca Grande, the symbolic landscape of this novel, functions as the imaginative epitome of the entrapment inherent in the nation's misdirected dream: it is the heart of darkness awaiting frontier exiles. As befits its status as the terminal frontier, Boca Grande is a country lacking any record of its past. Its isolation instills in casual visitors a weightless ennui. The "flat bush" and "lifeless sea" seem to absorb all light, "then glow morbidly." Attempts to cultivate or utilize the land are mocked by its inevitable return to equatorial rot and infestation. The Progreso causeway, built to connect the mainland with a projected capital, collapses after the President who favored its construction is assassinated during one of the arbitrary power struggles among the members of the ruling family. Its successor, a route into the interior, is likewise abandoned when the American investors learn that their bauxite find is a chimera. In the hell of Boca Grande, highways lead nowhere. The Carretera del Libertador was to have provided a "real" access back to the world beyond the country's borders, the America forsaken by its restless pilgrims and now in some sense lost to them. Significantly, this route exists only on Boca Grande's inaccurate maps, another reminder of the corruption which characterizes the internecine political "games" of the Strasser-Mendana family and an even more telling metaphor for the closure of the frontier. The futility of America's search for a new place and time and the inescapable frustration of what Turner saw as its "expansive character" are stressed in *A Book of Common Prayer* as Didion's imaginary Central America assumes the darkest traits of the original frontier: the blood betrayals, the sudden and pointless violence, and the paralysis of spiritual resignation. It is to this "place," Didion claims, that the West and, through it, America has come; and so Charlotte Douglas' "blind course south" ends in a country without a history, where the familiar tale of primal transgressions is on eternal replay.

The unconscious pattern of Charlotte's life is a poignant reflection of what it can mean to inherit the unresolved tensions of America's disturbing ideals. In order to sustain a "realistic and optimistic" outlook, she "revises" her memory of experiences, "erases" all knowledge of the debts left unpaid: family deaths, estrangement, divorce. When Marin becomes a revolutionary, Charlotte's shock at the loss of her child to "history" drives her into an hysterical repetition of this pattern of dissociation, and finally into exile. Charlotte's fear of the backward glance is writ large on the broad canvas of *Common Prayer*. She becomes in the novel a latter-day type of the "innocent abroad," an imaginative vehicle for Didion's exploration of the cultural heritage of the Far West.

When Charlotte arrives at her final destination, a place where she has no ties, she is referred to only as "*la norteamericana*." This ironic and hostile ascription of the status of "*de afuera*" to Didion's Californian suggests, however, a deeper truth. In Boca Grande, more clearly than in the American settings of *Run River* and "When Did Music Come This Way?" individual identity is subsumed by the national character and personal destiny merely re-enacts the course of choices already made. Charlotte Douglas is, then, representative of her culture, and never more so than in her unexamined decision to abandon the place of her origins and begin again in a country whose options are as closed as the world she leaves behind. It is Grace Strasser-Mendana who understands, because she too is an American in exile, what the designation *norteamericana* signifies:

> As a child of comfortable family in the temperate zone she had been as a matter of course provided with clean sheets, orthodontia, lamb chops, living grandparents, attentive godparents, one brother named Dickie, . . . as well as with a small wooden angel, carved in Austria, to sit on her bed table and listen to her prayers. In these prayers the child Charlotte routinely asked that "it" turn out all right, "it" being unspecified and all-inclusive, and she had been an adult for some years before the possibility occurred to her that "it" might not. She had put this doubt from her mind. As a child of the western United States she had been provided as well with faith in the value of certain frontiers on which her family had lived, in the virtues of cleared and irrigated land, of high-yield crops, of thrift, industry and the judicial system, of progress and education, and in the generally upward spiral of history. . . . It occurs to me tonight that give or take twenty years and a thousand miles Charlotte Douglas' time and place and my time and place were not too different.

Unlike Charlotte, however, whose innocence of history and politics is a function of her need to sustain the faith in progress instilled by her upbringing, Grace remains an attentive, self-styled "student of delusion" and, significantly, a woman in "putative control" of the Republic of Boca Grande. *A Book of Common Prayer* opens with a striking opposition between the undiscriminating *norteamericana* and this shrewd, perceptive observer of her fatal sojourn. Grace knows, as Charlotte never learns, that the conspiratorial politics of this closed frontier merely mask through their unceasing activity the real absence of change or purpose in the frustrated lives of its ruling family. Politics here are arbitrary "games," indices of entrapment expressed as a confused hatred of blood ties. The *guerrilleros* of the interior are empty theorists. The cynical Strasser-Mendana family in fact finance their insurrections; the victor then quells the revolution and puts his own "marker" in the Ministry of Defense—to be replaced a year later through another violent ouster when the ritual of "transition" is repeated.

The apparent superiority of Grace's understanding of Boca Grande's irresponsible revolutions and misdirected energies is nonetheless threatened by her recognition that the import of Charlotte's involvement with this "place" eludes her methods of definition. Was Charlotte's decision not to leave the country during the October Violence evidence of a deluded optimism or is her story one of passion? Who or what leads her to her fate? The contrast between a life lived "in the now" and one whose predominant strain is elegiac and disillusioned collapses when Grace learns of Charlotte's political murder, for she discovers herself to be no better equipped than the childlike *norteamericana* to confront the pain of grief and irretrievable loss. Even in the retrospective light cast by her own impending death from cancer, Grace must admit that she does not understand the "real points" of Charlotte Douglas' history and death. She is left in the end a solitary writer of a "letter" from Boca Grande, an act of remembering that brings her only the knowledge of the futility of her longing to comprehend the story which haunts her.

If the world of Boca Grande and the lives of the protagonists of *A Book of Common Prayer* are metaphors for the necessary failure of America's dream of frontier expansion, Didion's novel also asserts the dignity of Charlotte Douglas' final acceptance of the frontier's close. The Californian who arrives in Central America has, like the frontier children of *Run River* and the other fiction, erred in abdicating her primal responsibilities. Her "rambling" husband Warren rebukes the wife and daughter who leave him to die alone (and it is a charge Charlotte knows to be true, even though she never receives the message): *"You were both wrong but it's all the same in the end."* What distinguishes Charlotte's last days and sets her death apart from the accidents of the past is her decision not to leave Boca Grande. When Leonard Douglas tries to convince her of her vulnerability in the imminent revolution, her reply is the undeceived *mea culpa* of a woman who understands the implications of betrayed trusts, her own and others: "I walked away from places all my life and I'm not going to walk away from here." Less than a month later Charlotte is murdered and her body thrown on the lawn of the American Embassy. Grace, whose inability to protect this "child" from harm continues to obsess her, can see only the pointless absurdity of the suffering, yet *Common Prayer* suggests through Grace's narrative, with its disturbed perception of the equivocal nature of evidence, that Charlotte's choice is as well an individual act of courage, a separate peace made with the past.

For Didion, and it is important to recognize this, the writing of fiction itself constitutes a retrospective act involving the choice of a conservative, "démodé" form.[11] Her novels attempt to recover through an act of imaginative tenacity the mythic truth of worlds now lost to us, and she remains fascinated by

landscapes of the mind. In a recent article, Didion returned to the ideas
proposed in the early review of Cheever's fiction: "A place belongs forever
to whoever claims it hardest, remembers it most obsessively, wrenches it
from itself, shapes it, renders it, loves it so radically that he remakes it in
his own image, . . . It is hard to see one of these places claimed by fiction
without a sudden blurring, a slippage, a certain vertiginous occlusion of the
imagined and the real. . . ."[12] This description of the nature of literary possession of a place and time provides an explanatory key to Didion's imagined
territories, not only the California of *Run River, Play It As It Lays,* and *A
Book of Common Prayer* but also the latter's Boca Grande, the fictional
landscape of frontier exile. Fiction, she asserts, assumes as one of its basic
tenets the "irreducible ambiguities"[13] of human experience through time.
Indeed its very form acknowledges the sense in which the remembered past
synthesizes the imagined and the real. The novel is, for that reason, an ideal
medium for her to link the contemporary West with its frontier past. Didion's
fiction transforms the original ideal of pioneer self-determination by staking
another kind of claim on the last frontier her ancestors struggled to own, the
"flat fields" of the Sacramento Valley which her "great-great-grandfather had
found virgin and had planted" (*STB*) after the overland crossing. If the Eldorado
of the 1840's was forfeited as a reality, it is a world which remains accessible
to the imaginative claim of the novel, and Didion has established a place for
herself as the West's contemporary mythographer through her stubborn love
for and memory of its mythic past.

NOTES

[1]Joan Didion, "The Way We Live Now," rev. of *The Wapshot Scandal,* by John Cheever, *National Review,* 24 March 1964, pp. 237-40.

[2]Joan Didion, rev. of *America America,* by Elia Kazan, *Vogue,* 1 Feb. 1964, p. 64.

[3]John M. Peck, *A New Guide for Emigrants to the West* (Boston: Gould, Kendall, & Lincoln, 1837), n. pag.

[4]Frederick Jackson Turner, *The Frontier in American History* (1920; rpt. New York: Henry Holt and Co., 1948), pp. 37-38. All further references to this work appear in the text. See also the evaluation of Turner's contribution to American historiography in Richard Hofstadter, *The Progressive Historians* (New York: Alfred A. Knopf, Inc., 1968). I am grateful to E.D. Craven for her generous assistance in formulating the connections be-tween Didion's fiction and historical theories of the frontier experience.

[5]Kevin Starr, *Americans and the California Dream: 1850-1915* (New York: Oxford Univ. Press, 1973), p. 126.

[6]Didion, "The Way We Live Now," p. 238.

[7]Starr, p. 39.

[8]Joan Didion, "When Did Music Come This Way? Children, Dear, Was It Yesterday?" *Denver Quarterly,* 1, no. 4 (1967), 54-62.

[9]Joan Didion, "The Diamond Lane Slowdown," *Esquire*, Aug. 1976, pp. 35-37.

[10]Joan Didion, "Thinking About Western Thinking," *Esquire*, Feb. 1976, p. 10.

[11]Joan Didion, "Questions About the New Fiction," *National Review,* 30 Nov. 1965, pp. 1100-1102.

[12]Joan Didion, "Good-bye, gentleman-ranker," rev. of James Jones, *Esquire,* Oct. 1977, p. 50.

[13]Joan Didion, "The Women's Movement," *New York Times Book Review*, 30 July 1972, p. 2.

The Limits of History
in the Novels of Joan Didion
Thomas Mallon

JOAN DIDION'S ADMITTED "predilection for the extreme" (*STB*) and the gothic trappings of her imagination (rattlesnakes and the Donner Party are perhaps more referred to in her writings than any other phenomena) have helped win her books a good deal of popular attention in the last decade. Her ironic and ethical sharpness, as well as the severity of her prose, have gained critical respect. Didion is, it usually goes, among the best recorders of the beautiful and bizarre life of present-day California. Didion's ancestors went West during the pioneer migrations of the mid-nineteenth century, so she is a Californian with a well-developed sense of history. She has written that "time past is not believed to have any bearing upon time present or future, out in the golden land where every day the world is born anew" (*STB*). She does not want to believe this, and her preoccupation with the past in her novels—the individual pasts of her characters, the pasts of her region and the nation—makes her an unusual observer of her own place and time. To a certain extent she is, like Gràce Strasser-Mendana, the narrator of *A Book of Common Prayer*, " '*de afuera*,' an outsider."

In *Play It As It Lays*, Maria Wyeth admits to having "trouble with *as it was*." All of Didion's heroines have trouble with history, personal and otherwise, and each of her novels is an attempt at travelling backwards in search of various historical explanations. It is a tentative operation—she only grudgingly appreciates "all the opiates of the people, whether they are as accessible as alcohol and heroin and promiscuity or as hard to come by as faith in God or History" (*STB*). A willingness to seek explanation in the past, and to invite disappointment, is the impetus of each of her novels, as well as the basis for their narrative structures. All three books open immediately after a disaster— Everett's murder of Ryder Channing and his subsequent suicide in *Run River*; Maria's breakdown and hospitalization in *Play It As It Lays*; Charlotte Douglas' death in a Central American revolution in *A Book of Common Prayer*—and then take the reader backwards in time to show him what triggered the catastrophe. The effect of the technique is not only to erase immediately any grounds for optimism in the reader—he knows that the book can only take him back to the bad end he has already glimpsed—but to prepare him for an historical test: is the view of the past he is about to get sufficient explanation of the disaster he has already witnessed? This question is one that Didion repeatedly asks of history in these books. Her faith in her own exploration and method is much tried and ultimately very limited, but her looking backwards remains compulsive.

The heroines of all three novels share an unusual number of similarities. Physically, each has what is called for Lily Knight McClellan in *Run River* a "compelling fragility" or for Charlotte an "extreme and volatile thinness." An inability to cope with the day-to-day, a dreaminess, forms a large part of their sexual attraction. Charlotte's career at Berkeley, like Lily's, is uneventful: "she had read mainly the Brontes and *Vogue*, bought a loom, gone home to Hollister on weekends and slept a great deal during the week. In those two years she had entered the main library once." Charlotte settles problems by ignoring them or lying to herself; as Grace tells us, "She dreamed her life." Maria comes to feel "that her life had been a single sexual encounter, one dreamed fuck, no beginnings or endings, no point beyond itself."

The sexual realm is for each heroine completely removed from the daily world in which they achieve communication with such awkwardness and difficulty. For Lily, "things said out loud had . . . an aura of danger so volatile that it could be controlled only in that dark province inhabited by those who share beds." Maria, according to her husband, Carter, "has difficulty talking to people with whom she is not sleeping." As for Charlotte, "So dark and febrile and outside the range of the normal did all aspects" of the sexual contract seem to her that she was "incapable of walking normally across a room in the presence of two men with whom she had slept."

Even though each of these heroines has extraordinary resources in an emergency, even a kind of violent energy—Lily saves her bleeding son's life; Maria steals a car to escape from an intolerable sexual encounter; Charlotte performs an emergency tracheotomy at the dinner table—they cannot organize and sustain such energy into successful conduct of the lives they find themselves in. What Everett McClellan says about his wife applies to Maria and Charlotte as well: Lily was "peculiarly tuned for emergency. What eluded her was the day-to-day action." Instead of rational and routine action, each relies on the vague and shaky hope that there will always be "some way to make it all right, make everyone happy." They are almost unsure that their existences are real. Lily, for example, feels that "her entire life with Everett was an improvisation dependent upon cues she might one day fail to hear, characterizations she might at any time forget"; during a climactic conversation with Carter, Maria must remind herself that "Something real was happening: this was, as it were, her life"; as a child, we are told, Charlotte prayed "that 'it' turn out all right, 'it' being unspecified and all-inclusive, and she had

been an adult for some years before the possibility occurred to her that 'it'
might not."

Such delicate faith breaks down for all three. They each reach a point,
difficult to locate, where, as Didion once wrote of her own early career, "the
heroine is no longer as optimistic as she once was" (*STB*). The behavior
(particularly the sexual behavior) of each becomes more random and desperate.
They become less able than ever to do anything practical towards making "it"
come out right, and, particularly with Maria and Charlotte, veer toward breakdown. The "reserve of hysteria" (*Run River*) in each is called up. Maria tries
to fight off wave after "wave of the dread" by driving the freeways; Charlotte
plants herself with no logical reason in a mean and obscure country on the
verge of a revolution. Each attempts a hopelessly difficult commitment to
another as a way of again finding the road to where "it" is all right: Lily to
Ryder Channing, the seedy ex-suitor of her sister-in-law, a suicide; Maria to
Kate, her brain-damaged child; Charlotte first to her sardonic, dying ex-husband, Warren Bogart, and then to her daughter, a terrorist being pursued by
the FBI. None recovers her optimism, her faith in "it." Lily ends up cradling
the body of her husband after he has shot himself; Maria writing a notebook
at the request of the hospital psychiatrist; and Charlotte lying dead, murdered
by one or the other side during the revolution in Boca Grande, on the lawn
of the American Embassy.

To a large extent, the vague "optimism" these women initially possess is
based on ignorance and evasion of their own pasts. Only when the diffusion
of their security and good faith begins do they apprehend their own histories,
obtain a sense of where they come from and what they are; the more sharply
that new sense of history focuses itself, the more each realizes how irrecov-
erable the past is. In turn, that realization, having come too late, adds to their
despair and accelerates their decline. A number of Didion's essays have been
concerned with the idea of "home," which, after all, is the most vivid part
of anyone's personal history. Her observations in those pieces provide a kind
of thematic key to her novels insofar as the three books concern themselves
with their characters' lost pasts. She has written of herself as having been
"born into the last generation to carry the burden of 'home,' to find in family
life the source of all tension and drama" (*STB*). She knows that anyone of
her generation—and her heroines are all roughly of it—travels at one's peril
any real distance from home and the past; for herself, she knew that her early
attraction for New York "would cost something sooner or later—because I
did not belong there, did not come from there" (*STB*). Finally, she has expressed her belief that "we are well advised to keep on nodding terms with
the people we used to be, whether we find them attractive company or not.

Otherwise they turn up unannounced and surprise us, come hammering on the mind's door at 4 A.M. of a bad night and demand to know who deserted them, who betrayed them, who is going to make amends" (*STB*).

The past comes calling in each of the novels. Its arrival is least shocking for Lily, whose marriage to Everett McClellan has moved her the shortest distance from it—geographically and otherwise. She recognizes its force when things begin to go wrong: "She wanted now only to see her father, to go back to that country in time where no one made mistakes." The past brings her an increasing sense of helplessness; she and Everett and Ryder Channing seem "afflicted with memory." Each incident and encounter on the river in the last two decades is realized to have led to the shot Everett fires at Ryder: "she could hear it still, crackling reflexively through all the years before." Lily makes a surrender to history—personal, family, and local; such strict determinism becomes the excuse for drift and quietism. History consumes her thoughts. When she considers the reasons for her sister-in-law's suicide, she comes on "the pattern there all along, worked through it all as subtly and delicately as, in a drawing she had loved as a child, the tiger's face had been worked into the treetops. Once you had seen the tiger's face, you could never again see the treetops."

The past catches Maria in an even more virulent way; she begins to see not tigers' heads, but rattlesnakes—which prove equally implacable. The year her mother died she "had not been able to eat . . . because every time she looked at food the food would seem to arrange itself in ominous coils. She had known that there was no rattlesnake on her plate but once the image had seized her there was no eating the food." The past is discovered—as it is in each novel—too late for it to be of any use; it becomes simply an added form of devastation. Maria has no sense of her mother or of her own childhood until her mother dies, just as Lily has no sense of her father until he is dead, and Charlotte no sense of her actual relations to her first husband and child until Warren is dying and Marin is wanted in connection with murder. The past comes back merely as a taunt—it may explain things, but it gives no peace or guidance for the future; as Maria says, "it leads nowhere." She ends up anesthetizing herself, determined only to "watch a hummingbird, throw the I Ching but never read the coins, keep my mind in the now." She occasionally fantasizes about living in a seashore house where "there were only three people and none of them had histories."

Until catastrophe strikes, Charlotte is "immaculate of history, innocent of politics"; until her daughter disappears with the terrorists, she arranges her days to avoid "*the backward glance*." Grace tells us that she has never known "anyone who led quite so unexamined a life." Only when Charlotte is in the safe-deposit vault of the Wells-Fargo Bank after her daughter has disappeared (and the family business manager is explaining to her that she ought to have Marin declared legally dead so that she will not have to forfeit quarterly stock dividends of $807 from certificates on which Marin's name appears as joint tenant) does she understand that her own mother and father have actually died: "People did die. People were loose in the world and left it, and she had been too busy to notice." Again, the knowledge comes too late to bring anything but pain. The careless habits of a lifetime cannot be overcome. Charlotte continues to subject her own history to "revisions and erasures"; even after her flight has begun, she finds it easier to let the newspapers explain her life than to trust her own understanding of it:

> In the coffee shop of a Holiday Inn outside New Orleans one morning in May or June Charlotte read another Associated Press story in which Leonard was again quoted as saying that Charlotte was "travelling with friends." This time Charlotte read the story several times and memorized the phrase. It occurred to her that possibly she had misunderstood the situation. Possibly Leonard and Warren and the Associated Press were right.... Soothed by this construction Charlotte had another cup of coffee and worked the crossword in the *Picayune*.

As Grace records: "When I think of Charlotte Douglas apprehending death at the age of thirty-nine in the safe-deposit vault of a bank in San Francisco it occurs to me that there was some advantage in having a mother who died when I was eight, a father who died when I was ten, before I was busy." So overdue is Charlotte's sense of history, and, partly as a result, so premature is her death, that Grace tries to pay off, once and for all, Charlotte's debt to the past: "I will be her witness" is the opening sentence of *A Book of Common Prayer*.

Each of the heroines loses what Maria calls "the point." Each has a confrontation with the past made inevitable because, in a sense, she no longer has any future, certainly none that is linear or logical. All three novels make the attempt to connect the loss of the point, the arrival at a spot where personal history can only fall back on itself, with the fate of the nation—more specifically, the history and destiny of the American West. Didion has attributed John Wayne's appeal to his ability to absorb "the inarticulate longings of a nation wondering at just what pass the trail had been lost" (*STB*)—the point, as it were. The hippies she met in San Francisco in 1967, the first generation no longer to carry the burden of home, were "less in rebellion against the society than ignorant of it": "At some point between 1945 and 1967 we had somehow neglected to tell these children the rules of the game we happened to be playing. Maybe we had stopped believing in the rules ourselves, maybe we were having a failure of nerve about the game" (*STB*). Didion's essay on the Sacramento Valley (*STB*) is filled with a nostalgia that is less personal than broadly historical. She has lived with a sadness at the loss of frontier strength; her childhood "was suffused with the conviction that we had long outlived our finest hour." Around 1950 Sacramento "lost, for better or worse, its character." For worse, actually, because "character" here means not only the place's look or feel, but its moral strength. The history of the area is now just a useless rebuke; the "Valley fate . . . is to be paralyzed by a past no longer relevant."

Didion's concern is with what happens when one breaks down on the evolutionary road between Mrs. Minnie S. Brooks and Mrs. Lou Fox—each the subject of a single jotting in the notebook she keeps:

> In the basement museum of the Inyo County Courthouse in Independence, California, sign pinned to a mandarin coat: "This MANDARIN COAT was often worn by Mrs. Minnie S. Brooks when giving lectures on her TEAPOT COLLECTION."

> Redhead getting out of car in front of Beverly Wilshire Hotel, chinchilla stole, Vuitton bags with tags reading:
> MRS LOU FOX
> HOTEL SAHARA
> VEGAS

Mrs. Brooks's collection reminds Didion of "the souvenirs my Aunt Mercy Farnsworth brought back from the Orient. . . . Might not Mrs. Minnie S. Brooks help me to remember what I am? Might not Mrs. Lou Fox help me to remember what I am not?" (*STB*)

In *Run River*, Lily realizes, as her husband is dying of a self-inflicted gunshot wound, that the history of her own family and of Everett's is the history of the frontier. Their lives have run out, lost the point, because the frontier has run out:

> they carried the same blood, come down through twelve generations. . . . They had been a particular kind of people, their particular virtues called up by a particular situation, their particular flaws waiting there through all those years, unperceived, unsuspected. . . . It had been above all a history of accidents: of moving on and of accidents. What is it you want, she had asked Everett tonight. It was a question she might have asked them all.

The town of Silver Wells, Nevada, where Maria grew up, is now a missile range. Even when it existed, it was a kind of illusion, kept pumped up by the pipe dreams of her father and his friend, Benny Austin, but it is recalled by Maria with a kind of puzzled reverence. Even when she is convinced of "the answer"—"nothing"—she remains "*Harry and Francine Wyeth's daughter and Benny Austin's godchild. For all I know they knew the answer too, and pretended they didn't. You call it as you see it, and stay in the action.*" The implication is that we now lack the strength to pretend, or only arrive at it, as Maria does, after breakdown and nightmare. Maria's husband's producer, BZ, and Lily's husband, Everett, both get the answer in some form and then kill themselves.

Charlotte, too, finds herself at the attenuated end of the frontier. She grew up on a ranch in Hollister, California, and as "a child of the western United States . . . had been provided . . . with faith in the value of certain frontiers on which her family had lived, in the virtues of cleared and irrigated land, of high-yield crops, of thrift, industry and the judicial system, of progress and education, and in the generally upward spiral of history. She was a *norteamericana.*" After she "apprehends" the past in the bank vault, she goes to see her brother, who senses the importance of the ranch to himself and his sister, even though he believes it is "No good remembering," and does not want it sold. It is now a suburbanized place with too many telephones—Charlotte has understood its significance too late; it might as well be, like Silver Wells, part of a missile range—there is no going back to it.

The women in these novels have remnants of a conservative personal morality, enough to make Maria "sick of everybody's sick arrangements" or to make Grace find an American flag for Charlotte's coffin (the only one she can find is one stencilled on a T-shirt), even though there "were no real points in that either." They no longer have a connected ethical code; its remains can only be called upon fitfully, confusedly. Even though Grace knows that "it is never enough to be right . . . it is necessary to be better," a lesson of her own upbringing in Colorado, she chooses to stay in spectacularly corrupt Boca Grande—because, she tells us, she likes the way the light falls. Ethical coherence, the "point" of having a code and the ability to live it with consistency, has vanished for the characters and the country, somewhere between the worlds of Mrs. Minnie S. Brooks and Mrs. Lou Fox.

The last sentence of *A Book of Common Prayer*, "I have not been the witness I wanted to be," is Grace's admission of the limits of historical explanation and of her surprise at discovering them so severe. Where, as Maria asks, *does* the point lead? Not in a spiral upward or downward; despite the quotations from Toynbee and Yeats in her essay on the hippies, Didion adheres to no historical schema. Her mind, a frontier mind, is distrustful of the general and the abstract. As she has written, it "veers inflexibly toward the particular"

(*STB*). The writer knows, and her characters become aware of, the influence and disturbing impact of history, but application of its "lessons" remains problematic. In a world where there is "not as much sedation as . . . instantaneous peril," Maria and, to some extent, her creator are forced to remain less "*engaged by the problems of what you might call our day*" than "*by the particular.*" History is limited perhaps most of all by the harsh pull of the specific, the phenomenal.

At the beginning of the story she tells, Grace does not doubt the necessity of her act of witness, but she approaches the task of historical explanation with skepticism, even distaste. A biochemist who abandoned anthropology after she "stopped believing that observable activity defined anthropos," a woman who uses the word "tragic" not "easily or with any great approval," she stays in Boca Grande not only because she likes the light, but because that land is so resistant to historical explanation that she can avoid it almost entirely: "Every time the sun falls on a day in Boca Grande that day appears to vanish from local memory, to be reinvented if necessary but never recalled." For Charlotte she feels, in the absence of "the molecular structure of the protein which defined Charlotte Douglas," the need for history. She is baffled and hurt (more than she explicitly admits) by her search for the determining force behind the story. Perhaps Charlotte engages her, as Gatsby engaged Nick Carraway or Lord Jim engaged Marlow, by a pull that is ultimately more emotional than analytical. Still, the possibility that the story can be unlocked by an historical key pushes her onward in her narrative even as she herself is dying of cancer: "Maybe there is no motive role in this narrative. Maybe it is just something that happened. Then why is it in my mind when nothing else is."

By the end of her story, however, she recognizes more than ever "the equivocal nature of even the most empirical evidence." So strong is that sense that she speculates that she is "more like Charlotte than I thought I was" and is "less and less certain that this story has been one of delusion. Unless the delusion was mine." As a most startling admission of history's limits, her view is shared, in a way, by each of these books which make so strong a point of the inescapable trauma of apprehending the past: the heroine's version of the world may be the true one after all. Lily's belief that it is a matter of "accidents," Maria's final "Why not?" in answer to BZ's "Why?" and Charlotte's calm awaiting of a death she need not suffer impress themselves on the reader, stay with him, as much as any "historical" explanation he has received from the novels. The particular distinction of these novels lies in the way they not only insistently face the idea and importance of history, but also present such full and sympathetic portraits of women who have ranged outside its orbit.

Narrative Technique and the Theme of Historical Continuity in the Novels of Joan Didion

Leonard Wilcox

DIDION SHARES WITH Nathanael West a fascination with California as the dead end of the American dream. Didion's California, however, is essentially different from West's. His bizarre and volatile landscape of "Mexican ranch houses, Samoan huts, Japanese temples, Swiss Chalets, Tudor cottages and every possible combination of these styles," against which "only dynamite would be of any use," becomes in Didion's fictional world an undifferentiated terrain of Ralph's Markets, Carolina Pines hotels, Taco Bells and forty-foot neon Thriftimart T's—a landscape of bleached lostness baked by the dead white blankness of a vacant sunlight, scorched by hot Santa Ana winds. There is no dynamite in Didion's world: the potential for explosion that characterized West's California is replaced by a propensity toward implosion, the dream of an obscene millennium replaced by a vacuous posthistorical world in which "time past is not believed to have any bearing on time present or future" (*STB*).

One of the most significant factors that differentiates West's and Didion's California is their respective historical imaginations. West's historical imagination is apocalyptic, and the "itch for apocalypse" that characterizes his California in part reflects the ambience of the thirties: Didion's historical imagination is postapocalyptic, emerging from the climate of the seventies. West's central image of history approaching some violent catharsis on the western shores of America grows in part out of a radical political sensibility; Didion's concern with a hiatus between the "then" and "now," and her pivotal image of history collapsing into a blank "quintessential intersection of nothing" grows out of a conservative preoccupation with the loss of "generational, cultural, and historical continuity."[1]

Didion's concern with history, as well as her preoccupation with the loss of an intact historical world, is part of her experience as a fifth-generation Californian. Her ancestors, destined to pursue the dream of an El Dorado further west, made the 1846-47 crossing part way with the Donner-Reed party, separating from them before their tragic end. If they did not find the elusive El Dorado in the Sacramento Valley, Didion's ancestors did the next best thing, creating its secular version in the form of a luxuriant farmland which in its "type and diversity" of agricultural products (Didion was taught as a child) "resembled the holy land" (*STB*). Didion's writings are informed with an awareness of this idyllic and pastoral past, and its tragic loss. The loss of Eden occurred for Didion during the nineteen-forties and fifties when the aerospace machine invaded the agricultural garden and real-estate development began to encroach upon family farmland. Oppressed by the sense of a "kind of functional obsolescence," the established Valley people lapsed into self-doubts, and became "paralyzed by a past no longer relevant." Didion observes that after 1958 Sacramento, burdened by historical knowledge that failed to "add up," stripped of a teleological sense by which to envision a future, "lost its raison d'être" (*STB*).

The simultaneous sense of exile from and paralysis by the past, the breakup of an old order, a loss of a sense of historical coherence—all experiences of the forties and fifties—constitute crucial aspects of the California experience which informs Didion's literary imagination. Another facet of the California experience Didion draws from the sixties. If the world broke in two for Willa Cather in 1922 it did so for Joan Didion around 1967, the year in which she wrote her essays on the "lost children" of Haight Ashbury. For Didion, the counterculture phenomenon is the final symbol of the fall from an intact historical world into a chaos of historical discontinuity. Appropriately, in "Slouching Towards Bethlehem," she describes the San Francisco youth drifting from city to city, "sloughing off the past as snakes shed their skins." The hippie youth are manifestations of a "social hemorrhage." From Didion's conservative perspective they signal a social crisis having to do with the transmission of traditions and values along generational lines: they are "children who grew up cut loose from the web of cousins and great aunts and family doctors and lifelong neighbors who traditionally suggested and enforced society's values."

Obsessed with the past, with cultural obsolescence and historical loss, Didion's novels and essays return to the question of "where the trail has been lost." In her essay on the hippies, Didion, the stern moralizer, suggests that it may have been in the recent past: "At some point between 1945 and 1967 we had somehow neglected to tell these children the rules of the game we happened to be playing." Yet in other essays she suggests that the problem lies deeper, lies perhaps at the heart of the dream of El Dorado, the dream of a world free of time and memory. Didion's relation to the past is profoundly ambivalent. On one level she exhibits a conservative nostalgia for an intact world, a lost past which she sees (with not a little irony) embodied in John Wayne, who "in a world we understood early to be characterized by venality and doubt suggested another world . . . where a man could move free and make his own code" (*STB*). Yet since she shares the syndrome of those at the closed frontier—the tendency to probe and reevaluate the past with disenchanted or perhaps disillusioned eyes—she realizes like Lily in *Run River* that the frontier past "had above all been a history of accidents, of moving on and accidents." The frontier past of California reveals not only accidents however, but grim horrors. Like the past of Hawthorne's Salem, California is blighted by some terrible primal sin; behind the myth of El Dorado lies some horrible historical reality. "The California myth we are talking about resembles Eden; it assumes that those who absent themselves from its blessings have been exiled by some perversity of the heart. Did not the Donner-Reed party, after all, eat its dead to reach Sacramento?" (*STB*). If paradise lies in California, it was obtained by a grotesque parody of the Eucharist. As Jennifer Brady has pointed out, the Donner Party debacle becomes, in Didion's imagination, the antimyth of the golden land in which "the promised land becomes the heart of darkness."[2]

Didion's conservative imagination at any rate seizes upon this secular version of original sin. Didion explains that: "My own childhood was illuminated by the graphic litanies of the grief awaiting those who failed in their loyalties to one another. The Donner-Reed party, starving in the Sierra snows, all that ephemera gone save the one vestigial taboo, the provision that one should not eat his blood kin" (*STB*).The tale of "failed loyalties" becomes the basis of Didion's conservative "wagon-train" ethics which are based on the notion that instinctual loyalties must be preserved, that blood kin must recognize their mutual value for survival. More than this, however, the Donner Party horror becomes another aspect of the California past that takes on metaphoric shape in Didion's literary imagination. The historical example of the Donner Party becomes Didion's deepest image of the flaw endemic in the frontier dream, the legacy of which survives in present-day California. It is her deepest image of the hubris of attempting to escape history, the catastrophic breakdown of the "magnetic chain of humanity" that awaits those who attempt to attain an El Dorado free of time and memory.

Indeed, the specter of the primal crime is ever present in the Didion landscape. Her protagonists, often pursuing an El Dorado of the mind, attempting to repudiate the emotional grip and power of the past, are condemned to repeat the primal sin of blood betrayal and to experience the "grief awaiting those who failed in their loyalties to each other" (*STB*). Having breached these loyalties they find themselves cut off from the primary sources of meaning in their life; attempting to escape the grief of their pasts they find themselves in a desolate existential landscape of a historical, suspended present plagued by a bewildering sense of inner loss. In the pursuit of an El Dorado further west they find themselves stranded not in the Sierra snows but in the blank whiteness of a world without temporal or ethical moorings. In flight from her past, Maria Wyeth drives straight into the "hard white empty core of the world"; Charlotte Douglas flees her past into the "dead white sunlight" of Boca Grande.

In a more general sense, the life of the Didion protagonists resonates with the history of the West. Often these protagonists share the collective sense of cultural obsolescence, often they are troubled by pasts that do not add up. Frequently they reenact the frontier pattern of "cutting clean" from the past (the "cutting clean that was to have redeemed us all," as Lily put it in *Run River*) only to be pursued relentlessly by the nemesis of their personal history. Attempting to "avoid the backward glance," they reach the final borders of self, where, as Thomas Mallon puts it "personal history can only fall back on itself, [and merge] with the fate of the nation—more specifically [with] the history and destiny of the American West."[3]

As Mallon also observes, each of Didion's novels "is an attempt at travelling backwards in search of various historical explanations."[4] To be sure Didion's novels reflect her sense that in the past lies the key to the present. Yet her novels are not only historical probes but statements about the value of historical knowledge, its redemptive capacity in a world of exiles from past and future.

II

If Didion's message is a profoundly conservative one, her technique is quite the reverse: Didion's prose, precise and analytical as it is, is at the same time oblique and diffused, and one has to be constantly on guard for the seemingly offhand or throwaway statement which, on a subsequent rereading, one realizes is an important clue or key to subsequent events. Encountering Didion the novelist for the first time involves the reader in the process of piecing together the chronology of the narrative and the relationships between the central characters. The author holds all the cards, but she deals them in a seemingly random and haphazard manner. In *Play It As It Lays*, for example, the introductory section consists of three character sketches of Maria: one from Maria herself and the other two from Helene, a former friend, and Carter, Maria's former husband. The discrepancies between the sketches—between Maria's bleak detachment, Helene's bitter condemnation and Carter's unfeeling dismissal—raise more questions than they answer. Why, the reader wants to know, does Maria have trouble with "as it was"? Why does she avoid the thought of "dead things and plumbing"?

After the series of provocative first-person disclosures, the novel shifts to the third person and begins the Didionesque journey back into the past. Even here, however, the reader is thrown into a world where antecedent cause and consequent effect seem suspended, a disjointed and temporally fragmented world whose "center is not holding." This is aptly suggested in the description of Maria talking to Carter by telephone explaining her move to a furnished apartment on Fountain Avenue, while watching a television news film of a house about to slide into the Tujunga Wash:

> "I'm not living here, I'm just staying here."
> "I still don't get the joke."
> She kept her eyes on the screen, "Then don't get it," she said at the exact instant the house splintered and fell.

Other aspects of the narrative further suggest this world beyond the boundaries of history. Didion's narrative is characterized by a sparse, economical and almost minimalist approach; narrative sections are so succinct they seem to end before they begin thus reinforcing the sense of temporal collapse.

Didion's inventive use of metaphor enables the reader to make sense of random information and fill in the narrative. Metaphor also reinforces Didion's thematic preoccupation: the poverty of life in a world like Hollywood where ethical coherence has vanished, where life is led without regard to tradition or posterity. Three major metaphors inform the narrative: the crap game, the compulsive freeway driving, and the abortion. All illuminate the condition of living in post-history, yet all reveal something about the trouble with "as it was" both in terms of Maria's life and the life of the nation. The crap game, for example, suggests Maria's predicament—and by extension the California predicament—of living in a world where the past fails to connect rationally to the future, where dreams of new beginnings are played out. She inhabits a world which seems "not to apply" (her home in Silver Wells, Nevada has literally vanished, replaced by a missile range). In a world where "nothing adds up," one "plays it as it lays," Maria concludes, rejecting her American dreaming father's optimistic teleology that "the next roll of the dice will always be better than the one that went out last."

Yet specific reasons in Maria's personal history account for her conclusion that life's events, like the roll of the dice, are utterly random, as well as her related determination to keep her mind "in the now." Her fatalistic yielding to an eternal present is also an evasion of the past as the classic freeway scenes as well as the abortion suggest. Maria's daily runs on the freeway are logical extensions of the idea of refuge in the present implicit in "playing it as it lays." Like the game of craps her freeway driving implies randomness and directionlessness. Each trip is without aim or goal; no one has a relation to another. Initiated each morning at ten with the Corvette and a boiled egg, it is a ritual of eternal renewal, a debased version of the journey west, a parody of the effort to find new passages in a land beyond history. Didion describes the freeway sequences with ironic echoes of a frontier past:

> She drove [the freeway] as a riverman runs a river, everyday more attuned to its currents, its deceptions, and just as a riverman feels the pull of the rapids in the lull between sleeping and waking, so Maria lay at night in the still of Beverly Hills and saw the great signs soar overhead at seventy miles an hour: *Normandie* ¼ Vermont ¾ Hollywood Fwy. 1. Again and again she returned to an intricate stretch just south of the interchange where successful passage from the Hollywood on to the Harbor required a diagonal move across four lanes of traffic.

Here the successful passage becomes not the forging of rapids but a lane change; more to the point, the successful passage is the passage out of the past. "On the freeway," the narrator notes, Maria "never thought about . . . what seemed already to have happened."

When not driving the freeway, Maria finds other means to deny the past. Lying awake at night she tells herself stories: "In the story Maria told herself at three or four in the morning there were only three people and none of them had histories." In the real world, however, she is relentlessly pursued by the past: by the breakup of her marriage to Carter, by the brain damage of her daughter Kate, by her mother in Silver Wells, by the aborted pieces of tissue left in the bedroom in Encino.

The abortion becomes the primary metaphor of amputating present from past, of severing, through "radical surgery," the continuum of personal history. The abortion is the chief source of Maria's problem with "as it was," the source of her accumulated guilt, the cause of her nightmares of hacked pieces of flesh in the plumbing. The abortion is the primary reason Maria's past no longer "adds up"; it is the root of her despair, the most immediate and personal reason for her sense of the collapse of cause and effect. With the abortion she cuts herself adrift from any sense of purpose. Her affair with Les Goodwin, the father of the unborn child, disintegrates because she had "left the point in a bedroom in Encino." The abortion leaves Maria stranded at the dead end of her personal history.

Indeed, the abortion evokes repressed memories of the past. Above all, the Didion protagonist is condemned to repeat the errors and miscalculations of the past, both personal and collective. The abortion calls to mind Didion's image of "cutting clean"—the image associated with the frontier dream; Maria has repeated the frontier nightmare of primal transgression, blood betrayal. In terms of her own past, this profound moral failure triggers memories of another primal betrayal—her failure to be with her mother at death. Immediately after the abortion, nightmares begin, evoking the horror of her mother losing control of the car outside Tonopah and "dying in the desert light, the daughter unavailable in the Eastern dark." This "unavailability" and the abortion are connected in Maria's mind. Moreover, the image of one act of primary betrayal—a failure of the past—becomes inextricably bound to the other—a failure of the future. More than a metaphor of severing personal history, therefore, the abortion implies a hiatus in generational continuity.[5]

Finally, Didion extends the metaphoric significance of abortion. Attempting to shield herself from the past and its accumulated guilts, Maria drives the freeway, involves herself in promiscuity, and finally submits herself to a "second abortion"—a self-inflicted emotional lobotomy, a "cutting clean" from all feeling. Maria explains to Helene that she knew "precisely what BZ was doing" when he took thirty seconal tablets and lay down on the bed beside her to die. "Fuck it, I said to Helene. Fuck it, I said to them all, a radical surgeon of my own life. Never discuss. Cut. In that way I resemble the only man in Los Angeles County who does clean work." Exiled from past and future, Maria is dissociated from the present after this second abortion. The temporal world in total collapse, Maria moves through an eerie world of historical zero gravity where life is "one dreamed fuck, no beginnings and no endings, no point beyond itself." Maria's ontological loss is strikingly suggested as she stares "as if in a trance" into the "heart of whiteness"—the "pervasive vacant sunlight," the "dead still center of the world," the "quintessential intersection of nothing."

The conclusion of the novel returns to the first-person narrative and the vacant present where Maria, in Neuropsychiatric Hospital, "watches the hummingbird." Her only hope of redemption, her plans to "get Kate" seem at once tragic and futile: Kate, like herself, is institutionalized, and the chances of Maria breaking out of her impasse seem bleak. Maria knows "what nothing means," but after such knowledge what forgiveness? Perhaps Didion hints at the way toward salvation when Maria states, almost in passing, that "after everything I remain Harry and Francine Wyeth's daughter and Benny Austin's godchild." Yet Maria continues to watch the hummingbird, idly throwing things into a swimming pool, dreaming of the "old ways" like bottling fruit, a dream that merely emphasizes the inaccessibility of the past. If *Play It As It Lays* is a search for historical knowledge, it is the burden of such knowledge Maria is condemned to live without.

III

Didion's *A Book of Common Prayer* resembles *Play It As It Lays* in many respects, yet it is an even stronger statement of the need for historical knowledge. In many ways Charlotte Douglas resembles Maria Wyeth: like Maria, she is estranged from a past that is "no good remembering," but that she is nevertheless condemned to recall. Her home, a ranch in Hollister, California, now suburbanized with too many telephones, has in effect vanished like Silver Wells—there is no going back. Like Maria, she loses two children, one to "history," and one to "complications." Like Maria, Charlotte Douglas reenacts the frontier pattern of cutting clean and moving on, again with consequent crimes of betrayed family loyalties. Her "blind course" to the Central American country of Boca Grande suggests metaphorically the "terminal" of the westward movement, the necessary failure of the dream of no past and new beginnings.

Didion's imaginary landscape of Boca Grande is in fact the West extended: it assumes the essential traits of California with its postapocalyptic ambience and its collapsed sense of history. As Grace tells Charlotte, "Boca Grande has no history." Revolutions, empty rituals financed by the ruling Strasser-Mendana family as political diversions, ironically sustain the existing political elite. The very idea of historical progress or development, a "teleological view of human settlement," is made ludicrous: roads built into the interior to enable the cultivation of land or the exploitation of mineral resources collapse and rot. A nine-hole golf course, built to attract tourists, reverts to swamp. Temporal events circle back on themselves under the blazing sun of a perpetual noon. The primal transgressions and blood betrayals, the horrors of the Western past, are here played out in an eternal present in the form of power struggles among members of the ruling family. The equatorial sun, "so dead white at noon," captures symbolically the timeless blankness, the historical "white hole" of this new American frontier: "Every time the sun falls on a day in Boca Grande that day appears to vanish from local memory, to be reinvented if necessary, but never recalled."

If Didion's narrative strategy in *Play It As It Lays* might be likened to dealing cards in an almost haphazard manner, the narrative strategy in *A Book of Common Prayer* might be likened to inviting the reader to assemble a jigsaw puzzle in which the composite picture of the protagonist—and the narrator—changes as the author adds new pieces. If the narrative focuses almost exclusively on the past in *Play It As It Lays*, the narrative in *A Book of Common Prayer* treats time in a non-linear fashion, as Grace, the narrator, continually mixes past and present, her situation in the Boca Grande present and Charlotte

Douglas's history. Such an approach to the narrative "jigsaw" reinforces Didion's themes of historical knowledge as well as the growing relationship between the novel's two central characters, Charlotte and Grace.

Thus at the outset Grace Strasser-Mendana first approaches her self-appointed task—to be Charlotte Douglas's "witness"—with a skepticism toward the past. A former anthropologist from Colorado who has abandoned the study of kinship structure and ritual—the study of human culture through time—she has taken up in its stead the objective study of biochemistry, a discipline, she explains, "in which demonstrable answers are commonplace and personality absent." At the beginning of the narrative she presents only the "objective data" about her subject, only the bare empirical narrative outline:

> Here is what happened: she left one man, she left a second man, she traveled again with the first, she let him die alone. She lost one child to 'history' and another to 'complications' (I offer in each instance the evaluation of others), she imagined herself capable of shedding that baggage and came to Boca Grande, a tourist. *Una turista.* So she said. In fact she came here less a tourist than a sojourner but she did not make that distinction.
> She made not enough distinctions.
> She dreamed her life.
> She died, hopeful. In summary. So you know the story.

Nevertheless Grace is drawn to the riddle of Charlotte Douglas's life, and to "the meaning of that sojourn [which] continues to elude me." Beginning in her capacity as a scientist with the most empirical artifacts of Charlotte's life—her passport and visa, her International Vaccination Certificate—Grace is pulled back into the complex nexus of Charlotte's history. Grace begins her story in a categorical tone of the objective scientist; many of her statements are prefaced by "for the record," "in fact," "in point of fact." She insists that as a narrator she plays no "motive role in this narrative, nor would I want to." Yet as the novel progresses this categorical tone gives way to a provisional tone as she discovers the complex history of Charlotte Douglas, a personal past that suggests "the equivocal nature of even the most empirical evidence." Moreover, her claim that she tells us who she is to "legitimize her voice," that "in no other sense does it matter who 'I' am," is undercut as she discovers the telling of Charlotte Douglas's story is coextensively a journey into her own past.

As Grace pieces together and recounts Charlotte's past she is forced to admit that "I am more like Charlotte Douglas than I thought I was." She finds she shares with Charlotte a "lost child"—lost if not to "history" to political corruption and indolence. Discovering some pages that Charlotte typed before her death, Grace reads the "commonplaces of the female obsessional life," concluding that "we all have the same dreams." And if Grace and Charlotte share in common dreams so do they in a common fate. Early in the narrative, Grace mentions "the smell of danger" in the house in conjunction with Charlotte's death. Such a juxtaposition suggests that in telling the story of Charlotte's passion and death Grace must come to terms with her own terminal illness and reevaluate her past life. For Grace, like Charlotte, a "pure product" of Western America, comes to recognize her own tendency to evade and deny the past, her similar propensity to remain wilfully ignorant of history and innocent of politics.

The conservative moral core of Didion's work again has to do with the consequences of breaking human bonds and severing the tissue of generational continuity. Again Didion's preoccupation with the primal transgression is the central issue. Charlotte Douglas, the Californian who has arrived in Boca Grande "avoiding the backward glance," has, like Maria Wyeth, abdicated some primal obligations, severed a blood link. And again narrative technique reinforces the idea. In this case the reiteration of certain phrases, which take on the quality of a liturgical chant (lending significance to the book's title), emphasizes the moral gravity of these lapsed obligations. Charlotte's "Marin and I are inseparable," for example, appears toward the end of the first section and later in a variety of contexts. Initially a statement apparently meant to be taken at face value, it later becomes clear as Grace assembles more data that the statement is delusionary, a protective deception arising out of the pain of a severed relationship between mother and daughter. Later, Warren's "tell Charlotte she was wrong," as well as Warren and Charlotte's "Tell Marin she was wrong," refer to the taboo of blood betrayal and the associated abandonment of a loved one at death. Because she is in flight from the past, Charlotte fails to be with her ex-husband Warren Bogart at the time of his death, and this crime is repeated by Charlotte and Warren's daughter Marin, who, wiping the slate of personal history and becoming a revolutionary, also abandons Bogart at his death. Having severed her past and her blood links, Charlotte, like Maria, faces the blankness of the tabula rasa world of Boca Grande.

What distinguishes Charlotte Douglas from Maria Wyeth is her final acceptance of her past and its moral failures. Her statement "tell Marin she was wrong," indicates her realization of her own similar moral failure. What further distinguishes her is her decision to stay in Boca Grande. Having arrived with a typically American teleological optimism, seeing the "green light" of possibility in the equatorial landscape, Charlotte realizes frontiers are closed; she can no longer run from the past. Having exhibited a self-deluding romanticism, she now takes a grim existential stand. Her decision to stay is "absurd" ("you have to pick the places you don't walk away from," Leonard admonishes her), yet it is "absurd" in the existential sense, a positive act of defiance and courage. Moreover, it implies an individual act of accepting the past, a reconciliation with personal history: "I walked away from places all my life and I'm not going to walk away from here." Thus, if Maria succumbs to the still point of madness outside history, Charlotte accepts her history and thereby gains self-knowledge in her last stand in Boca Grande.

Confronting death, Grace, like Charlotte, must accept her own past and her self-deception about it. Perhaps the single incident which forces her to recognize her own "innocence" about the past is Grace's discovery of the emerald ring, the ring given to Leonard by a man in Bogota, the "man who financed the revolutionary Tupamaros." Leonard identifies this man as Grace's deceased husband Edgar. Grace is thus forced to relinquish her guise as an objective scientific observer, forced to recognize she is hopelessly entangled in the events she is recording and in the histories of the characters she is relating. She can no longer claim to have "no motive role in this narrative," no longer insist that it does not "matter who 'I' am": Grace's narrative is one of self-discovery. Such discovery leads her to recognize the characteristics she shares with Charlotte, the Western *Norteamericana* tendency to make "revisions and erasures," and the discovery also suggests Grace's own capacity for self-deception about the past: "I am less and less certain this story has been one of delusion. Unless the delusion was mine."

Moreover, the discovery of the emerald ring suggests Didion's larger theme of the "commonality" of human life and human history, the notion that to live in history is to live as functioning interdependent organs of the world's body. Didion juxtaposes this concept against the futile dream, shared by Grace and Charlotte, of living in a tabula rasa world, innocent of history. Her novel is nothing if not a complex meshwork, a tissue of interlocking history and destiny. The emerald ring serves as a focal point of this "meshwork." The ring binds characters together in power and political corruption (Leonard, the radical chic lawyer and gun-runner, and Edgar, plantation-owner and founder of diversionary uprisings). It also binds them in death: if Leonard obtained the ring he gives to Charlotte from Edgar in payment for guns for the Tupamaros, it is such revolutionaries, using Leonard's hardware, that ultimately kill Charlotte. Leonard is thus implicated in Charlotte's death, and the ring suggests the fatal bond. Finally, the ring suggests the interconnection of the lives of the women in the novel. When Charlotte is arrested during the revolution she mails the ring to Grace along with Marin's address. After Charlotte's death Grace attempts to return the ring to Marin, realizing now that she and Marin are bound together through Charlotte in common histories and a kind of generational nexus, that she and Marin are (in Charlotte's words) truly "inseparable."

In another sense, the theme of the "commonality" of human history is implied in the very process of the narrator's reconstruction of Charlotte Douglas's history. From this reconstructive process Grace learns not only about her own past and its link through Charlotte to a "common" American culture, but about the "common" nature of historical knowledge. Grace pieces together Charlotte's past from accounts by Victor, Gerardo, Leonard, from second- and third-hand sources, some of which she would rather "not know about." Thus Grace's probe of the past is tentative, provisional, hypothetical, but above all a collective activity. At the conclusion of her narrative, therefore, Grace admits she has not been the solitary or scientific "witness" she wanted to be:

> I am told, and so she said.
> I heard later.
> According to the passport. It was recorded.
> Apparently.
> I have not been the witness I wanted to be.

In a sense the quest to solve the riddle of Charlotte Douglas's history fails; Grace admits at the conclusion she retains her interest in the past but understands it no better. History remains inexplicable, ironic and full of "contrived corridors." Nevertheless if Grace, the narrator, remains puzzled by the riddle of history, the novel itself suggests that historical knowledge cannot be dismissed or ignored, for it provides the fundamental source of human meaning—the assertion of the continuity of life through time. Perhaps this realization brings Grace back from the blank heart of Central America, in a return journey reminiscent of that in Conrad's *Heart of Darkness*, in an attempt to convey to Marin, the middle-class revolutionary, something of the vital connection between generations. Yet Marin, whose understanding of her mother's life is formulated in terms of "class analysis," is unreceptive. Like the "beloved" in Conrad's novel, Marin would fail to comprehend Grace's message even if delivered. "Marin had no interest in the past," recounts Grace. "I do."

Grace's interest in the past is also Didion's. Both *Play It As It Lays* and *A Book of Common Prayer* seek explanations in personal history; both link the personal past with the collective history of the nation. Both have "conservative" messages insofar as they show the ravages of a failed sense of ethical coherence and generational continuity; both imply the redemptive capacity of historical knowledge for a world where the past is devalued and the future difficult to envision. In Didion's world neither the avoidance of the past nor a straightforward empirical understanding of the facts of history are enough to redeem the present. What is implicit in her often disjointed and oblique narratives is the absolute necessity for the individual, whether reader, "witness" or "analysand," to experience the process of reconstruction of the past in order to understand and learn from it. The reader is forced to go through the same process of reconstruction as, for example, Grace Strasser-Mendana does as narrator or "witness" in *A Book of Common Prayer*. The disjointed narrative conveys both the sense of being cast adrift from any fixed point of reference in the past and, by the end of the novel, the importance of being able to piece these fragments together—not only in terms of the world of the novel, but in the wider implications that the narrative has for recent American history.

NOTES

[1]Jennifer Brady investigates aspects of this loss of historical continuity, particularly with regard to the history of the West in "Points West, Then and Now: The Fiction of Joan Didion," *Contemporary Literature,* 20, 4 (1979), pp. 452–470. I am indebted to Brady's article for insights regarding the Western historical dimension in Didion's fiction.

[2]Brady, p. 452.

[3]Thomas Mallon, "The Limits of History in the Novels of Joan Didion," *Critique*, 21, 3 (1980), p. 48.

[4]Mallon, p. 43.

[5]I am indebted to Sally Harlan's excellent discussion of the significance of abortion in *Play It As It Lays* in her M.A. Thesis "The Lost Children of Joan Didion; A Reassessment of the New Sensibility" (University of Canterbury, 1978), pp. 43–44.

The Didion Sensibility:
An Analysis
Ellen G. Friedman

AN INSISTENT, DISTURBING yet elusive sensibility directs Joan Didion's essays and fiction. Her sensibility has been described in condemning terms—self-indulgent, neurasthenic, and immoral—and in more instructive, analytical terms—elegiac, anti-romantic, Existential after Sartre and Camus, Existential after Kierkegaard, nihilistic, and mythic. However, whether we approve of it or not, this sensibility compels our attention. We recognize our world in it, and for many, it is a recognition that illuminates and clarifies.

Didion's sensibility has provoked several critics into ad hominem attacks, and although these attacks are finally silly, she and her protagonists do have eccentric allegiances. In such an attack, Barbara Grizzuti Harrison condemns Didion for buying at I. Magnin in Beverly Hills the dress that Linda Kasabian wore at the Manson trial.[1] Somewhat less damning from this point of view is Didion's attraction to the seemingly trivial, to John Wayne and the Royal Hawaiian Hotel, or her adulation of orchid grower Amado Vazquez. Idiosyncratic defines her regard for the Hoover Dam and the likes of Michael Laski, General Secretary of the Central Committee of the United States Communist Party, and her fascination with Alcatraz, the "rock of ages," and the opulent Getty mansion. *Run River*'s heroine, Lily Knight McClellan, with whom we are meant to sympathize and do, takes as her lover a man who is blamed for the suicide of her husband's sister, who is an anathema to her husband, and whom she does not love. For those who condemn it, the Didion sensibility seems idiosyncratic, eccentric, or trivializing—perhaps because it is unfamiliar. Its morality is delicate; it is suspicious of universality—though Didion constantly speaks in metaphors.

Like the existentialists, Didion sees no hope for the meaning of existence in the way the world is organized. For her, the world is "atomized." As she puts it in "The White Album," there is no "narrative." There is no God, no dependable system governing the social order. For the existentialists, the "narrative" may be recovered by the individual. Didion, however, has no faith in the authority of individual choice and action. The individual in her view is not endowed with the power to recreate the world, imbue it with meaning, restore coherence and purpose. She shares the existentialists' sense of sickness and dread, but she does not believe in their, or in any, general cure. Indeed, compared with Didion, Camus and Sartre seem foolish optimists.

She is even more severe in some ways—to leap to another sphere—than that apostle of self-pitying and angry hopelessness, Sylvia Plath, who reduced the world to the self and then accused, often justifiably, those who tried to enter that world of being fascists, of being "daddy," of suffocating her being. Didion's heroines, on the other hand, have a less secure sense of self than Plath's personae generally have. The Didion world is in fragments rather than reduced to the isolated self. The Didion heroine generally lacks a well-defined enough sense of self to isolate from the world. She is continually establishing and reestablishing her selfhood in relation to others and to the past. Lily Knight of *Run River* is so "absent" that her dates compare her to a "deaf mute." Even after two children, Lily feels like a "house guest who had stayed too long." Her husband repeatedly compares her to a "refugee." The condition of Grace in *A Book of Common Prayer* is that of *de afuera*, outsider. Maria in *Play It As It Lays* is obsessed by thoughts of her dead parents, but when she meets their best friend, Benny Austin, in a Las Vegas casino, she escapes him as soon as she can. Carter, her husband, tries to find a pattern to Maria's behavior, but can find none.

One should not conclude that Didion's atomized world implies a nihilistic stance. Despite her repudiation of the efficacy of social and ethical systems, her dramatization of the pain that the obsolescence of these systems inflicts, and her conviction, expressed in "On Morality" (*STB*), that moral imperatives are the props of madmen, her works teach a stubborn clinging to life and are suffused with an obsessive nostalgia. It is a nostalgia for a romanticized, idealized past, the past as it should have been with all social and ethical systems in good working order—the past as she knows it never was. "Notes from a Native Daughter" (*STB*) expresses just that doubt about the reality of the remembered past for which she nevertheless yearns: It is "melancholy to realize how much of anyone's memory is no true memory at all but only the traces of someone else's memory, stories handed down on the family network." In a nostalgic mood, Didion makes this wish for her daughter at the end of "On Going Home" (*STB*): "I would like to promise her that she will grow up with a sense of her cousins and of rivers and of her great-grandmother's teacups . . . but we live differently now and I can promise her nothing like that." However, other things Didion says about the past argue that this gentle past is largely legend handed down on the family network.

California history has the value of myth to Didion. It is, though, a myth of loss in which the promise that drove the pioneers resonates in every evidence of its failure. Didion's picture of California, in "Notes from a Native Daughter," is pervaded by a sense of determination "that things had better work here, because here . . . we run out of continent" and by proof that things are not working. The Donner-Reed party is Didion's symbol for the spirit that built and haunts California: "In one respect . . . the California we are talking about . . . resembles Eden: it is assumed that those who absent themselves from its blessings have been banished, exiled by some perversity of heart. Did not the Donner-Reed Party, after all, eat its dead to reach Sacramento?" This statement is deeply ironic. On the one hand, it implies that the survivors must have built Eden to justify such sacrifice. On the other hand, such an act pollutes and dooms the goal for which it is committed. It is a singular, astonishing, and unredeemable history of Eden. This is the history against which Didion measures contemporary California. She describes people and draws characters who have inherited their commitment to the original myth, who are now victims of this myth, and who seem not to remember that the cost of the leap from myth to reality was cannibalism—of one sort or another. The last tale she tells in "Notes from a Native Daughter" presents such a victim:

> A few miles out of [Sacramento] is a place, six or seven thousand acres, which belonged in the beginning to a rancher with one daughter. That daughter went abroad and married a title, and when she brought the title home to live on the ranch, her father built them a vast house—music rooms, conservatories, a ballroom. . . . They are long dead, of course, but their only son, aging and unmarried, still lives on the place. He does not live in the house, for the house is no longer there. Over the years it burned, room by room, wing by wing. Only the chimneys of the great house are still standing, and its heir lives in their shadow, lives by himself on the charred site, in a house trailer.

Whatever else the son's condition may represent, it represents California—its distance from its own dream and its strategies for pretending that the dream is realized.

Didion is obsessed with the Donner-Reed story. Her ancestors travelled with the party, though they left it before the cannibalism took place. In "On Morality," she reports that as a child she was offered the Donner Party story as a cautionary tale that illustrated what happens when people fail "in their loyalties to one another." It recurs in *Run River* in which both the McClellans and the Knights are related to members of the Donner-Reed expedition. As children the main characters of *Run River* play "Donner Party" instead of house. They prophesy the doom they will fulfill as adults. It is an ancestry Didion offers as a cryptic explanation for Martha McClellan's suicide over the betrayal of her carpetbagger lover, Ryder Channing; her brother Everett's murder of this lover when he discovers that his wife, Lily, has arranged a tryst with Ryder; and Everett's subsequent suicide. As Everett is about to commit suicide, he thinks, "Everything seemed to have passed from his reach way back somewhere; he had been loading the gun to shoot the nameless fury which pursued him ten, twenty, a good many years before. All that had happened now was that the wraith had taken a name, and the name was Ryder Channing." Like the Furies who pursue that older house, the house of Atreus, also soiled by cannibalism, Ryder, a modern Fury, pursues the McClellans to their doom. His death sentences Everett—who accepts responsibility for everyone's errors, perhaps including his ancestors'—to suicide. Near the end of the novel, Lily says of all of them, "They seem afflicted with memory."

Not the place promised in the myth of the West, Didion's California is a land known to require of those who wish to possess it, surrender of the last and most tightly held idea about what it means to be human. Despite Didion's nostalgia, her history of California is not, at bottom, elegiac. Rather, this history is an ugly fact, immutable and unredeemable.

Perhaps Kierkegaard's ideas in *Either/Or* concerning the aesthetic and the ethical existences are useful to an understanding of Didion's sensibility, though Kierkegaard's and Didion's visions do not coincide at many points. Kierkegaard proposes that "one either has to live aesthetically or one has to live ethically. In this alternative . . . there is not yet in the strictest sense any question of a choice; for he who lives aesthetically does not choose, and he who after the ethical has manifested itself to him chooses the aesthetical is not living aesthetically, for he is sinning and is subject to ethical determinants even though his life may be described as unethical."[2] Kierkegaard believes that there is an ethical pattern to the universe imposed by God. The individual must awaken and recognize the pattern and then choose to live by it. Once the individual recognizes the existence of this pattern, he is defined in relation to it, whether he defies it or accepts it. However, if he lives aesthetically, he lives in the immediate, without awareness of this larger pattern. He lives, in Didion's terms, as if there is no narrative.

In contrast to Kierkegaard, Didion believes there is no large, coherent, ethical pattern against which to measure all individual choices. Near the end of "On Morality," she argues against moral imperatives: "You see I want to be quite obstinate about insisting that we have no way of knowing . . . what is 'right' and what is 'wrong,' what is 'good' and what is 'evil'." Despite these denials, Didion's sensibility is stubbornly moral. However, one senses the existence of a moral force in Didion the way physicists discover a new elementary particle—by the traces it leaves behind as it disintegrates.

In an intelligent analysis of *Play It As It Lays*, C. Barry Chabot argues that the world of the protagonist, Maria, is driven by Kierkegaard's aesthetic mode—"immediate pleasure seems its sole imperative."[3] Among the many examples of the aesthetic mode's domination of this fiction, Chabot cites Maria's statement, "I try to live in the now and keep my eye on the hummingbird." But this attempt to live aesthetically, in the immediate, fails. Maria retreats, Chabot claims, into "complete indifference" except for obsessive thoughts of her brain-damaged daughter. It is perhaps this exception that colors the world of the book with the ethical, the other Kierkegaardian mode. Maria retires from life lived in the immediate because she is helplessly awake to the ethical, by which she gauges individual action. The loyalty and love for her daughter, who must remain institutionalized, are fed by an ethical sense, as is Maria's revulsion against abortion and her resistance to the fact of her husband's mistress. Unlike the Kierkegaardian existentialist who, having come to a recognition of the ethical, would—if he were to take the next step—choose to define his life in relation to God, Maria winds up in Neuropsychiatric Hospital. Kierkegaard's options are not open to Maria. In her afflicted world, there is no God waiting to be chosen so that he can bestow meaning on her life; Maria cannot choose to organize the universe meaningfully.

Didion has no faith in universal systems. For Kierkegaard, the answer to life's meaning is God. For Maria, on the other hand, the answer is "nothing." In the last words of the book Maria reflects, "One thing in my defense, not that it matters. . . . I know what 'nothing' means, and keep on playing. Why, BZ [a friend who committed suicide in Maria's arms] would say. Why not, I say." Maria's "why not" does not, of course, express a celebratory affirmation of life, but she does choose life and she does refuse the nihilistic option. In "The White Album," Didion tells a story in which a question, similar in meaning to Maria's "why not," is asked. The story is of a Mormon motel manager who asks Didion as she checks out of his motel in Oregon: "If you can't believe you're going to heaven in your own body and on a first-name basis with all the members of your family, then what's the point of dying?" Didion offers this question as a "koan of the period," and the emotional understanding that there is less point to dying than to living provides the logic for much of Didion's fiction and some of her essays.

The Mormon motel manager's question also speaks to Didion's belief in personal relationships and personal loyalties. It is Didion's insistence on the personal rather than the universal that most separates her vision from Kierkegaard's and, more importantly, that accounts for her and her protagonists' idiosyncratic loyalties. The point of living is specific to each individual. It does not necessarily mean living in the immediate, in the aesthetic mode. It means that the only absolute is death. It means that the individual's commitments are determined by personal, inner compulsion and that these commitments are special to each individual. Unable to make sense of Everett's murder of Ryder Channing or of the doomed histories of the Knights and McClellans, Lily concludes: "Maybe the most difficult, most important thing anyone could do for anyone else was to leave him alone; it was perhaps the only gratuitous act, the act of love." Lily leaves Everett on the beach and stays in the house until she hears the second shot, signalling Everett's suicide. It is this philosophy that explains Maria's inaction in *Play It As It Lays* as BZ dies in her arms after taking a bottle of Seconal. In this contracted world, rescue is a violation of love. One bows to individual necessity.

Didion's sensibility navigates between two points: The first is the perception that the world is atomized, and it begins every book she has written. The second is a belief in what she calls "extreme and doomed commitments."
In the "Preface" to *Slouching Towards Bethlehem*, Didion explains that her experience in the Haight-Ashbury district of San Francisco during the sixties "was the first time I had dealt directly and flatly with atomization, the proof that things fall apart." Nearly every essay in the collection attempts to substantiate the perception in this preface. The opening essay, "Some Dreamers of the Golden Dream," speaks of January 11, 1965, a day on which

> A woman in Hollywood staged an all night sit-in on the hood of her car to prevent repossession by a finance company. A seventy-year-old pensioner drove his station wagon at five miles an hour past three Gardena poker parlors and emptied three pistols and a twelve-gauge shotgun through their windows, wounding twenty-nine people. . . . Mrs. Nick Adams said that she was "not surprised" to hear her husband announce his divorce plans on the Les Crane Show, and, farther north, a sixteen-year-old jumped off the Golden Gate Bridge and lived.

The title essay ends with the story of five-year-old Susan, who is in "*High* Kindergarten," along with two of her friends whose parents also give them acid and peyote.
Run River begins with the sentence "Lily heard the shot at seventeen minutes to one," announcing Everett's murder of Ryder, preceding his own suicide, marking the end of an era of Sacramento Valley farming aristocracy. The entire novel is a flashback explaining this final atomization. Lily reads the time, "seventeen minutes to one," on a diamond watch Everett gave her on their seventeenth anniversary, a watch too big for her thin wrist, too ornate to be worn every day, which she nevertheless wears every day, a watch that

is rusted because Lily refuses to take it off even in the shower, a watch that runs infrequently, but which accurately represents the atomizing effect of time on the McClellans.

The stunning, laconic opening of *Play It As It Lays* introduces a character who no longer expects the world to make sense. Maria's voice begins the novel's first paragraph: "What makes Iago evil? Some people ask. I never ask." In the novel's second paragraph, she says, "To look for 'reasons' is beside the point." In the third paragraph we learn that she answered a questionnaire for Neuropsychiatric Hospital, from which she narrates the opening chapter, with "nothing applies."

Similarly, Grace admits on the second page of *A Book of Common Prayer* that knowing the facts does not give one the narrative. She says, "I am an anthropologist who lost faith in her method, who stopped believing that observable activity defined anthropos." Charlotte visits the Boca Grande airport daily though she is neither meeting a flight nor catching one, and she reads *Revista Boca Grande*, written in Spanish, though she cannot read Spanish very well. She visits the airport because that is where a mother would go if her daughter were arriving, and she reads the paper because that is how one passes the time until the flight arrives. But her daughter, Marin, has no intention of coming to Boca Grande. Charlotte invents a narrative in which people are directed by motives of love and loyalty. She attempts to live within this narrative, selectively disregarding the real world, a world broken apart, which neither honors nor recognizes Charlotte's values but moves somewhat by accident and somewhat by deliberate cruelty, as when Antonio and Carmen destroy crates of cholera vaccine.

The White Album's first line reads "We tell ourselves stories in order to live" and it proceeds to argue that stories are impositions on the "shifting phantasmagoria" of actual life. Didion says, "In what would probably be the middle of my life I wanted still to believe in the narrative and in the narrative's intelligibility, but to know that one could change the sense with every cut was to perceive the experience as rather more electrical than ethical." This collection of essays catalogues numerous attempts, benevolent and malevolent, to impose a narrative line on experience. However, the evidence of narrative breakdown is pervasive, personal as well as external: the neurologist who tells Didion that she should "lead a simple life" since she has multiple sclerosis adds "not that it makes any difference." Didion sees it as "another story without a narrative." Linda Kasabian, a member of the Manson tribe who turns state's witness, is an emblem of narrative breakdown, for her dream, Didion discovers when she interviews her in prison, has always been to open "a combination restaurant-boutique and pet shop."

In recording narrative incoherence in *Salvador*, Didion's voice is uncharac-
teristically filled with indignation and anger. The only piece that comes close
to matching her tone here is "Bureaucrats" in *The White Album* concerning
the California Department of Transportation's creation of a "Diamond Lane,"
the purpose of which is to increase the flow of traffic but that instead triples
traffic accidents while slowing traffic flow. *Salvador* is the most clearly polem-
ical of Didion's works. It takes an aggressive moral stand against Salvadorian
terrorism and against United States complicity in this terrorism. However,
what Didion dwells on in Salvadorian political life is the elusiveness of facts.
   In paragraph after paragraph, Didion registers the equivocal nature of facts
in El Salvador. Observe the openings of these several succeeding paragraphs:

> In the absence of information (and the presence often, of disinformation)
> even the most apparently straightforward event takes on, in El Salvador,
> elusive shadows, like a fragment of retrieved legend. . . .
> The crash occurred either near the Honduran border in Marazán or, the
> speculation went, actually in Honduras. There were or were not four people
> aboard the helicopter. . . .
> Questions about what actually happened to (or on, or after the crash of,
> or after the clandestine landing of) this helicopter provided table talk for
> days. . . .
> At one point I asked President Magaña, who had talked to the pilot, what
> had happened. "They don't say. . . ."
> All information was hard to come by in El Salvador. . . . Numbers tended
> to materialize and vanish and rematerialize in a different form. . . .

Although Didion doubts the *meaning* of facts, doubts "narratives," she has
always trusted in the particular, in the reality of facts. Even her understanding
of morality is in specific terms—for instance, her tale of a man who stays
with a corpse so that it will not be violated by coyotes is her illustration of
a "moral" act in an essay that argues against the meaning of "morality" as a
universal ("On Morality"). Thus the inaccessibility and unreliability of facts
in *Salvador* points to a complete breakdown of the individual's relation to
reality. If "what happened" cannot be determined, how much more removed
is the meaning of what happened.
   Didion redeems the nihilism that a vision of an atomized world invites,
allows meaning to penetrate her severe universe, with individual commitments
that give purpose to the life of the person making them. The commitments
are by definition "doomed and extreme" because there is no coherent order
into which they may be absorbed. These commitments do not necessarily
make sense in terms of the larger world; one is only compelled to make them.
As Didion writes, "I . . . appreciate the elaborate systems with which some

people manage to fill the void . . . whether they are as accessible as alcohol and heroin and promiscuity or as hard to come by as faith in God or History." "Comrade Laski, C.P.U.S.A. (M.-L.)," an essay in *Slouching Towards Bethlehem*, concerns a professional Communist Party revolutionary who has made such a commitment: "The world Michael Laski had constructed for himself was one of labyrinthine intricacy and immaculate clarity, a world made meaningful not only by high purpose but by external and internal threats, intrigues . . . an immutably ordered world in which things mattered." Didion writes that she is "comfortable with the Michael Laskis of this world . . . those in whom the sense of dread is so acute that they turn to extreme and doomed commitments. . . ." She speaks again of extreme and doomed commitments in "In the Islands" (*WA*) as she lists the values which she brought into adult life and which now seem irrelevant, but she refuses to surrender her faith in these commitments.

The eccentricity or perversity of some of the loyalties she and her protagonists form spring from this sense of commitment. Lily Knight—who is as selfless in some ways as Milly Theale, though more self-deluded than Milly, whom Didion offers as a model for taking on extreme and doomed commitments—follows a decidedly personal logic in taking Ryder Channing as her lover: "It was apparent that he needed someone, and as she drove out to the ranch she imagined that he needed not someone but her. Whether it was true or not did not much matter: she was already committed." Persisting in staying on in Boca Grande though she can surely expect to die a pointless death in the revolution, Charlotte uses a logic similar to Lily's: "I walked away from places all my life and I'm not going to walk away from here. . . ." The commitment of Amado Vazquez to orchids ("On the Morning After the Sixties," *WA*) is, of course, just as doomed and extreme in its fashion as are Charlotte's and Lily's commitments. Vazquez, who finally establishes his own orchid business, is nearly ruined by a fire.

Didion is interested in the specific, the particular, the personal, the individual because having come of age in the fifties, in the "silent" generation, that is how she experiences the world: "We were silent because the exhilaration of social action seemed to many of us just one more way of escaping the personal, of masking for a while that dread of the meaningless which was man's fate." Didion stops just short of solipsism; her protagonists and the voice of the essays reach out to Other through personal commitments. For the existentialists, commitments have worth in the external world as they are manifested in actions that are recognized by Other; such recognition confirms the existence of the actor. For Didion, the value of and justification for commitments are emphatically internal and personal.

When Didion paints paradise, however, it is solipsistic. Paradise is a self-contained, self-sustaining system in perfect working order, usually free of the burden of meaning. Her admiration for John Wayne rests on the fact that "in a world of ambiguities, he suggested . . . a place where a man could move free, could make his own social code and live by it. . . ." The Hoover Dam is a paradise about which Didion is particularly eloquent: "a dynamo finally free of man, splendid at last in its absolute isolation, transmitting power and releasing water to a world where no one is" ("At the Dam," *WA*).[4] Paradise is life lived according to the halcyon assumptions which maintain the exclusive Royal Hawaiian Hotel or the sumptuous Getty mansion or a place like Alcatraz, a world free of the mainland and sparsely populated. It is a bleak vision of earth that inspires such a vision of paradise.

Didion's work mirrors a melancholy and deprived world, a world that is without joy, suspicious of good works and optimism. As she says of herself, "You are getting a woman who somewhere along the line misplaced whatever slight faith she ever had in the social contract, in the meliorative principle, in the whole grand pattern of human endeavor" ("In the Islands"). Didion's is the most depressing writing I know. It is also among the truest and most brilliant.

NOTES

[1]Barbara Grizzuti Harrison, "Joan Didion: The Courage of Her Afflictions," *The Nation*, 29 September 1979, p. 277.

[2]Søren Kierkegaard, *Either/Or*, trans., Walter Lowrie, II (Princeton: Princeton University Press, 1949), p. 141.

[3]C. Barry Chabot, "Joan Didion's *Play It As It Lays* and the Vacuity of the 'Here and Now'," *Critique: Studies in Modern Fiction*, 21, 3 (1980), p. 55.

[4]Maria, the protagonist of *Play It As It Lays*, shares Didion's sense of the Hoover Dam: "She wanted to stay in the dam, lie on the great pipe itself, but reticence saved her from asking."

Run River: Edenic Vision
and Wasteland Nightmare
Katherine U. Henderson

◆━━━

Run River received only a handful of relatively brief reviews upon its publication in 1963, and neither the reviewers who scorned it nor those who praised
it fully understood the remarkable achievement of Joan Didion's first novel.
A reviewer who at least acknowledged that he did *not* understand much about
the novel was Guy Davenport, who wrote his piece for the *National Review*
in the form of a dialogue between "Reader," who praised Didion's superb
prose and "uncommon grasp of place and character," and "Critic," who found
the book "too even, too smooth," and complained that "all humor, all irony,
have been pared away." Reader insists that the story is a fine one and accuses
Critic of wanting the book "to be what it isn't." But Critic persists in raising
questions, especially the crucial question of the novel's organization: "I don't
fail to recognize the novelist's insights. Nor her power to show us all these
matters of the heart. But what do they mean? The details of a pattern are
organized and organization is a principle. What's that principle?"[1]

Since 1970, when Didion's second novel *Play It As It Lays* was nominated
for a National Book Award, *Run River* has received a modicum of serious
critical attention. Probably the most systematic attempt to deal with the novel's
principle of organization is that of Jennifer Brady, who sees the subject of
the novel as the continuity and contrast between the past and the present of
two old California families, the Knights and the McClellans. Brady asserts
that the novel concerns "a society in transition": the Knights, McClellans,
and their neighbors who in the 40's and 50's are forced by rapid social and
economic change to recognize "the timebound quality of the frontier experiment." Explicating one of the epigraphs to the novel—"the real Eldorado is
still further on," from Peck's 1837 *New Guide to the West*—Brady argues
that the lives of the Knights and the McClellans "dissipate into indecision
and crippling self-doubts when the mantle of Eldorado slips from their grasp
and they have to confront the obsolescence of their old world."[2]

Brady's arguments are persuasive, and she is right in asserting that their
ancestral past has an obsessive and damaging hold on many of the main
characters of *Run River*. But she has read the novel at only one level, as a
period piece, and she ultimately perceives Didion (as, indeed, many critics
do) as a regional author. Many crucial details of the novel are simply not
explained by Brady's thesis. If the novel's central theme is the eroded ideal

of the Western experience, how does one account for its *first* epigraph, from Robert Lowell's "Man and Wife," a poem set on Marlborough Street in Boston? What is the meaning of the Christian prayers spoken by all the major characters at christenings and funerals?

The themes of *Run River* are not primarily regional or narrowly historical; they are deeply moral and universal. They are expressed by the integration of traditional myths with the private history of the novel's characters and the public history of their community and nation. This integration of myth and history, which is the principle of the book's organization, creates a double dimension of time in the novel. While historical time traces a series of tragic circles through the lives of the Knights and the McClellans, mythic time contains and defines the experience of their lives within a second series of larger, transcendent circles. The novel's complex moral statement unfolds as the experience of the characters validates the myths and resides finally in the pattern of concentric circles which ties together the historic and the mythic dimensions of time.

The book's title and two epigraphs prefigure its interweaving of history and myth. The wording of the title was probably suggested by Ecclesiastes 1:7 ("All the rivers run into the sea . . ."), but it also refers to the Sacramento River on whose banks the action of the novel takes place and alludes, finally, to the river that God placed in Eden ("And a river went out of Eden to water the garden" [Genesis 2:10]).[3] The connections among these rivers will obtain in the novel itself. Although the Sacramento River, like the river in Eden, irrigates a fertile and fruitful land, the Sacramento Valley belongs not to paradise, but to the fallen world in which all man's efforts are "vanity and vexation of spirit" when measured against the enduring pattern of nature (Ecclesiastes 2:26). Didion probably intended the reader to recall the entire passage from which the title is taken, verses well known for their evocation of the circular, repetitive pattern of nature:

> One generation passeth away, and another generation cometh; but the earth abideth forever . . . The sun also ariseth, and the sun goeth down, and hasteth to the place where he arose. The wind goeth toward the south, and turneth about unto the north; it whirleth about continually, and the wind returneth again according to his circuits. All the rivers run into the sea; yet the sea is not full; unto the place from whence the rivers come, thither they return again. (1:4-7)

The passage is familiar in American literature as the source of Hemingway's title *The Sun Also Rises*; this connection is doubtless not a coincidence, for the novels share a similar mythic structure.

The river in Eden was a source of luxuriant life; after the fall, when time and death entered the world, the river became a symbol of time, affecting man and yet continuing relentlessly after the individual man "passeth away." As the novel progresses the river acquires additional mythic meaning, for it becomes the home of the wounded Fisher King whose domains lie wasted. In contrast with the title, heavily weighted with mythic significance, the first epigraph to the novel is taken from Robert Lowell's autobiographical poem "Man and Wife":

All night I've held your hand,
as if you had
a fourth time faced the kingdom of the mad—
its hackneyed speech, its homicidal eye—
and dragged me home alive . . .

The poem describes the private history of a troubled marriage between a man given to episodes of madness and a wife who habitually rescues him during those episodes. This circular pattern of emotional rescue, as well as other details of the poem from lines not quoted (the tranquilizers, the bed as the locus of both love and quarreling), anticipates the "story" of *Run River*, the tragic course of the marriage of Lily Knight and Everett McClellan.

The second epigraph to the novel, from John Peck's 1837 *New Guide to the West*—". . . the real Eldorado is still further on"—exists in ironic relation to the first epigraph, with its description of an interior hell, "the kingdom of the mad." Didion is invoking both the mythic and the denotative content of Peck's statement. While on the denotative level Peck was informing his reader that fertile land and opportunity lay in the unsettled territory of America's Far West, he was also (Didion believes) appealing to an unconscious motive for the westward migration, a childish desire for an earthly paradise, the legendary "Eldorado" where all discontents would be magically erased. When the first settlers arrived in the Sacramento Valley, they found fertile land, but not the effortless happiness they had anticipated. This chapter of American history is repeated in *Run River*, as a new wave of migrants pours into the Valley after World War II—not farmers this time, but real-estate speculators and engineers, many of them men like Ryder Channing who succumb to the same myth of Eldorado that drew the nineteenth-century pioneers, the promise of easy riches and easy living. Didion sees Peck's statement as finally about the connections between time, place, and human restlessness, a reflection of the delusion that one can discover an ideal tomorrow by moving on.

The circular pattern of time in *Run River* is announced by the frame of the novel, which begins and ends in August, 1959. (The central and longest

section of the novel covers the twenty-one-year period preceding this date.)
The importance of time is clear from the opening paragraph:

> Lily heard the shot at seventeen minutes to one. She knew the time precisely
> because, without looking out the window into the dark where the shot
> reverberated, she continued fastening the clasp on the diamond wrist watch
> Everett had given her two years before on their seventeenth anniversary,
> looked at it on her wrist for a long time, and then, sitting on the edge of
> the bed, began winding it.

Lily Knight McClellan, married at the age of seventeen, given a diamond
watch on her seventeenth anniversary, hears the shot that effectively ends her
marriage at seventeen minutes to one. Guessing that the shot is her husband's
revenge on her lover, she nevertheless winds the watch, for she knows and
accepts the truth that Everett does not—that time cannot be halted. Only the
author of fiction can freeze time or turn it backward; in chapter one Didion
freezes the moment when Lily discovers that Everett's gun is not in the drawer
where it belongs while Lily recalls each incident of the day with which the
novel begins and ends.

Didion scrupulously maintains the sense of precise historical time in *Run
River*. The reader knows not only the month and year of major events, but
the exact date (December 6, 1848) on which the first Knight died in California,
even the year (1933) in which Walter Knight's mistress sold him 120 frontage
feet of a downtown block in Sacramento. This insistence on history enables
Didion to clarify the chronology of events, a clarification made necessary by
the constant use of flashbacks; equally important, it serves to balance the
numerous passages and scenes of a non-literal, mythic character (e.g., Everett
remembers driving the river road on hot summer nights: "Lost in the night
fields, his body, Lily's body, the house ahead: all one, some indivisible
trinity"). Through the intricate interlacing of two styles which reflect two
dimensions of time Didion gives dramatic substance to myths of sin and
redemption while simultaneously expanding individual history to express universal truths.

Two myths are thematically and structurally incorporated into *Run River*:
the Biblical myth of Adam's original sin and fall from grace, with the New
Testament sequel of redemption through Christ's sacrifice; and the pagan myth
that was Christianized in the medieval period, that of the Fisher King whose
wound renders his whole kingdom a wasteland. The Edenic myth of Adam
is one of the most persistent traditions in the American novel, and Jennifer
Brady has pointed out the use of the myth in *Run River* to characterize the

way in which the Knights and the McClellans idealize and romanticize the Sacramento Valley. But the myth is more crucially used in the novel to inform the characters' sense of personal *time*, in particular their nostalgic remembrance of childhood.

All three of the novel's major characters idealize their childhood as an Edenic time of unconditional love and total freedom from pain or danger. Of these three characters Lily is the one whom the reader comes to know best (more than half of the novel's twenty-six chapters are narrated from her point of view), and in scenes between Lily and her father we see his overprotectiveness, his reluctance to let her grow up. Walter Knight places his daughter in the role of Daddy's little girl. When she cries over his failure to be reelected to the legislature, he soothes her, "Now Lily. Lily-of-the-valley. . . . You're still my princess." When on her sixteenth birthday she confesses to her father that she does not know what she wants from life, he tells her, "I'll do the worrying. . . . You know that." Thus Lily as an adolescent is taught that she needn't struggle or make choices, since someone will always be there to care for her. Having allowed herself to be defined as her father's princess, Lily responds to the news of his fatal accident with terror at the prospect of her lost identity: "I'm not myself if my father's dead." Months later, aware of something wrong in her marriage, Lily "wanted now only to see her father, to go back to that country in time where no one made mistakes."

Despite her reluctance to abandon her childhood role, Lily does develop a capacity for emotional responsibility; she successfully raises two children (both born before her twentieth birthday), and tries, although often without success, to give support and encouragement to her mother and sister-in-law. Everett and Martha McClellan, on the other hand, refuse to accept the emotional risks and responsibilities of adulthood; thus time is for them an enemy that must be guarded, resisted, and—if possible—halted. Their mother died at Martha's birth, and Lily recalls that their father, a tense and volatile man, "had always spoken to them as if they were puppies. Down, Martha. Sit, Martha." In idealizing their childhood, Martha and Everett recall not their parents, but their (perhaps fantasized) closeness to each other. Six months after returning from the army Everett learns that Lily is pregnant and not (she thinks) by him; turning his back on the problem, he spends the night drinking bourbon and studying an old photograph of himself and his sisters taken at Lily's birthday party. When the sun comes up he is still holding the picture,

as if by tracing his finger down the crack in that yellowed snapshot he could recoup all their mortal losses, as if by merely looking long enough and hard enough he could walk back into that afternoon, walk back into Lily Knight's house, holding Martha by the hand, and begin again; could run with Martha up from the dock to where Lily cried beneath the lilac in the twilight and be home free.

Unable to deal with Lily's betrayal of him (and his own betrayal of her, his refusal to come home during his two years in the army), Everett takes refuge in an Edenic vision of childhood in which problems were simple and easily solved, in which everyone could be reassured, could be "home free."

Martha shares Everett's need to deny the complexities of adult life. On the day that she learns of her lover's engagement to the daughter of a wealthy construction owner, Martha pretends with Lily and Everett that she doesn't mind, that she is in fact happy for him. The date is December 18, and as she plays Christmas carols on the piano that at one level foretell her own death ("Above thy deep and dreamless sleep the silent stars go by"), she reminds Everett of the "happy" Christmases of their childhood: "Remember before Sarah got married when we used to go to Carmel at Christmas time. . . . I always think about how nice it was at Christmas. . . . And we always took that same house on the point? . . . And you always carried me upstairs to bed?" Martha repeatedly regresses to an idyllic remembrance of childhood in which her brother took care of her, as a mother (the mother she never had) would care for a small child.

The line between childhood fantasy and adult responsibility is indicated in *Run River* by the image of a snake that in mythic terms represents the loss of Eden. For each of the three major characters, the encounter with the snake is his moment of truth, the moment at which he chooses to grow up, with all that that entails, or the moment at which he chooses death. Lily feels the presence of the snake while running in the irrigation ditches with Everett, and she knows at that moment that her childhood has ended:

> When she screamed beneath him, remembering that snakes infested the ditches, he neither told her that there was no snake nor told her that the snake (if there was one) was harmless, but picked her up and held her until she was quiet and until the snake (if there was a snake at all) had gone away. Shortly before noon she told Everett that she would marry him. . . . It seemed as inescapable as the ripening of the pears, as fated as the exile from Eden.

Implicit in the passage is her expectation that Everett will help to protect her from the "evil" of adult responsibility; she has yet to learn that the most crucial moral choices one makes alone. But she does accept the inevitability of "exile from Eden," of moral and psychological adulthood. Having accepted the loss of childhood, she is then able to deal with subsequent losses, even with the death of her beloved father: "Things change. Your father no longer tells you when to go to bed, no longer lulls you with his father's bourbon, brought out for comfort at Christmas and funerals. Nobody chooses it but nothing can halt it, once underway; you now share not only that blood but that loss." Lily learns and grows a good deal in the course of the novel—not enough to save her marriage, perhaps not even enough to nurture self-esteem— but, as Didion shows, to be an adult among the old families in the Sacramento Valley at a time when all was being changed by the war was no easy matter. How does one relinquish the Edenic myth of childhood for responsible adulthood when most of the adults one knows are using sex and alcohol to conceal the moral poverty of their lives? It is to answer this question that (as we will see) Didion employs the myth of the Fisher King.

Lily's adulthood is limited by her passivity and her promiscuity, but unlike Everett and Martha she does attempt to reflect upon her life and understand it; and she does make emotional commitments to her parents, to Everett, to her children, and (as much as she can) to Martha. Everett, on the other hand, will not take the risk of an adult emotional commitment. He chooses to marry Lily specifically because she was part of his childhood on the ranch: "Lily required no commitment: Lily was already there. . . . To risk losing her would be to risk losing Martha and Sarah and himself as well. . . . She alone could retrieve and keep for him the twenty-one years he had already spent." Lacking a genuine commitment to Lily, Everett does not hesitate to enlist in the army in 1942, leaving her with two babies and a querulous father-in-law. Didion has Everett stationed at Fort *Bliss* to suggest that for this emotionally unresponsive man his stint in the army provided an almost Edenic interlude in life: "He missed her and the babies, but not as much as he told her he did, and then only in an abstract way. They were safe, and his absence from them was more than blameless; it was blessed by all the Allied Powers."

From his two years in the army, as from his four years at Stanford, Everett— because he gives nothing of himself—learns nothing about himself or the world. Because these experiences leave no mark on him, he assumes that other people and places also remain static. But when he returns home from the army after his father's death he finds that the ranch has fallen into disrepair and that Lily has been having an affair with a neighbor, Joe Templeton. Determined to regain his childhood by putting the ranch in order, Everett does so—obsessively—and is then frightened to ever again leave (with the exception of two weekends, he never does). But over the course of the next fifteen years the outside world invades the ranch relentlessly. In the real-estate boom that follows the war, taxes on their eight thousand acres double, and Everett, who identifies the integrity of the ranch with that of his childhood, must resist the rational arguments of his sister Sarah, who feels that they should sell some of the less profitable acreage. Ryder Channing, the handsome captain from Tennessee, has an affair with his sister Martha that Everett suspects is linked to her drowning; four years after Martha's death Channing commences an affair with Lily. Everett's domain is assailed from within his family, too, when his only son, who regards ranchers as old-fashioned, makes clear that he rejects the destiny of eight generations of McClellans, that he has no intention of spending his life on the ranch.

Everett's characteristic mode of resolving conflicts with other people is neither rational discourse nor emotionally charged argument, but denial of the conflict by removing from his presence what he perceives as the source of the problem. When he and Lily are not getting along he invariably suggests that she and the children go on a trip. His shooting of the rattlesnake on the lawn is not irrational in realistic terms, but in mythic terms it demonstrates his attempt to deal with a problem by removing its symbol. After he has killed Ryder Channing with the same .38 with which he killed the rattlesnake, he has a partial insight into the truth about himself: "Everything seemed to have passed from his reach way back somewhere; he had been loading the gun to shoot the nameless fury which pursued him ten, twenty, a good many years before. All that had happened now was that the wraith had taken a name, and the name was Ryder Channing." He fails to see, though, that the "nameless fury" is his own inability to confront the emotional complexities of adulthood by letting go of his memory of childhood as an Edenic state of grace and innocence.

His suicide is as much in character as the murder; since *he* has now become the problem, he must eradicate himself. True, there is an element of nobility in the act (for the alternative is a trial in which Lily's adultery would become public knowledge), but the mode of heroism of his suicide is that of a child; he will save Lily from the consequences of her behavior at the same time as he saves himself from the consequences of his: "His entire commitment to Lily had become an unbreakable promise to protect her from the mortal frailties which were, since they were hers, his own." He did love Lily, did have a kind of commitment to her, but he could not act upon that commitment by engaging in a reciprocal emotional relationship on a daily basis; he could only act upon it through dramatic gestures like the giving of diamond watches—and his life.

For Martha McClellan, too, time is essentially circular and repetitious, taking her ever backward into childhood and ultimately to death. Martha's emotional life consists of a series of destructive involvements with cold and unresponsive men—first her father, then Everett, and finally Ryder Channing. Failing to get the affection and approval she desperately craved from any of them, she forced them to pay attention to her through a pattern of hostile provocation that worked especially well with her father and with Ryder. Because of her own relentless suffering, she enjoys—in the fashion of a child—making men suffer; after her death Lily finds in her room a notebook which includes not only three pages with the headings, "REASONS NOT TO LOVE RYDER," "REASONS NOT TO LOVE EVERETT," "REASONS NOT TO RE-MEMBER DADDY WITH LOVE," but also a triumphant list of techniques that she has discovered to enrage and embarrass Ryder.

Martha enjoyed her academic success because she felt that it pleased Everett, but when Channing helped her to land a job with a Sacramento television station, Martha worked only eight days. She walked off the job partly because it did not meet her ideal of "a nice ordered life right here on the river," but principally because of her profound emotional resistance to playing any adult role. What made the job really intolerable, she explained to Everett, was the "enormous clock with a second hand that never stopped":

> She knew clocks weren't supposed to stop, don't be silly. She knew they needed a clock. But she could not work with it going every second. When it was going every second that way she could not take her eyes off it, and because it made no noise she found herself making the noise for it in her mind.

What Martha wants to do is to transform the very nature of time, to make it stop until the deprived infant that lives within her receives the unconditional love it persists in demanding. But no one can give this form of love to a woman in her twenties.

On the day that she walks off the job (in the way that a child turns its back on responsibility, without speaking to her boss), Martha drives to Yuba City, climbs on the rocks, and watches the rapids in the Feather River, where she sees a dead rattlesnake caught in a backwater. Didion inserts this symbolic scene here to indicate that Martha has failed her moment of truth; she, like the rattlesnake, is caught in the backwater of her own past. At the moment of sighting the snake Martha enters an emotional wasteland. Her relationship with Channing degenerates into verbal combat, and his rejection of her comes as no surprise to the reader. Less than two months after his marriage to the heiress—on St. Patrick's Day, 1949—Ryder stops by the ranch, finds Martha alone, and seduces her without love or tenderness. Four days later she takes a boat out on the river at high flood and drowns.

For Martha, both personal and historical time have come full circle. As he did in the house at Carmel on the Christmases she remembered, Everett carries her body upstairs to bed. Her coffin is a long sea chest from which Lily unpacked Mildred McClellan's linens and the "ivory fan carried by Martha's great-great-grandmother Currier at Governor Leland Stanford's Inaugural ball in 1862." Over the loud protests of the sheriff, Everett insists on burying her beneath the cherry tree near the levee on the ranch which she had made her brother promise that he would never, never sell.

Everett and Martha McClellan take their own lives because they cannot accept or confront the responsibilities and betrayals of adult life in a fallen world. Didion's use of Biblical myth does not end with the Old Testament, however; through the responses of the living to the dead, she shows the New Testament circling back to and fulfilling the Old, as in Christian belief Christ through his sacrifice redeemed the loss of Eden. While the lives of the characters in *Run River* are not guided by profound faith, all of the major characters take comfort and hope from the rituals and the language of Christianity, especially in times of crisis. What is striking, too, is the degree to which the prayers spoken at such times are appropriate to the person whose loss is mourned. At the funeral of her father, a man who had a strong sense of both change and continuity in human history, Lily memorizes a passage from the Order for the Burial of the Dead in the Book of Common Prayer—"For a thousand years in thy sight are but as yesterday when it is past, and as a watch in the night." Everett speaks a child's prayer over Martha's body: "Gentle Jesus, meek and mild . . . look upon a little child. Pity her simplicity and suffer her to come to thee." Lily, unable after the murder to dissuade Everett from suicide, aware of the "nameless fury which pursued him," identifies with his pain and isolation and prays, "Drive far away our ghostly foe and thine abiding peace bestow." Although they have both fallen far from grace and innocence, the final images in the novel are of rising. Lying beside Everett's body on the dock, Lily speaks to him of specific occasions on which they shared ordinary pleasures: "She hoped that although he could not hear her she could somehow imprint her ordinary love upon his memory through all eternity, hoped he would rise thinking of her." When she hears the sirens from the Highway Patrol she stands up, thinking already of the future, planning what she will tell the children. At the novel's conclusion Didion counterpoises the two dimensions of time: historical time, in which one must struggle with human weakness and the tragedy that is consequent upon weakness, and eternal time, through which human weakness is redeemed and historical time vanquished.

The prayers that Lily and Everett speak for their dead offer the hope of redemption in a non-historical dimension of time; this hope is supplied by the Christian myth of the sacrifice of Christ which makes salvation possible for the descendants of the fallen Adam. Didion used another myth in *Run River* to address the parallel question of redemption in *this* life, in historical time. One of the reasons that Lily, Everett, and Martha had such difficulty in relinquishing their Edenic fantasy of childhood was that to cross the threshold into adulthood in that particular time and place was to step into a moral and emotional wasteland. Their parents owned vast ranches and orchards, but their lives were barren of spiritual, aesthetic, and intellectual values. The marriage of Lily's parents was sustained by outward forms of family harmony, while Walter Knight spent his days in town with his mistress and Edith Knight spent hers planning or recovering from huge parties. The conversation of John McClellan, Everett's father, was composed almost entirely of clichés about "property rights and . . . the American way" and condemnations of all Easterners ("goddamn pansies and goddamn Jews") and non-white ethnic groups ("goddamn wetbacks and . . . goddamn Filipinos"); he repeatedly called Martha "strange little creature" because of her childhood interest in books and ballet dancing.

While Lily, Everett, and Martha rejected many of their parents' prejudices, they neither inherited nor acquired a coherent set of moral values; Everett developed an obsessive attachment to his land, while Lily sought desperately for a sustaining value-system, envying her mother, who was content to play the role of river-matron-and-hostess, and her cousin Mary Knight, who had become a nun, a decision her family never forgave her. With the exception of Mary Knight, Lily's peers in the Valley were also morally bankrupt; Francie Templeton became an alcoholic, and her husband, like Lily, became promiscuous.

As Didion used the myth of Eden to describe an ideal of childhood whose loss her characters mourned, she chose another myth to characterize the decadent society of the Sacramento Valley in the pre- and post-war years, and also to define a way of escape from this wasteland. This originally pagan myth is that of the Fisher King whose domains were fruitful so long as his own sexual and procreative powers were intact. When he was injured in battle, however, his lands became barren and remained so until he was magically cured or replaced by a younger figure. In the thirteenth century this myth became Christianized and absorbed into the legend of the quest for the Holy Grail. In the best of the Grail romances, the *Parzival* of the German Wolfram von Eschenbach, the wound of Anfortas, the Fisher King, is caused by his sensual love for his mistress Orgeluse. In his first visit to the castle of Anfortas, the knight Parzival, although he sees the suffering of the King, fails to ask the magic question—"What ails you, uncle?"—because he has been taught that a true knight does not ask personal questions. After much suffering and many adventures Parzival realizes that he has unwittingly hurt many members of his own family through rigid adherence to the *form* of the courtly code rather than its humane spirit. So he returns to the Grail Castle, asks the sympathetic question, and Anfortas is cured.[4]

As Eliot in *The Waste Land* merged many literary and mythic figures, so Didion in the character of Lily Knight echoed both the Fisher King and the questing knight Parzival. Like Anfortas, Lily receives a wound caused by sensuality—the abortion resulting from her adulterous affair with Joe Templeton. The wound is prefigured during her first sexual experience with Everett. After they swim across the Sacramento River and he pulls Lily out of the current, she notices "a long scratch on her left thigh, gradually turning bruised where Everett had pulled her across a submerged root into the shallow water." She forgets about the bruise while they make love on the riverbank, but "later the scratch on her thigh became infected from the river water and left a drawn white scar." Purely symbolic, this scar is never mentioned by Didion again, but it clearly prefigures Lily's abortion five years later. The abortion, which renders Lily sterile, leaves a deep scar on her marriage. Lily thought that she was having the abortion for Everett's sake, but he wanted the child, and the event becomes in subsequent fights "the heaviest weapon in both their arsenals." The abortion is both a cause and a symptom of the wasteland within and around them.

Run River, like Eliot's poem, abounds with imagery of water, fire, aridity, and heat from which there is no shelter. On the bus trip going home after the abortion Lily observes out the window "field after dry yellow field"; the Valley towns all look alike:

> The streets looked abandoned and the frame buildings as fragile as tinder: . . . three-story houses in need of paint, each fronted by a patch of dry grass, maybe a tricycle overturned on the cracked concrete walk. The afternoon heat could bleach these towns so clean that the houses and the buildings seemed always on the verge of dematerializing.

When Eliot entitled a section of *The Waste Land* "Death by Water" he had in mind the kind of baptism and rebirth experienced by Alonso in Shakespeare's *Tempest* when his ship sinks. Three people in *Run River* die by drowning— Walter Knight, Rita Blanchard, and Martha McClellan; although there is in Didion's novel no Prospero to magically rescue them, their deaths (as well as that of Channing, who falls into the river after being shot) are occasions of insight for the people close to them.

The moral of Wolfram's *Parzival*—that a true knight should sympathize with another's pain—deeply influenced Eliot's poem; the commands spoken by the thunder at the close of *The Waste Land* may be translated as "Give," "Sympathize," and "Control." In *Run River* Lily is the only character who gives and sympathizes. On the night after Martha's burial, in a scene that recalls Lowell's "Man and Wife," she took Everett "to bed and held him against the night and the rain and Martha lying outside." When Julie is upset because her brother has run away, Lily sits by her bed smoothing her hair and trying to reassure her. Lily is not entirely blameless, however; she resembles less the mature Parzival than the immature one who wants to do what will help others but does not know how. When Martha is rejected by Channing, Lily tries to cheer her with a candlelight dinner but never directly confronts her pain, never asks, "What ails you?" Like Parzival, Lily mistakes the gestures of courtesy for its essential core.

There is a potential Parzival for the next generation in *Run River*: Lily and Everett's son (named, of course, Knight). Although his spirit is one of anger rather than sympathy, he essentially asks his father, "What ails you?" when he demands to know why Everett pays no attention to any member of his family, why he pretends they don't exist, why he ignores Lily's affairs. He later apologizes to his parents, bringing Lily roses, and the entire incident leads them all to the unspoken awareness that "that was the day they began to be very polite to one another. . . ." Knight also resembles Parzival in unwittingly contributing to the death of a parent. Parzival's mother did not want her son to become a knight, and when he left home in quest of the Arthurian court without looking back, she died of a broken heart. Knight McClellan is also leaving home to seek a future that is alien to his father, and his rejection of the ranch contributes to Everett's despair and subsequent murder/suicide. Although a brash and even obnoxious adolescent, Knight is also a speaker of truth. While *Run River* does not conclude with a magical healing of either Lily's sterility or the wasteland around her, the very presence of a younger generation (not to be found, for example, in *The Sun Also Rises*) is grounds for hope: Knight may learn, as Parzival did, to become sensitive to the pain of others, to "give, sympathize, and control."

While the myth of Christ as successor to Adam gives hope in *Run River* of eternal life in a world to come, the myth of the Fisher King serves to answer the question of how a person can preserve his own integrity and console others in a fallen world. Each of the two myths traces a transcendent circle of spiritual loss and redemption which encompasses the tragic histories of Lily, Everett, and Martha McClellan. The interweaving of myth and history in *Run River*

places Didion in the oldest traditions of European and American literature
and establishes her "region" as that of the human spirit.

NOTES

[1]Guy Davenport, "Midas' Grandchildren," *National Review* (May 1963), p. 371.
[2]Jennifer Brady, "Points West, Then and Now: The Fiction of Joan Didion," *Contemporary Literature*, 20 (Autumn 1979), pp. 457–58.
[3]There is another possible source for Didion's title—the first sentence of *Finnegans Wake* ("riverrun, past Eve and Adam's, from swerve of shore to bend of bay, brings us by a commodius vicus of recirculation back to Howth Castle and Environs"). The possibility that Didion had Joyce's opening sentence in mind is intriguing, in view of its allusion to Adam and its image of circularity. However, both biographical evidence—Didion has said that she learned "how sentences work" by copying entire chapters from Hemingway at the age of fifteen—and internal evidence—both the themes and the mythic structure of *Run River* resemble those of *The Sun Also Rises*—indicate Hemingway's epigraph from Ecclesiastes as the more likely source.
[4]For an excellent analysis of the merging of pagan and Christian elements in Wolfram's *Parzival* see W. T. H. Jackson, *The Literature of the Middle Ages* (New York: Columbia University Press, 1960), pp. 115–35.

Nothingness and Beyond:
Joan Didion's *Play It As It Lays*

David J. Geherin

WHAT WE PROBABLY do not need in American fiction is yet another "Hollywood novel." Hollywood as metaphor for everything that is tawdry, artificial, and superficial about America has become a cliché in contemporary fiction. Those novels about Hollywood which are still read—West's *The Day of the Locust*, Mailer's *The Deer Park*, Fitzgerald's *The Last Tycoon*, Schulberg's *What Makes Sammy Run?*—succeed by transcending the limitations of their subject matter. Countless other ones have faded as quickly as the sunset in the West they describe because their voyeuristic concern was with Hollywood as Hollywood, their fascination with tinsel as tinsel.

Joan Didion's *Play It As It Lays* belongs to that former group of novels which enlarges upon the limited nature of its material. Although its setting is Hollywood, its heroine is an actress, and movie-making figures prominently in its action, the novel is as much "about" Hollywood as *Heart of Darkness* is "about" Africa or *The Stranger* is "about" Algeria. Like those novels, *Play It As It Lays* depends upon an intimate connection between setting and theme; but also like them, its overriding thematic concern is man's relationship with himself and with existence in general. Didion's novel is neither primarily a sociological commentary on the values of contemporary American society nor a psychological case study of its heroine. It is, rather, a picture of personal dread and anxiety, of alienation and absurdity lurking within and without. For although Hollywood is her setting, nothingness is Didion's theme.

The novel presents a harrowing picture of Maria Wyeth, a thirty-one-year-old actress and former model, and her encounter with an existential nothingness which envelops her like a coastal fog. Her marriage to Carter Lang, an egocentric, ambitious young film director, is breaking up; her four-year-old daughter, Kate, is institutionalized with some sort of brain damage; her casual affairs are many but mechanical and lifeless. When Maria discovers she is pregnant, probably not by her husband, she has an abortion. Her closest friend, BZ, a homosexual who produces her husband's movies, commits suicide by taking an overdose of pills while cradled in her arms. Finally, Maria herself is hospitalized for what is usually loosely described as a "nervous breakdown."

The facts of Maria's life are the basic material of thousands of soap-opera situations. What saves *Play It As It Lays* from degenerating into banality is Didion's control over her material, her skill in focusing attention not on the events in Maria's life so much as on her cumulative response to them. The real action of the novel takes place in the mind and heart of Maria as she is forced to deal with her experiences. Viewed from a medical point of view, she might well be classified as a near-schizoid personality whose experiences have precipitated a severe emotional crisis resulting in the loss of an integrated personality. In a more profound sense, however, her sickness is neither emotional nor psychological; it is ontological. She is suffering not from a nervous breakdown, but from the breakdown of a world around her which threatens to engulf her whole being with nothingness.

Although narrated in third person for the most part, the novel begins with Maria's first-person account of her situation, written, she tells us, at the urging of the doctor who is treating her. Her statement is lucid, perceptive, and sensitive. It reveals Maria's response to her personal encounter with nothingness, which the rest of the novel details. Maria says she answers "Nothing applies" to the battery of psychological tests put before her, indicating neither evasion nor unwillingness to cooperate and nothing less than the naked truth. "What does apply, they ask later, as if the word 'nothing' were ambiguous, open to interpretation, a questionable fragment of an Icelandic rune." With an arrogance characteristic of the initiated, Maria displays impatience at the obtuseness of others because she has "been out there where nothing is," as BZ puts it. Unlike him, Maria lives on; her encounter with nothingness does not completely defeat her but forces her into a new awareness. Her confinement in the sanitarium is not to be viewed as a solipsistic retreat but as a temporary withdrawal from the world in preparation for a future re-emergence, wounded but wiser, with a wisdom born of pain.

In this way, *Play It As It Lays* is closer in spirit and theme to the works of Camus and Sartre than to those of Nathanael West. In *The Myth of Sisyphus*, for example, Camus writes:

> In certain situations, replying "nothing" when asked what one is thinking about may be pretense in a man. Those who are loved are well aware of this. But if that reply is sincere, if it symbolizes that odd state of soul in which the void becomes eloquent, in which the chain of daily gestures is broken, in which the heart vainly seeks the link that will connect it again, then it is as it were the first sign of absurdity.[1]

Play It As It Lays testifies on every page to this eloquence of the void as Didion relentlessly explores the emotional shock of the encounter with absurdity. The refrain "Maria said nothing" is repeated with increasing persistence throughout the novel until it takes on the characteristics of a ritual chant. In its silence, the statement itself becomes eloquent, illuminating the almost palpable nature of Maria's dread. That Maria cannot articulate her experience to others, can say nothing, only makes more poignant and intense her experience. To her husband, her friends, her doctor, she appears vague, evasive, withdrawn; for herself, she sees no ambiguity whatever. She has heard the silence of the void, has encountered that absurdity Camus describes, and has learned the truth of Beckett's observation that there is nothing more real than nothing.

For the title to her collection of essays, *Slouching Towards Bethlehem*, Joan Didion chose the final line of Yeats's "The Second Coming." Her overriding concern in those essays and in her two published novels—the first was *Run River*—is with the broken center, with things falling apart, with "anarchy loosed upon the world." However, where the emphasis in the essays is primarily on the sociological impact of such fragmentation (the title essay, for example, deals with hippie life styles in San Francisco), *Play It As It Lays* focuses on a highly personal and private version of the broken center. Things are falling apart in Maria's world, the chain of daily gestures has been irrevocably broken. What results is the main concern of the novel, Maria's encounter with absurdity and nothingness.

Maria's painful journey toward perception begins with a nagging awareness of dread hovering over her. At the beginning of the novel, her perception has no real focus, no sharp delineation of its exact nature. Her ultimate fate is suggested early by a description of a documentary movie of her life as a model in New York, filmed by her husband. In the final scene of the movie, Maria's face is shown in negative image, foreshadowing the nothingness that will soon be her life. To ward off the increasing anxiety, Maria develops a compulsion to drive the freeways, to seek order and meaning to counteract her growing sense of disorder. In the hypnotic flow of the freeways, she is able, temporarily at least, to ignore the outside world. At night the sense of dread inevitably returns, but each morning brings the escape of the automobile once again. Only on the freeways is she able to feel the orderly rhythm of life that she finds nowhere else. The automobile becomes an appropriate symbol of her escape: self-contained and womblike. Driving is both free and tightly ordered; she can flow along aimlessly but only in the direction the road dictates. Ironically, the only source of the rhythm of life is mechanical; nature, the normal source of natural rhythms, is depicted as polluted, sterile, and lifeless. Maria's compulsion causes her to drive over seven thousand miles in one month. The freeway runs out in a scrap metal yard in San Pedro, and Maria soon discovers that driving is ineffective protection against the "unspeakable peril" she senses about her.

We discover the particular causes of Maria's anxiety only gradually: her marriage is breaking up; her daughter is institutionalized while doctors try to figure out "what went wrong"; she is haunted more and more by the sudden violence of her mother's death in an automobile accident in the Nevada desert some years earlier. Not only the facts distress her: uneasiness has arisen because she has asked "why" (her name should probably be taken symbolically; Wyeth: Why is). Asking questions sometimes prompts answers that the questioner is not prepared to handle. As Camus writes, "one day the 'why' arises and everything begins in that weariness tinged with amazement."[2] That weariness, which Camus says comes at the end of a mechanical life, is the beginning of the impulse of consciousness. In seeking answers to fundamental questions about her life, for an explanation for the unaccountable suffering of her child, for a logical reason for her mother's sudden death, Maria gains a new awareness. She discovers no answer, that *nothing* is the answer to all these questions. She is forced to confront irrationality and silence. The reader soon recognizes that her opening words in the novel, "What makes Iago evil? some people ask. I never ask," are not an evasion; instead, they clearly indicate her profound awareness that there is no answer. To explain Iago's evil is impossible and futile, since mere explanation cannot remove it. "To look for 'reasons,'" Maria confesses, "is beside the point."

Maria's knowledge of evil is symbolized by the frequent appearance in her dreams of the rattlesnake. As a girl, her father had warned her against turning over rocks for fear she might reveal a snake. She was unable to follow the advice, for the rattlesnake is revealed all too clearly in the harsh light of her reason. Once released, it never crawls back under the rock. "A man is always prey to his truths," said Camus. "Once he has admitted them, he cannot free himself from them. One has to pay something. A man who has become conscious of the absurd is forever bound to it."[3] Maria can have no turning back, no retreat to the comforts of innocence or ignorance; the rattlesnake pursues her everywhere, in her dreams, on the highways, even in the coiled shape of her food.

What distinguishes Maria's experience from that of most heroes of existential novels is that hers is uniquely feminine, not that Didion has written a blatantly feminist tract, nor that Maria's encounter with nothingness is ultimately qualitatively different from a man's. However, one must understand her experiences as a woman to appreciate fully the nature of her crisis. When Carter calls Maria to ascertain that she has made definite arrangements for the abortion, he is totally insensitive to what she feels emotionally as a woman about to abort her child: "Sometime in the night she had moved into a realm of miseries peculiar to women, and she had nothing to say to Carter." Just as Ralph Ellison's hero is shaped by the particular nature of his experiences as a black man in America, Maria is shaped by experiences uniquely feminine. Just as the Invisible Man could say, "Who knows but that, on the lower frequencies, I speak for you," Maria can speak for many who are neither women, nor actresses, nor residents of Hollywood.

By having a woman protagonist, Didion adds a heightened sensitivity and emotional impact to the encounter with nothingness. Maria's role as mother, for example, causes her to feel so deeply not only about Kate, but also about all the suffering innocents in the world. Such inescapable realities as "the four-year-olds in the abandoned refrigerator, the tea party with Purex, the infant in the driveway, rattlesnake in the playpen" convince her intuitively of the "unspeakable peril" in the everyday. That maternal sensitivity is further emphasized when Maria breaks down into uncontrolled sobs on the day the aborted baby would have been born; although she had deliberately avoided keeping track of the days, "she must have been counting them unawares, must have been keeping a relentless count somewhere." Maria is not afforded the luxury of deciding whether or not to confront absurdity; it is thrust upon her as a result of the nature of her situation. Once begun, the confrontation moves inexorably toward a crisis. In no way does an intellectual awareness of absurdity, general disorder, and cruelty debilitate her; her feminine (and maternal) sensitivity to things such as the unreasonable suffering of children and the inexplicable ailment afflicting her daughter leads her to see "the dead still center of the world, the quintessential intersection of nothing."

Maria's visceral awareness is complicated and intensified by her abortion. Although repelled by the idea, she agrees to have the operation to satisfy Carter, who threatens to take Kate away if she refuses. Her guilt, her sense of complicity in that suffering of the innocents which she detests, only serves to strengthen her growing awareness of the absurdity. Her guilt, both moral and psychological in origin, is expressed in a dream in which she acts as an attendant at a gas chamber where children file by on their way to execution. Her job is to whisper words of comfort to the reluctant children because "this was a humane operation." Her abortion was to be a "humane operation" too, but she could not escape persistent thoughts of the fetus in the garbage. Her inability to deal with guilt associated with the abortion is perhaps the strongest single factor in her emotional collapse, the culmination of her deepening awareness of the irrationality and absurdity of life.

Maria may well be compared with Esther Greenwood, the heroine of Sylvia

Plath's *The Bell Jar*. Both characters undergo a severe emotional crisis as a result of specifically feminine problems (for Maria an abortion, for Esther an attempted rape) and both are hospitalized as a result. Plath is much more concerned with the specific details of Esther's crisis and, in fact, wrote the book as therapy relating to her own psychological problems. Didion, however, is purposely vague about the exact details of Maria's breakdown because she is more interested in the metaphysical rather than the psychological implications of her illness.

Both Maria and Esther suffer from what existential psychologist R. D. Laing calls "ontological insecurity," a condition in which the individual lacks a firm sense of his own identity in a world which seems to be threatening him at all times.[4] Laing suggests that such insecurity can lead to insanity which, from the point of view of the individual involved, can be seen as a perfectly rational adjustment to an insane world. Esther exemplifies an extreme form of ontological insecurity and madness; her emotional problems drive her to several suicide attempts and eventually to a complete breakdown. While Maria exhibits some of the recognizable symptoms of schizophrenic behavior, Didion apparently does not want the reader to dismiss her simply as mentally or emotionally disturbed. Her sickness is metaphysical, a manifestation of her difficulty in adjusting to her newly discovered consciousness of absurdity.

As Maria's awareness of absurdity deepens, she finds herself in a desperate search for meaning, for escape, or for values of some kind. She soon discovers she can find no relationship between cause and effect, no meaningful explanation for the way things are, for such things as suffering, random violence, and death. Although she throws the I Ching in the sanitarium, she does it only to pass the time; she never bothers to read the coins because she now knows that nothing can be predicted, everything is random. Her various attempts to escape her perceptions also fail. Driving the freeways did not work. Love as a solution is futile, whether sought for in her husband, who loves himself, in BZ, who is homosexual, in casual lovers, who invariably treat her as an object, or in her daughter, who is emotionally incapable of returning her love. She gets no pleasure from any of her affairs and is unable to achieve satisfaction even at the purely physical level.

Religion, a traditional source of consolation in time of stress, is represented in the landscape of the novel by the giant red T of the Thriftimart, under which the attendant meets Maria to take her to the place for her abortion: "For miles before she reached the Thriftimart she could see the big red T, a forty-foot cutout letter which seemed peculiarly illuminated against the harsh unclouded light of the afternoon sky." The attendant, who unfeelingly tells Maria how nice the neighborhood they are driving through is for raising children, ironically describes himself as "a regular missionary." When she is lonely, Maria turns to Dial-a-Prayer, only to fill the silence with an available voice. She becomes fascinated with the story of the man who went out walking in the desert to find God but finds a rattlesnake that kills him. Religion for Maria leads to the same dead ends the freeway did.

Most desperate of all is her search for the past. When memories of the immediate past become unbearable, Maria turns to thoughts of her childhood and seeks to discover the roots which can give her support. Her parents are dead, and Silver Wells, her home town, no longer exists, replaced by a missile range. She even goes so far as to attempt to return to her mother's womb through hypnosis, but to no avail. The only living link with her past is Benny Austin, an empty failure pumped full of unrealized dreams, but his memories usually differ from Maria's. Significantly, Maria's search takes her to the barren deserts of Nevada, a state whose name suggests *nada* itself. In the end, she is forced to admit that the past no longer exists; she rejects "as it was" and learns instead to play it as it lays.

The only consistent value Maria retains throughout the novel is Kate, who represents a kind of talisman against peril; whenever things get bad, she dreams of Kate. On one occasion, she goes to Kate's bed, clutches her pillow to her and fights off "a wave of the dread." When she has been stripped of everything—her optimism, her humor, her past, her husband, her illusions, even her emotional stability—she still has Kate: "Why bother, you might ask. I bother for Kate." More than simply a mother's stubborn instinct, her concern for Kate is a positive gesture, a reaching out of love, a celebration of value in a meaningless world.

Play It As It Lays is not a nihilistic novel. Although Maria encounters nothingness, she survives: "Now that I have the answer, my plans for the future are these: (1) get Kate, (2) live with Kate alone, (3) do some canning. Damson plums, apricot preserves. Sweet India relish and pickled peaches. Apple chutney. Summer squash succotash." Not much of a future, since Kate may not ever be able to live with Maria outside the institution. But this future and its resolution, however precarious, are meant to be taken seriously. In another context, Didion has written: "I know something about dread myself, and appreciate the elaborate systems with which some people manage to fill the void, appreciate all the opiates of the people, whether they are as accessible as alcohol and heroin and promiscuity or as hard to come by as faith in God or History" (*STB*). Maria's system for salvation lies somewhere between the extremes of heroin and history. Nevertheless, she has found an answer to nothingness and a reason for continuing to play the game. The novel ends with Maria playing solitaire and looking at the hummingbird, whose frenetic wing activity allows it to appear motionless, at rest in the center. After the swirling experiences of the previous months, Maria has achieved a similar stasis, an inner peace which enables her to confront existence and prepare for the future once more.

Maria's encounter with nothingness is contrasted with BZ's, whose confrontation with the void destroys him. In the most intensely moving scene in the novel, BZ, having reached the end of his endurance, commits suicide by taking an overdose of pills while Maria holds his hand. Unable and perhaps unwilling to stop him, Maria nonetheless comforts him maternally as she comforted the doomed children in her dream. BZ's suicide is shocking but not unexpected, for he has lost his resilience and desire to continue. Stripped of a name, reduced almost to a cipher, BZ is never even physically described in the novel; he exists only as a voice, a presence, a shadow. He has gone all the way to Z, to the end where there is nothing more, and he can find no reason to live one moment longer. BZ and Maria provide alternate answers to the question raised by Camus in the opening words of *The Myth of Sisyphus*: "There is but one truly serious philosophical problem, and that is suicide. Judging whether life is or is not worth living amounts to answering the fundamental question of philosophy."[5] BZ tries to convince Maria that nothing matters, that playing the game has no point any more. His name also suggests a parallel with Beelzebub, a Satanic tempter who seeks to corrupt Eve from her innocence. Maria loses her innocence but ultimately refuses BZ's offered apple, the Seconal pills which kill him. Through Maria, Didion endorses Camus' conclusion that living is better than dying, even if one must live with nothingness. Why? "Why not," Maria says, in the final words of the novel. Humanity is won by continuing to play in the face of defeat, even if the odds against the player are overwhelming. Maria understands that although life may have no meaning, it is still worth living.

If Maria's last name suggests her questioning of existence, her first (pronounced, she tells us, Mar-EYE-ah) suggests an enduring self-identity. Despite the numerous threats to her fundamental existence, her sense of "I" endures. At one point in the novel, she confronts non-being and finds herself threatened with personal annihilation: "By the end of a week she was thinking constantly about where her body stopped and the air began, about the exact point in space and time that was the difference between Maria and other." She senses the same fundamental threat to her existence that Roquentin does in Sartre's *Nausea* when he discovers his contingency and his nothingness in the world of things. (Maria's own personal version of nausea is graphically illustrated by her constant vomiting; her physical revulsion at the way things are should be seen as more than a simple case of nerves or a chronically weak stomach.)

Although Maria loses selves—Maria as actress, Maria as Carter Lang's wife, Maria as Francine and Harry Wyeth's daughter—she never loses her real self, that enduring sense of "I," the source of all the false selves, whose continued existence ultimately prevents a feeling of total annihilation.

Maria's encounter with nothingness is set in a world which Didion pictures in vivid images as bleak, sterile, and hostile—where houses fall into canyons, where men seeking God are killed by rattlesnakes, where towns are replaced by missile ranges. It is a random world of chance, suggested in the novel by recurring references to gambling (including the title). It is a nightmarish burning world, where fire and destruction always threaten: "In the aftermath of the wind the air was dry, burning, so clear that she could see the ploughed furrows of firebreaks on distant mountains. Not even the highest palms moved. The stillness and clarity of the air seemed to rob everything of its perspective, seemed to alter all perception of depth, and Maria drove as carefully as if she were reconnoitering an atmosphere without gravity." It is a world devoid of natural beauty and comfort: "She drove to the beach, but there was oil scum on the sand and a red tide in the flaccid surf and mounds of kelp at the waterline. The kelp hummed with flies. The water lapped warm, forceless." It is a world inhabited by the dead and the dying: "A woman in a nurse's uniform wheeled a bundled neuter figure silently past the hedges of dead camellias."

As Maria's awareness of nothingness deepens, the action of the novel moves from Hollywood to the desert, to a town "on a dry river bed between Death Valley and the Nevada line" where Carter is filming. Here in the desert BZ discovers absolute zero and kills himself; here Maria has her "breakdown." Didion describes the town: "By late day the thermometer outside the motel office would register between 120° and 130°. The old people put aluminum foil in their trailer windows to reflect the heat. There were two trees in the town, two cottonwoods in the dry river bed, but one of them was dead."

But all is neither desolate nor hopeless. One tree is dead (BZ), but one is still alive, even in the inhospitable desert. The ability to survive is personified by the waitress at the local diner who invites Maria to her trailer, set on a concrete foundation, surrounded by a split-rail fence and a hundred miles of drifting sand. She comforts Maria, who is crying, by telling her that since she made her "decision in '61 at a meeting in Barstow," she has not shed a tear. She has found a reason to go on. Throughout her conversation with Maria, she continues to sweep the sand: "The woman picked up a broom and began sweeping the sand into small piles, then edging the piles back to the fence. New sand blew in as she swept." An endless, frustrating, almost ridiculous gesture, sweeping back the constantly blowing sand; no more hopeless and endless than Sisyphus' eternal task of pushing the rock to the top of the hill. Both activities embody a stubborn refusal to submit to the way things are, to admit defeat by surrendering to meaninglessness. Even if she cannot keep the sand away, the woman refuses to stop trying; even if Maria cannot have Kate, at least not now, she refuses to stop planning. The ending of the novel is not optimistic—nor is it nihilistic. For, as Camus wrote about Sisyphus, "The struggle itself toward the heights is enough to fill a man's heart. One must imagine Sisyphus happy."[6] Similarly, one must imagine Maria happy.

Didion's narrative technique recalls Eliot's line from *The Waste Land*, "A heap of broken images," images of alienation and desolation, fragments of banal conversations, the minutiae of everyday life joined in a mosaic of nothingness. Instead of a flowing narrative, a broken and disordered pattern is brought about by frequent juxtaposition of past and present, important and trivial scenes, and first- and third-person narration. What emerges through Didion's careful selection and rendering is a bleak and haunting picture of nothingness. Since so many chapters are short, some only a few lines long, the reader is struck most profoundly by the empty spaces, the blankness on the pages of the book. These silences between the chapters become as disturbing and eloquent as the emptiness of the void itself, as significant as the refrain of "Maria said nothing" in communicating vacuity.

The novel is an acutely sensitive record of Maria's mind, moods, and emotions. Although she is the narrator only at the beginning and end of the novel, she dominates every page. Everything—events, other characters, objects, even the weather—is seen from her point of view, measured by her response. Even her abortion is presented not for the objective details of the operation, but rather for her subjective reactions; the color of the wallpaper, the noise of the air-conditioner, the sound of the television set in the next room are the things that count; her mind records them as she desperately tries to ignore the reality of the abortion. We share her emotions because we see them from within her experience.

Although the narrator's gaze at Maria is unflinching, it is never unfeeling, never completely a detached camera-eye. A chapter which opens in a clinical manner, "On the tenth day of October at quarter past four in the afternoon with a dry hot wind blowing through the passes Maria found herself in Baker," soon becomes internalized as the point of view quickly moves into Maria's mind where she debates whether or not to call Carter on location. The detached point of view enables us to focus on Maria, to escape temporarily the claustrophobic confines of her mind. We are invariably drawn back into Maria, forced to share with her those experiences which she cannot escape. We care about Maria because we are with her so intimately. We care because the narrator cares.

The character of Maria's mind dictates the structure of the novel. The lack of continuity between chapters reflects the randomness and disorder that Maria perceives. Just as she is unable to discover connections between cause and effect, no obvious logical connection is often made between one chapter and the next. Where Maria can make connections, the structure reflects them; for example, Chapters 27 through 29, seemingly unrelated on the surface, are closely related by their concern with motherhood. These chapters follow immediately after Maria's abortion, when thoughts of motherhood naturally loom large in her consciousness.

Above all, Didion's laconic prose style communicates Maria's situation both powerfully and movingly. Her style is reminiscent of Hemingway's in its surface simplicity, its concreteness, its avoidance of abstractions and artificiality. Like Hemingway, Didion understands that less is frequently more, that understatement can often communicate more emotion than overstatement. A typical paragraph from the novel will illustrate: "The heat stuck. The air shimmered. An underground nuclear device was detonated where Silver Wells had once been, and Maria got up before dawn to feel the blast. She felt nothing." With precision and economy (three of the sentences are only three words long), she subtly communicates the ennui of Maria's life, her anaesthetized feelings, the hostility of the world as she perceives it, and her failure to recapture the past. When Didion writes, "At four that afternoon, after a day spent looking at the telephone and lighting cigarettes and putting the cigarettes out and getting glasses of water and looking at the telephone again, Maria dialed the number," she vividly illustrates the desperate, mechanical ways Maria seeks to fill up time—here because of an unwillingness to make arrangements for the abortion. Throughout the novel, numerous passages like these resonate with unstated but nonetheless powerfully wrought emotional significance.

Another element of that emotional message is the sense of loss which is so prominent in *Play It As It Lays*. The opening sentence of Chapter One, "In the first hot month of the fall after the summer she left Carter (the summer Carter left her, the summer Carter stopped living in the house in Beverly Hills), Maria drove the freeway," introduces the elegiac tone which encompasses the entire novel and is characteristic of all of Didion's writing: in the painful regret over a broken marriage and a lost past in *Run River*; in the poignant realization that things are not the way they used to be, or ought to be, in the essays of *Slouching Towards Bethlehem*; in Maria's loss of innocence and naiveté as she realizes the high cost of her encounter with nothingness in *Play It As It Lays*. Sadness is as much a part of the novel as silence.

With relentless attention to telling detail, a perceptive eye for sharply etched characters, an unerring ear for the absurdities and non sequiturs that pass for daily conversation, and a diamond-hard unsentimental style, Joan Didion has fashioned a remarkable novel which never misses in its portrayal of a modern woman caught in a mid-twentieth-century crisis. She has cast anew, in her unique idiom, one of the prevailing concerns of modern literature: confrontation with the void. Despite its preoccupation with death, suffering, boredom, and despair, *Play It As It Lays* is always fresh and alive. The novel not only touches the heart of its reader through its sensitive treatment of Maria Wyeth but also assaults the mind in its investigation of the heart of darkness too often discovered lurking behind the fundamental questions about existence in the modern world.

NOTES

[1]Albert Camus, *The Myth of Sisyphus and Other Essays*, trans. Justin O'Brien (New York: Alfred A. Knopf, 1955), p. 12.
[2]*Ibid.*, p. 13.
[3]*Ibid.*, p. 31.
[4]R. D. Laing, *The Divided Self* (New York: Pantheon Books, 1969), p. 40.
[5]Camus, p. 3.
[6]*Ibid.*, p. 123.

Joan Didion's *Play It As It Lays* and the Vacuity of the "Here and Now"

C. Barry Chabot

"THEY SEEMED AFFLICTED with memory," thinks Lily Knight McClellan of herself, her husband, and her most recent lover near the end of Joan Didion's first novel, *Run River*, a Faulknerian story of the inner dissolution of landed California families. That affliction exacts considerable costs, and try as they might either to forget, to forgive, or to move on, however lamed, no remedy seems sufficient. A woman of quite different familial and material circumstances, Maria Wyeth of *Play It As It Lays* pushes the tendencies of these earlier characters to their logical limits, becoming at last *"a radical surgeon of my own life,"* and thereby effecting a cure of sorts. So radical is Maria's surgery that she would sever herself not only from the past but from the future as well, leaving her to inhabit solely the immediate present: "I am working very hard at not thinking about how everything goes. I watch a hummingbird, throw the I Ching but never read the coins, keep my mind in the now." *Play It As It Lays* seems to demonstrate that, whatever the deftness of Maria's surgery, the operation itself offers only an illusion of relief, while it renders her condition irremediable, terminal.

Although more sparse, the structure of *Play It As It Lays* is reminiscent of that of *Run River*. It begins with a prologue of sorts with three sections, each from the point of view of a specific character, concerning the situation as it exists in the narrative present. Maria is institutionalized, and from some casual phrasings we are led to think that she has been for a considerable time, for a year at the very least. Maria seems bemused by her surroundings, perhaps a trifle regretful, but were it not for the absence of her daughter, Kate, she would by and large be content with her present lot. On the other hand, her former husband, Carter, seems defensive, as though he feels the need to explain his role in bringing about Maria's fate; and Helene, perhaps the most acidulously drawn woman in recent fiction, is accusative, believing that she, not Maria, is the true victim of the piece. The prologue is followed by eighty-four numbered, extremely terse chapters, many of them no more than a few sentences. Most of the chapters are narrated in the third person; they go back in time to relate the sequence of events which culminates in Maria's being institutionalized. Seven chapters entirely in italics punctuate the final quarter of the narrative proper; they are told from Maria's point of view and seem to record her ruminations while in the sanitorium. In a sense, therefore, the narrative present brackets the main narrative, which in turn seems addressed to the question of how this particular situation came to be; the novel asks what turn of events brought Maria to her present impasse.

The novel itself needs to ask such questions, for Maria will not, "not any more." One way of reading the novel would be to trace the series of steps through which she came to the conviction that such questions are always fruitless because the answers are not adequate. For Maria now "there are only certain facts"; they lead nowhere, have no entailments beyond themselves: "I am what I am. To look for 'reasons' is beside the point"; the notion of cause-effect is worse than bootless—it is a positive misconstruing of the way things come about. Maria believes, or would believe, that she inhabits a world composed of dissociated facts, a world in which one thing follows another in an utterly random fashion.

Maria implies that she has come to this view as a result of a series of observations and that, therefore, it represents the result of considered judgment: "Why should Shalimar attract kraits. Why should a coral snake need two glands of neurotoxic poison to survive while a king snake, *so similarly marked*, needs none. Where is the Darwinian logic there." While these arcane matters have their point, one supposes that they were dug up under the pressure of more immediate, but no less inexplicable, concerns. Why, for instance, should her daughter be afflicted with "an aberrant chemical in her brain"; why should her mother have driven off the highway; and why should her body have been discovered first by coyotes, which tore it almost beyond identification? What is the logic, the necessity (however grim), of such events? More to the point, what sort of world makes provision for such traumatic events? It could only be, Maria reasons, a world in which the human scale is marginal, of little consequence, a world without reason, which distributes events at random, a material world in which nothing finally matters. Given such a world, one should not trouble oneself with searching out the reasons or causes for actions; in a capricious world, one could do worse than accept the cogency of Maria's father's advice: "*it goes as it lays, don't do it the hard way.*"

Maria's social world offers her scant comfort from the harsh natural realm, for it is apparently ruled by what Kierkegaard called the aesthetic mode—immediate pleasure seems its sole imperative. Everything becomes an exclusively aesthetic concern: blue movies have "extraordinary technical quality"; a woman watches her home slide into the Tujunga Wash and only comments to newscasters about their "really outstanding camera job"; Helene's concern for Maria's impending divorce devolves upon whether to have lunch before

or after court—"Day of days, Maria. Of course lunch"; and BZ dresses up
for suicide. In such a world truth and concern have been displaced by pleasure
as the norm for discourse: "If it's not funny don't say it," Helene instructs
Maria. Because Maria believes that the entire city operates on this principle,
she worries as she waits to see her agent: "If Freddy Chaikin thought she
carried trouble with her he would avoid her, because trouble was something
no one in the city liked to be near. Failure, illness, fear, they were seen as
infectious, contagious blights on glossy plants. It seemed to Maria that even
the receptionist was avoiding her eyes, fearing contamination."

Left to its own devices, fulfilled repeatedly, desire tends to require elaboration
if it is to be satisfied; its old objects no longer serve, and gratification slides
into boredom. New arrangements must constantly be sought; sex becomes a
group activity with new players in new positions, amplified, as in BZ's
menagerie, by sadism and voyeurism. The genius of BZ seems to have been
to recognize the logic of the life they were leading and to act on that knowledge.
Whether he simply ran through the available combinations faster than others
or actually penetrated the logic of their lives, BZ is emblematic of the society
in *Play It As It Lays*: having narrowed the range of social values to the receipt
of pleasure, he cares only for the alleviation of boredom. When that no longer
seems possible, BZ prefers suicide to ennui—and why not, for apparently
nothing remains that can redeem his tiresome days. Maria's social world,
therefore, hardly seems designed to offer her solace for the griefs inflicted by
the natural world; her world seems calculated to become a replica of the
natural order, for it makes human relations, too, matters of chance and of
long-term indifference.

If by the end of the narrative Maria can agree with BZ that nothing matters,
if she can be so indifferent as to fall asleep as he dies beside her in a bed,
she had only recently come to hold those attitudes. Only if she thinks things
matter could she be so traumatized by her mother's death or Kate's affliction;
only on the condition that she thinks her marriage with Carter of some importance could she be so troubled by its dissolution, could she care whom Carter
was with on location, or if he was present when Susannah Wood was beaten.
If she did not care, she could simply shrug off such events and resume the
round of her days. So painful are all these things to Maria that she resorts to
a series of desperate, magical gestures—driving the freeways, paying her
bills—by which she hopes to reassert at least the illusion of control over her
life.

However battered Maria may have felt by one and all of these events, none
precipitated her eventually acceding to the view that nothing matters. The
novel suggests that the crucial event was the abortion.[1] Before it she was

able, although tentatively and with considerable effort, to get from day to day; subsequently, she is increasingly troubled by dreams, distraught, unable to neutralize the rebuffs of daily life. Maria initially reacts to her pregnancy just as she does to other unwelcomed events in her life: she ignores it, hoping that it will not be the case; and when that does not work, she resorts again to magical gestures—sleeping between clean white sheets, purchasing a wicker bassinette in a futile effort to ward off the unwelcomed, to "court miscarriage." Nonetheless, she appears unwilling to take more forthright action and, in effect, is only blackmailed into having an abortion when Carter suggests that he will contest her custody of Kate if she does not.

The matter-of-fact behavior and mundane conversation of the man who takes Maria to the place where the abortion is to be performed assist her in minimizing the impact of what is to take place:

> Maria turned off the ignition and looked at the man in the white duck pants with an intense and grateful interest. In the past few minutes he had significantly altered her perception of reality: she saw now that she was not a woman on her way to have an abortion. She was a woman parking a Corvette outside a tract house while a man in white pants talked about buying a Camaro. There was no more to it than that.

Such dissociation from the train of events is altogether congenial to Maria. As she enters the bedroom where the operation is to be performed, she happens to recall a tableaux from her childhood; she recognizes that if she could concentrate on it, that would be a time "during which she was not entirely party to what was happening in this bedroom in Encino." During the operation itself, her dissociation becomes complete: "No moment more or less important than any other moment, all the same: the pain as the doctor scraped signified nothing beyond itself."

While the operation was technically a success, Maria was not so successful in rendering it an accomplished fact, in seeing it as merely another of the unaccountable events which collectively constituted her life. At first she was troubled by bleeding she would have welcomed shortly before; then, she was visited by the horrifying dreams she could not simply disregard, dreams which featured plumbing stopped up by human tissue. To avert them Maria first moves into a furnished apartment, only to return to the house in Beverly Hills after the shower drains slowly one morning, demonstrating that there "would be plumbing anywhere she went." She arranges to spend an evening with her lover, Les Goodwin, but their meeting is to no avail. They tell themselves that things will go better another time and offer one another all manner of excuses: "They mentioned everything but one thing: that she had left the point in a bedroom in Encino."

Maria is suffused with guilt for having done so. Her thoughts obsessively return to the question of what the doctor had *"done with the baby. The tissue. The living dead thing, whatever you called it."* As this series of appositions suggests, Maria reviles herself for having transformed mattering—that is, caring—into dumb matter. So insistent are these self-castigations, so feeble all efforts to lay them aside, that she finally seeks relief through the drastic measure of aborting her own life: *"Fuck it, I said to them all, a radical surgeon of my own life. Never discuss. Cut. In that way I resemble the only man in Los Angeles County who does clean work."* In a desperate effort to cope with the aftermath of the abortion, she finds in it a pattern for her own life. She would convince herself that no moment is more or less important than any other, that all are the same, that no single moment either entails or looks back upon another, that no moment bears consequences beyond itself. Maria would convince herself, were she able, that nothing finally matters.

In a crucial sense Maria greets the notions that nothing matters and that events follow upon one another in random fashion with relief rather than distress. She fashions these notions precisely to shield herself from a long accumulation of guilts, however just any of them may be: if nothing finally matters or if events do follow upon one another utterly at random, then Maria could not hold herself accountable for anything she may have done. She would think herself innocent, absolve herself for her every act, have nothing to regret. The surgery necessitated by her ambition involves nothing less than amputating her entire past. Therefore, when Maria says that she has "trouble with *as it was*," we must understand that difficulty as not only having been endured but sought out as well. While she suggests that the trouble with the past is that it leads nowhere, she actually wishes that were true. She would amputate the past so as to absolve herself for past actions; what is troubling is the limited extent that she can do so. Although Maria can soothe herself with fantasies of an idyllic life by the sea for herself, Les Goodwin, and Kate, a life in which "none of them has histories," she is also troubled by dreams of clogged plumbing.

The attempted surgery is still more radical, since it involves giving up the future as well. If, as Maria would believe, events occur at random, then one can do nothing to bring about a happier future; one can only submit to the course of events, play it as it lays. Maria repeatedly says she wants to be united with Kate; however, she has apparently been institutionalized for a considerable time and takes no concerted actions to bring about that union, suggesting the extent to which that hope is merely a residual gesture from her former life. Maria would live, then, cut off from a past she cannot undo and a future she feels helpless to make; she would exile herself to the narrow confines of the present: "I try to live in the now and keep my eye on the hummingbird."

Whether by intention or not, Maria ends up dissociated from the present as well. When she returns home from an evening of driving the freeways to find Ivan Costello, a former lover from New York, she apparently resists his advances, for later they have this exchange:

> "Oh Christ," he said. "Baby. I just came to make you remember."
> "I can't remember."
> "You remembered all right the last three hours."
> She wrapped her arms around her bare shoulders. "That hasn't got anything to do with me."

Maria's self-protective gestures apparently extend so far that she is dissociated even from physical actions of the present: she is numb to her world. She can overcome her initial scruples—"Don't start faking me now," says BZ—and do nothing as he quietly commits suicide while lying beside her on a bed. Her ability to fall asleep in such a circumstance testifies to the extent to which she has immunized herself to the batterings of her world. Her refusal of BZ's course of action cannot be read as an affirmation: it would simply be a redundancy, for she has already effectively aborted her own life.

Finally, Maria conspires in being institutionalized; the passivity of sanitarium life represents for her a haven from a world that appears to offer only causes for grievance. In a fine irony, she effects her escape from an inhospitable world precisely by perfecting and carrying to their logical limits the very attitudes which rendered that world intolerable to her initially. If the people in her world chronically shy away from the distress of others, Maria comes to cast a cold eye on their comforts and pains alike. If little concerns her associates beyond securing their immediate pleasures, Maria herself eventually finds pleasure in making herself immune to pleasures beyond the contemplation of a hummingbird hovering immediately before her. She would take her pleasures as they come, in the ready to hand; the others at least work for them, however languidly. The "*nothing*" Maria takes some pride in having faced is at least partially the product of her own labors: having systematically stripped her life bare, willed her own indifference to the things of this world, this most abstracted of characters, not surprisingly, finds herself before this barest of abstractions. The problem is not so much that Maria cannot feel, nor surely that she has nothing to feel, as that she feels so painfully; so raw are her nerves that she will not let herself feel any further—that is her haven as well as her grief.

Aside from the foolishness of the doctors and the annoyance of occasional visitors, the only deprivation Maria seriously feels in the institution is the absence of her daughter: "*Except when they let Carter or Helene in, I never minded Neuropsychiatric and I don't mind here. Nobody bothers me. The only problem is Kate. I want Kate.*" Maria's residual concern for Kate is the sole imperfection in her otherwise successful excision of anything which might matter; she is still afflicted by memory, yet she languishes in the sanitarium, doing nothing that might bring about their reunion. Only concerted effort could make good her wish; only if she could muster the resources necessary to put her life again at stake—risking failure and pain—could Maria reasonably hope to break out of her present impasse. Her final prospects seem bleak indeed: she will not relinquish the comforts of her present estate for the mere chance of achieving something more substantial. She no longer gambles for such high stakes.

NOTES

[1] On this point—and little else—my reading of the novel is in accord with that of David J. Geherin, "Nothingness and Beyond: Joan Didion's *Play It As It Lays*," *Critique*, 16, No. 1 (1974), pp. 64–78. I find it particularly hard to credit Geherin's depiction of Maria as a character beset by fate who nonetheless wins through to some sort of "celebration of value in a meaningless world." I fear that the mere presence of resonant words like "nothingness" is too readily taken as a sure sign that we are on the track of existential profundities.

Play It As It Lays: Didion and the New American Heroine

Cynthia Griffin Wolff

◆

IT IS TROUBLING that we have found Joan Didion's fiction so easy to dismiss. Often it is dismissed with lavish praise: praise for the style, so idiosyncratic and spare; praise for the sensitive portrayal of neurotic women whose anarchic interiors seem unable to connect with the outside world. "*Play It As It Lays* focuses on a highly personal and private vision of the broken center," one critic writes. "Things are falling apart in Maria's world, the chain of daily gestures has irrevocably broken. What results is the main concern of the novel, Maria's encounter with absurdity and nothingness."[1] Surely without intending to do so, Didion's champion has concocted a fatal scenario. Didion is a talented woman writing a nicely turned prose style; her subject is really an up-dated version of the passive heroine of the sentimental novel, interesting because of the tenderness of her sensibilities, but doomed to destruction because of her inability to translate these feelings into meaningful action. Such a reading of Didion's fiction comes dangerously close to applauding the author for having produced an aesthetic/emotional "set piece," artistically effective, perhaps, but not "significant." And Didion's detractors, most of whom agree with the "set piece" interpretation of her intentions, pillory her for what they see as artistic self-indulgence. "Now, unlike the heroines of Didion's fiction, I do not regard memory as an affliction; I remember. I remember in part because I have no choice, but also in part because (unlike Didion's heroines, whose fate depends less upon memory and volition than upon selective amnesia), I believe that without memory there is not civiliza-tion. . . . Part of Didion's appeal, I am convinced, lies in her refusal to forge connections (notably between the personal and the political or between the personal and the transcendental). In spite of the sense of dread that suffuses her work, it contains this implied message of (false) comfort: if Didion—who is so awfully smart—doesn't trouble to make connections, why should we?"[2] The debators agree on the nature of Didion's work; they disagree only about the value one should set upon such an enterprise.

Ironically, the argument thus waged is *itself* meaningless: both sides have entirely missed the deeply moral intention in Didion's novel, responding to a naive reading—where the heroine's simplest statements and most negative self-evaluations are taken at face value—rather than to the author's complex artifice. To be sure, Maria Wyeth, the central figure in *Play It As It Lays*, rehearses her faults as if they were a litany or a Gregorian Chant, seeming to confirm her own essential disconnectedness: "I have trouble with *as it was* . . . I try to live in the now . . . NOTHING APPLIES." Yet not even Maria can disengage her mind from the past. It crowds upon her in not-altogether disconnected fragments. And the *novelist*, Didion, has an even larger scheme in mind.

Maria may begin by renouncing the activity of questioning: "What makes Iago evil? some people ask. I never ask." Nonetheless, she concludes with a question after all, "Why not, I say," the very last words of the novel. Her very name insists upon the inescapable necessity of this activity—Wyeth (Why is)—and only a very gullible reader will fail to see that the questing and questioning elements are at the very core of this fiction. We are not meant to rest satisfied with the delicate nuances of Maria's emotional life; quite the contrary, Didion demands that we use Maria's agonized explorations as a vehicle for the examination of nothing less than our heritage as Americans. The tensions in this work, which professes so disingenuously to ignore temporal connections, are always between past and present—Maria's past and present, and the past and present of a once-great culture. Echoes from the past drop in and out of the novel: different literary and cultural strategies are alluded to and discarded, or perhaps tried again and again in the stubborn effort to make the present comprehensible in terms of the past. Didion has a ruthless memory, and she recalls all of the most poignant dreams of the American experiment. In the end, she compels us to seek a definition for the chaos of our society, a cause for the restlessness and despair. Her achievement as novelist lies in the power with which she summons this modern "wilderness" and in the skill with which she defines its meaning, using as medium Maria, who professes to know nothing but nothingness itself.

One critic, Katherine Henderson, has been shrewd enough to understand the extent to which *Play It As It Lays* is a novel that deals with our inheritance from the "fathers"; and it is typical of Didion's compression that this theme embraces both the whole set of ideals that Americans identify with "Fathers"— Puritan Fathers, founding fathers—and the literal legacy of Harry Wyeth to his daughter. "My father advised me that life itself was a crap game: it was one of the two lessons I learned as a child. The other was that overturning a rock was apt to reveal a rattlesnake." Henderson writes:

> Harry Wyeth's philosophy is a perversion of the religious belief of early Americans that . . . they were objects of God's special grace. . . . In Wyeth's version of this belief God is absent, and the optimism inherent in the belief

is tied to games of chance. . . . The second lesson that Wyeth teaches his
daughter, that anyone who overturns a rock is "apt to reveal a rattlesnake,"
is a secularization of the dark side of the American religious heritage, the
Calvinistic sense of lurking evil.[3]

The important thing is that the moral concern persists even after it has become
detached from a belief in the Deity. Maria's initial question, which appears
to dismiss the question of evil altogether, actually serves to focus our attention
on the "Hawthornian" fascination with evil that pervades this entire work;
and on the second page of the novel, Maria drops unthinkingly back into
language that is morally, even prayerfully framed. These moves are not incidental to the novel's concern: Didion would claim that no one can speak
meaningfully unless he employs such categories and language. Any other
form of rhetoric can deal with only instrumental behavior: one thinks of the
precise, merely denotative, non-judgmental language that renders Carter's
casual amorality. Ironically, Didion would agree with her acidulous critic: we
must make connections between the personal and the transcendental; if we
altogether relinquish that effort, we might as well choose BZ's way of death.
    The mythology of our Puritan Fathers was predicated upon their certainty
that the things of this world will always yield to the combined forces of time
and death, the Grace of Election standing as the only defense against those
twin predators. The godless glitter of Didion's America still shadowboxes
with the same old enemies in its search for "happiness" or "fulfillment," and
Maria's crowd pursues the apparition of eternal youth—gleaming, unlined
bodies—"as if they had an arrangement with mortality." These people are
always in motion, moving from party to party, bed to bed; but theirs is motion
without direction or purpose. Its frenzy recollects the haphazard movement
of that earlier "lost" generation, just as the anxious dread of time's passage
summons the ghost of Robert Cohn to bleat: "Do you know that in about
thirty-five years more we'll be dead?" Hemingway's nightmare (values van-
ishing as time plunges ahead) presides visibly in Didion's novel, with this
important difference: Hemingway never altogether confronted despair. His
heroes could still pray, could still discover quiet moments of peace that hinted
at a "great good place," could still formulate dreams that suggested the genuine
possibility of heroic activity. Didion's fictional world does not offer these
consolations.
    So it is with Didion's adaptation of the "Hemingway style." Hemingway
had banished that literary god, the omniscient narrator, and had pared away
the opulence of Victorian sentence structure to reveal the beautiful bare bones
of syntax. It was a verbal loss of sorts, but it recollected the literal "Puritan"

impulse that lay at the heart of American culture. In Didion, this impulse is no longer purifying. It is lethal. Hence Didion's redaction of Hemingway prose is no more than fragments of language, clipped almost beyond recognition and reduced to the point where coherence itself is nearly lost. This mutilation of verbal structures renders the moral starvation of a society that has dispensed almost entirely with the freight of ethical intention.

Within the framework of the novel, this same habit of discarding moral and emotional values is rendered with a bizarre literalness: Maria and her friends equate beauty with "thin," and women starve themselves into grotesquely skeletal shapes. The horror of modern amorality is echoed and emphasized, then, in the detachment of the doctor's coolly clinical appraisal of Maria just before the abortion: "You don't weigh enough." It is reiterated in self-punishing fetishes designed to control weight; and it is apotheosized in the other half of Maria's inheritance, the bones which are all that remain of her mother. "The night my mother ran the car off the highway outside Tonopah I was with a drunk rich boy at the old Morocco, as close as I could figure later: I didn't know about it for a couple of weeks because the coyotes tore her up before anybody found her and my father couldn't tell me."

Hemingway's linguistic rites of purification were morally encoded. The banished omniscient narrator was the voice of Victorian standards (that is, the standards of a *female* ruler), and the "good places" for Hemingway men resemble the pastoral retreats of Twain's runaway boys. Both were places from which women, and especially "mothers," had been excluded. The strategies for happiness that were invented by these runaway boys never fully succeeded; nonetheless, the response to their inadequacies was not a reexamination of the runaway mentality, but rather a conviction that perhaps our failures were due to the fact that our heroes had not run far enough. Robotlike, Maria tries to assuage her pain by imitating the American heroes thus formulated: she drives the highway "as a riverman runs a river, every day more attuned to its currents, its deceptions, and just as a riverman feels the pulls of the rapids in the lull between sleeping and waking, Maria saw the great signs soar overhead at seventy miles an hour." But now we have run so far that there is no longer even a river, just the "flawless burning concrete" of the open road. It is an arid world, bereft specifically of the nurturing element that had sustained Victorian pieties. Even Maria intuitively understands the nature of this loss, and she weeps in the dark for her own lost mother, helpless to repair the desolation.

Maria's mother, Francine, has died before the novel begins, but the destruction of those nurturing elements that had combined to make "motherhood" began well before Francine's body served as supper for coyotes. She had been a good cook; it had been one of her ways of giving comfort to her daughter. But the men had other notions about the use to which Francine's talents should be put. "Franchises, you rent out your name and your receipt," Benny said; "Franchised services, that's where the future lies." Nourishment, care—these are no longer in the picture; clipped Hemingway prose becomes perfect advertising copy in a world where "Francine" can be so quickly transformed into "Franchise." The mother's moral and emotional concerns must yield to the father's monied dreams: " 'She can't win if she's not at the table, Francine.' Harry Wyeth threw down his napkin and stood up. 'You wouldn't understand that.' " The dinner table does a slow fade into a craps table, and food is transformed into fecal matter without even the intermediary process of digestion.

Repeatedly throughout the novel, Didion demonstrates the moral derangements of modern society by patterns of images, sometimes even by abstract verbal patterns or by patterns of association, which capture the inherent distortion of value. Gold which has given way to silver, silver which has given way to even baser metals: this ancient pattern is a traditional way of suggesting that the present has fallen away from the greatness of the past. Didion deploys this pattern with a wry twist. Even California's past has dubious moral implications, and its future is little short of apocalyptical. Hence there are echoes in Maria's story of that earlier gambler, "The Girl of the Golden West." There is even the faint afterimage of some "golden era" in filmdom—Erich von Stroheim's *Greed* (to choose the apposite example), which rendered the moral debasement of the gold-rush days quite literally, thousands of frames of film with the "golden" objects in them gilded by hand so that in the otherwise black-and-white picture, gold flickered obscenely across the screen. Now the corruption has begun to expand and dominate: Maria is a girl of the silver screen; she was reared in the town of Silver Wells, a town where the "wells" have never had water and where the silver stopped flowing long ago. But silver still drifts in and out of the fiction—in echoes of her mother's longing to cross the ocean in a silver plane, in the silver vinyl dress that Maria buys to help herself forget the abortion, in the "Silverlake home" of the charlatan hypnotist. And just ahead, an even more terrifying moral epoch awaits, for the moral disease has now apparently spread even into the political world beyond California. The silver age has by and large played itself out: Benny and Maria's father have begun buying zinc futures, and the town of Silver Wells has disappeared altogether. "There isn't any Silver Wells today. . . . It's in the middle of a missile range."

Patterns of this sort run throughout the novel, yet our concern is less with the patterns themselves than with what Maria makes of them. Her quest is to comprehend, even though she so often disclaims that quest.

The novel begins with her assertion that she is telling her story only to be an agreeable player of the game; yet almost at once, this mein of good-natured passivity fades before the blaze of genuine passion. "Why bother, you might ask. I bother for Kate. What I play for here is Kate." The love for her daughter, like the longing for her lost mother, comes from the depths of her nature and is authentic. Carter, who seems by comparison to Maria so patently normal and efficient, never bothers to keep track of people and their relationships; "feelings" have no meaning for him. Thus when Maria tells Carter of her unexpected pregnancy, he has only one thought: "he was going to give her the telephone number of the only man in Los Angeles County who did clean work." Clean abortions. Erase the fetus, eliminate the problem; forget it.

Maria cannot take these events with such cold, matter-of-fact competence. She has trouble with time: she forgets appointments, she forgets to call the answering service, she forgets to pay her bills; in all the things that "matter" to Carter, Maria is hopelessly inept. But in the more vital elements of life, she is the *only* person in this world who takes account, the only keeper of the record. She remembers her mother, even dreams about her. She remembers the daughter whom Carter has consigned once and for all to the doctors, and then forgotten. And after the abortion, she is the only one who remembers the fetus that was flushed down the drain.

> Once in her car she drove as far as Romain and then pulled over, put her head on the steering wheel and cried as she had not cried since she was a child, cried out loud. She cried because she was humiliated and she cried for her mother and she cried for Kate and she cried because something had just come through to her, there in the sun on the Western street: she had deliberately not counted the months but she must have been counting them unawares, must have been keeping a relentless count somewhere, because this was the day, the day the baby would have been born.

By the conclusion of the novel, we realize that Maria has lived in order to tell the tale. At some level, even Maria understands this role, for she alerts us to it at the very beginning: "My name is Maria Wyeth. That is pronounced Mar-*eye*-ah, to get it straight at the outset." If Carter is the *camera's* eye— clicking neutrally and impartially open and close, one "take" after another, absorbed only in the mechanical arrangement of shot after shot—Maria keeps track of the *human* relationships. And though the intention is usually expressed in her sense of "charms" or superstitions, she is also attempting to determine the moral implications of what she has seen, to find some larger, transcendent meaning to the memories she cannot forget. It is a mission in which she repeatedly attempts to include Carter, without success.

"What do you think about it," Maria asked Carter . . . "About the man at the trailer camp who told his wife he was going out for a walk in order to talk with God."

"I wasn't listening, Maria. Just give me the punch line."

"There isn't any punch line, the highway patrol just found him dead, bitten by a rattlesnake."

"I'll say there isn't any punch line."

"Do you think he talked to God?"

Carter looked at her.

"I mean do you think God answered? Or don't you?"

Carter walked out of the room.

Like the opening questions which echo that Hawthornian preoccupation with evil, so this passage suggests that insofar as the novel is a ransack of American culture, a search for some viable moral/aesthetic strategy, Didion has located a system which will serve.

Maria embraces "NOTHING." She appears to deny even self itself in this pursuit, and still she assaults us with the power of her unrelentingly moral vision in "Mar-*eye*-ah." She is, of course, echoing Emerson. "I become a transparent eyeball; I am nothing; I see all." And as Maria searches with the beacon of her sight, she responds intuitively to another Emersonian maxim. "1. Words are signs of natural facts. 2. Particular natural facts are symbols of particular spiritual facts. 3. Nature is the symbol of spirit."

Carter and the rest of the Hollywood crowd use language as no more than an instrument; Maria cannot always comprehend the moral implications in the common coinage of California slang, but she reacts to them. One meaning is already apparent: "silver" and even "gold" signify fraud and greed. There were "rush" periods for both silver and gold in the old days of California; and if, as Maria's father advised her, a snake lurks under the rocks of this area, the poison of the snake is palpable embodiment of the Evil inherent in the hectic fight to gain silver and gold. The term "rush" has pretty much dropped out of the mining trade, where great fortunes no longer wait to be captured by brutality and greed; nevertheless, the term lives on. It has been absorbed into the film industry, and with it have come the grinning forms of deathless Evil, Brutality and Greed. Such are the transcendent spiritual "Truths" which the jargon of film language signifies.

"Cut" is one of Carter's words. Technically, it means the piecing together of scenes in one or another order, no more than a neutral term, he would say. But Maria knows differently; she learned as she watched Carter make that initial, experimental film. "Carter had simply followed Maria around New York and shot film. . . . Maria asleep on the couch at a party, Maria on the telephone arguing with the billing department at Bloomingdale's, Maria cleaning some marijuana with a kitchen strainer." Eventually, as the single shots accumulated and "Carter began cutting the film" Maria could begin to understand the violation that was taking place. Carter was assembling and reassembling "Maria," putting her together so that he could exhibit her. Not a person anymore, Maria has become a *property*: anybody can look at her whenever he wants—speed her up, slow her down, run her backwards, perhaps. Most of all, this notion of "the cut" denies any intrinsic order to Maria's identity; the film, "Maria," can be "cut" many different ways, whatever makes for good box office, Carter would say. The *girl herself* counts for nothing. It is a form of rape, and Maria reacts with increasing moral horror. "Carter took her to BZ and Helene's one night when BZ was running the picture and she had to leave the house after the titles, had to sit outside on the beach smoking cigarettes and fighting nausea for seventy-two minutes."

Like Carter, Maria's father had accepted the notion of a "cut," but for him it had been a cut of the cards. Maria had been his ticket to fortune, and like Carter, he had high expectations for the profit to be made from her.

Both Carter and Maria's father are really part of some larger social perversion. The "cut" is a violation of self, and modern America is a society that daily permits such violations: humanity has come to be held in very little regard. Eventually in Didion's fictional world, the "cut" is translated into the literal wound of abortion, an acceptable, antiseptic negation of humanity. " 'Hear that scraping Maria?' the doctor said. 'That should be the sound of music to you . . . six weeks from now you'll have a normal period, not this month, this month you just had it, it's in that pail.' " Maria quite consciously understands the ominous undercurrent in this victory of expedience over moral commitment, comprehends without having the means to redress the Evil. Her language indicates that she understands (less consciously, perhaps) the connection between this violation and those other forms of "cutting" which had nauseated her; and it is the enraging powerlessness of this understanding that leads to madness. *"Fuck it, I said to them all, a radical surgeon of my own life. Never Discuss. Cut. In that way I resemble the only man in Los Angeles who does clean work."*

"Scene" is another of Carter's words. The very beginning of his opening remarks suggests that this term is central to his way of ordering not only his work, but his experience as well: "Here are some scenes I have very clear in mind." The term "scene" denotes a brief, often choreographed bit of action between two or more characters; a single scene is nothing in itself, of course. A single scene tells no story. The flexibility of Carter's art, the making of films, resides in the fact that he can move "scenes" in relation to each other as the final print is "cut." Yet this way of ordering life has a hidden moral implication: like the use of the word "cut," the more general use of language which would define not only the plot in a film, but also the sequence of an individual life or the coherent moving chronicle of interaction among people as no more than a concatenation of "scenes" denies essential meaning to all of these. It is a way of looking at the world which tacitly asserts that there is no intrinsic, inherent meaning in the relationship of the part to the whole. Carter's creation of a series of "scenes" which can be shifted radically in their relationship to each other does not have the same kind of unyielding moral significance that the "seen" world has for the visionary. Carter's camera eye has no power in and of itself to perceive the relationship between the personal and the transcendent, and Carter the film-maker has so thoroughly debased his capacity for moral insight that he cannot create what his mechanical camera's eye has never recorded. Maria's monitoring eye seeks to discover precisely that vision that the camera's eye cannot record, yet at every turn, this essentially moral impulse is thwarted by the destructive conventions of the modern world.

Maria tries over and over again to forge a different kind of "story" from that offered on the silver screen. When Carter returns to their home after they have formally separated, Maria is puzzled. She attempts to dispel the confusion by summoning a plot with a moral component: "Something real was happening; this was as it were, her life. If she could keep that in mind she would be able to play it through, do the *right* thing, whatever that meant" (my emphasis). But Maria has fatally little material to work with. In order for Maria really to construct more than a series of essentially separate "scenes" as the story of her life, society would have to offer support for some sustaining social ethic. Language would have to contain at least the possibility of moral implication. "Husband" and "wife" would have to be more than merely denotative nouns; they would have to indicate as well a transcendent and on-going moral commitment. "Mother" would have to name something that could never be franchised. Hence even Maria's vision and language are compromised by the abbreviated, free-floating relationships that modern society breeds. Her summonings of Kate's memory, for example, are always tainted with the rosy images of advertising copy: they will do some canning in the kitchen and sell the products of their labor (Maria's way of fulfilling both her mother's and her father's ambitions for her). And again, when Maria's yearning for an ordered family with Carter seeks expression, it inevitably falls into the corrupted, disconnected patterning of the popular media. "Kate fevered, Carter sponging her back while Maria called the pediatrician. Kate's birthday, Kate laughing, Carter blowing out the candle. The images would flash at Maria like slides in a dark room. On film they might have seemed a family." In the end, Maria is not strong enough to withstand compromise, and she can offer no sustained alternative to this way of conjuring and naming life's processes.

Thus moral principles are never directly or articulately or forcefully enunciated; and in this absence, widespread corruption occurs. Poison is in the air, and it infiltrates Maria's relationships with all of the most important people in her life. It works silently and invisibly, and Maria's most consistent and powerful allusion to the notion is made through a series of images of some deadly gas. Her life with Carter makes her feel like Ingrid Bergman in *Gaslight*. And her memories of the abortion—perceived obliquely, for they are so horrific that Maria is seldom able to recall the events themselves—fall into hallucinations of the Nazi holocaust.

> "This way to the gas, ladies and gentlemen," a loudspeaker kept repeating in her dreams now, and she would be checking off names as the children filed past her, the little children in the green antechamber, she would be collecting their lockets and baby rings in a fine mesh basket. Her instructions were to whisper a few comforting words to those children who cried or held back, because this was a humane operation.

An accursed land, perhaps this is after all no more than a condemned race to which Maria belongs. The water has gone. Everything that should soothe or refresh or create anew has dried and blistered in the desert heat. The river to be navigated is a stream of burning concrete; the springs and the lake are "silver"; when Carter goes on location to shoot, he sets up in a dry river bed between Death Valley and the Nevada line. Maria does search for healing liquidity, but she can find it only when it is encased in concrete; thus she creeps out at night to sleep by the swimming pool, having no other source of water available.

One heroic vision that comes out of the American past is that of the diver-hero, Ishmael the wanderer, the man who rides the coffin up and lives to tell the tale, the man who plunges into the uttermost recesses of his nature to discover the meaning of "self" and "life." Such a form of heroism, growing as it does at least in part from Emersonian transcendentalism, is congenial to that image of herself which Maria insists upon so vehemently in her assertion of Mar-*eye*-ah. Indeed, throughout the novel, Maria gives many indications that she longs for this kind of heroic possibility, but none exists in the desert wilderness to which Fate and History have consigned her. She struggles valiantly, nonetheless; and when her life begins to reach that crisis of identity when she is no longer certain about "where her body stopped and the air began, about the exact point in space and time that was the difference between *Maria* and the

other,"[4] she makes the only sort of "heroic dive" available in the aridity
which signifies the wilderness of modern America. She tracks the eerie depths
beneath the Hoover Dam.

> She began to feel the pressure of Hoover Dam, there on the desert, began
> to feel the pressure and pull of the water. When the pressure got great enough
> she drove out there. All that day she felt the power surging through her own
> body. All day she was faint with vertigo, sunk in a world where great power
> grids converged, throbbing lines plunged finally into the shallow canyon
> below the dam's face, elevators like coffins dropped into the bowels of the
> earth itself. With a guide and a handful of children Maria walked through
> the chambers, stared at the turbines in the vast glittering gallery, at the deep
> still water with the hidden intakes sucking all the while, even as she watched;
> clung to the railings, leaned out, stood finally on a platform over the pipe
> that carried the river beneath the dam. The platform quivered. Her ears
> roared. She wanted to stay in the dam, lie on the great pipe itself, but
> reticence saved her from asking.

It would be wrong to say that Maria comes away with no answer, for she
does live, and she does tell us her tale.

As a result, we can understand, as she does not, that the looming mechanism
at the heart of the dam sums and confirms the conflation of plumbing fixtures
with the process of feminine reproduction that has haunted Maria's thoughts
ever since the fetus fell into the drain, amniotic fluid and incipient life indis-
tinguishable from waste. Thus this monumental damming of water with its
life-giving force stands as emblem for all of those processes which have
offered "nothingness" where vitalizing moral and emotional commitment ought
to be. It is a horrific and compelling confirmation of Henry Adams' vision
of the Dynamo which has replaced the Virgin. The Virgin is surely gone—
Maria's namesake utterly without meaning now. This is a new way of life:
Maria warns us at the beginning of her tale. "Everything goes. I am working
very hard at not thinking about how everything goes." It is a bitter irony.
With the freedom to do "everything," "everything of value" entirely disappears.

Maria spends a lot of time riding the freeway. It is an activity which captures
the essence of many American dreams. The open road has always seemed a
"sign" of the opportunity for betterment: for Puritans, the pathway to Paradise,
for Alger the road to riches. Rush hour had been Jay Gatsby's emblem for
the Magic of the New World ("It was the hour of a profound human change,
and excitement was generating on the air"). And now Maria drifts out and
back, going nowhere in particular, because although her father has told her
that she's holding all the aces, he has not told her exactly what she is going

to win. She has no home to signal respite and safety and domestic order, only that missile range where Silver Wells used to be. Thus the freeway, with its formless aridity, becomes the definitive sign that when "everything goes," "everything of value" really disappears.

In America, the notions of "freedom" and "constraint" have always been precariously balanced: founded through an act of violent, filial rebellion, the United States has been in something of a quandary when it came to delimiting the exact nature of our freedom and the precise constrictions of our duty. Now Maria Wyeth's world has tumbled into unrestricted chaos. It may be desirable, even necessary, for children to leave the family and seek their own fortunes; but it is not "free." The rancor that can come between husband and wife may require the desperate measure of divorce; but divorce is not "free." Abortion may be no more than "induced menstruation" or a "humane operation," but abortion is far from "free." We have eased the old, crippling restrictions, and we have introduced flexibility and choice; however, we have not expanded our moral categories to include such easements. Instead, we have behaved as if moral categories were simply no longer relevant. The result has been not the Utopia we had hoped for, but rather a nightmare world in which identity itself has been lost in the shuffle. Such is the burden of Didion's fiction. It seems to be the case, she argues mordantly, that we need moral categories if we are really to "be."

Presented with the bleak message of Didion's analysis of modern America, we are not left entirely without hope. This ransack of our American heritage does, finally, yield an apposite exemplum for the nothingness of Maria's life: Hester Prynne in Hawthorne's *The Scarlet Letter*. Moreover, the ruthless disclosure of Evil that Didion's novel provides is a modern-day equivalent to Hawthorne's intricate dissection of the many forms Malignancy may take. Hawthorne, who may not have believed in an omniscient Divinity, had nonetheless an unshakable faith in the necessity of understanding the transcendent meaning of the immanent world. One simplified way of understanding *The Scarlet Letter* is to see it as a study of that Evil which results from the iron grip of a dour and inflexible church-state, a portrayal of a society that has lost the balance between freedom and duty. Heroism in such a society necessarily entailed violation, the breaking of rigid rules and the exertion of "lawless" freedom. Hawthorne did not intend for his audience to infer that lawlessness was correct; rather he wanted us to recognize that Hester's sin had wrought good after all, that the relationship between freedom and duty is not simple and may even be paradoxical, that a "fortunate fall" can herald the beginning of a new era of moral endeavor. And the scarlet "A" itself iterates the paradox: adultery/beginning.

By the time Maria has to attempt heroism, the world of Hester Prynne has been turned upside-down: where there was once an iron rule, there is now license; where adultery was once branded, marriage and motherhood have become obsolete. Clearly, Maria cannot adopt Hester's mode of heroism, the heroism of violation. Still, she is unwilling to consign herself and her daughter to the drifting, amoral world that Carter navigates so well. Maria has fatal knowledge: "She could not read newspapers because certain stories leapt at her from the page . . . the rattlesnake in the playpen, the peril, unspeakable peril, in the everyday." Maria does more than take note of these macabre facts; she understands that they have meaning.

Within the fiction, Maria's vision is the only one which comprehends the fact that this liberated society is in fact a wasteland; however, she has few tools to combat the forces of Evil around her. Hence Maria often "sees" something which she cannot precisely interpret. She begins the central episode of the abortion looking for "signs." Soon afterwards, a sign appears, but like so many things in this desolate world, what was once endowed with dignity has become vulgar and commercial. " 'Get it right, Maria,' the voice on the telephone said. 'You got a pencil there? You writing this down? . . . Maria, I told you, you can't miss it. Under the big red T.' " Thus the quest begins, and Maria scans the sky. "For miles before she reached the Thriftimart she could see the big red T, a forty-foot cutout letter which seemed peculiarly illuminated against the harsh light of the afternoon sky." Maria cannot read the "meaning" of that giant red letter scorched against the Heavens, but the reader, whose moral intelligence is less fragmented than Maria's, will recall the relevant scene in Hawthorne's great work: Hester, Dimmesdale, and Pearl, mounting the scaffold together at night, the sky suddenly ablaze with a preternatural illumination, and a letter appearing as divine sign. ". . . the minister, looking upward to the zenith, beheld there the appearance of an immense letter,—the letter A,—marked out in lines of dull red light."

Maria follows her "sign," and although she seems oblivious to its implications, she persists restlessly in searching for the meaning of this nightmare experience. Subtly, the red letter which has guided her to the place of violation merges with the increasingly portentous images that suffuse her imagination. She may be undergoing no more than "induced menstruation"; however, all of her associations are dominated by archetypal images of evil and disaster.

> She knew a lot of things about disaster. She could manage. Carter could never manage but she could. She could not think where she had learned all these tricks. Probably in her mother's *American Red Cross Handbook*, gray with a red cross on the cover. . . . If she could concentrate for even one minute on a picture of herself as a ten-year-old sitting on the front steps of

the house in Silver Wells reading the gray book with the red cross on the cover (splints, shock, rattlesnake bite, rattlesnake bite was why her mother made her read it).

The cruciform of the "sign," the red-illuminated T, collapses into this one living memory of a mother who had tried to nurture, of a mother who had known of evil and who had offered as defense against it the gray manual with the red cross on the cover.

Maria cannot parse the meaning of this emblematic red cross, and Didion declines to explicate it for us. Indeed, she even relinquishes the authority of giving her fiction a strong closure, judging perhaps that the evil she has drawn is so pervasive and so powerful that any reassuring "resolution" would only falsify.

Nonetheless, some things are very clear. The red cross here does not signify a beginning; it is in general (as it is concretely for Maria) the emblem of some earlier age, an age whose loving mercy had been founded upon an acknowledgement of suffering, an age when freedom and duty had been more meaningfully balanced. This is no answer. It is, instead, the diagram of an answer, the assertion of the *need* for some answer, some alternative to the "free way" that has led to that nothingness which Maria alone can recognize and understand. And in such an age, perhaps it is enough to merely keep on playing.

NOTES

[1]David J. Geherin, "Nothingness and Beyond: Joan Didion's *Play It As It Lays*," *Critique*, 16, No. 1 (1974), p. 67.

[2]Barbara Grizzuti Harrison, "Joan Didion: The Courage of Her Afflictions," *The Nation* (29 September 1979), pp. 277–279.

[3]Katherine U. Henderson, *Joan Didion* (Frederick Ungar: New York, 1981), pp. 20–21. Henderson's first-rate introductory study of Didion and her work is the best comprehensive work on the author now available.

[4]Maria's last name (Lang) suggests that Didion had the categories of R. D. Laing in mind when describing the world Maria must live in. Didion's implications are not entirely clear; however, it seems most probable that the "Laingian" implications of Maria's *husband's* name (which she must take on) direct us to a public world, indeed a culture, which supports none but vitiated relationships. Thus, although it is of course *Maria* who seems to "break down" or become "crazy," Didion wants us to perceive that Maria's reaction is in some manner a reasonable one—indeed, that it is the only way to evade the *depersonalized* relationships which have become the norm.

A Taut Novel of Disorder
Joyce Carol Oates

IN THE TITLE ESSAY of her superb collection, *Slouching Towards Bethlehem*, Joan Didion draws back briefly from her painful study of the Haight-Ashbury dropouts to comment on the possible meaning of the "social hemorrhaging" she has been observing at close range. The drifting, inarticulate children of the 1960's, drug-besotted and prematurely aged, take on for Didion an almost allegorical significance. They are the pitiful casualties of an immense and perhaps inexplicable social change—an "atomization" prophesied by such visionary poets as Yeats, who wrote in "The Second Coming," "Things fall apart; the center cannot hold;/Mere anarchy is loosed upon the world." Such apocalyptic murmurings have always been with us, the complacent or indifferent are quick to say; what genuine evidence have we for making such statements? Joan Didion's books offer the evidence. Her third and most ambitious novel, *A Book of Common Prayer*, investigates the consequences of this breakdown over the past two decades, particularly on parents and children.

"At some point between 1945 and 1967 we had somehow neglected to tell these children the rules of the game we happened to be playing," wrote Didion in *Slouching Towards Bethlehem*. "Maybe there were just too few people around to do the telling." Charlotte Douglas, the heroine of *A Book of Common Prayer*, is one of the adults who failed to explain the rules of the game to her child. Marin, Charlotte's 18-year-old daughter, was seen with several other young people detonating a crude pipe bomb in a San Francisco office building and later hijacking a plane to Utah, where they burned it in time for the incident to interrupt the network news. Now a fugitive, she participates in revolutionary activity, mainly by making tape recordings in which she speaks of "expropriation" and "firepower" and the need to destroy imperialist symbols. "The fact that our organization is revolutionary in character," Marin says with solemn, mindless circularity, "is due above all to the fact that all our activity is defined as revolutionary."

But perhaps Charlotte Douglas's failure to explain the world to her daughter is a consequence of her own failure to understand it. She is, in Didion's imagination, a not untypical North American who simply revises history, personal and collective, as she goes along. In her stupefying ignorance she is almost innocent, almost a victim; a martyr, perhaps, to our "generally upward spiral of history."

"As a child of comfortable family in the temperate zone," writes Didion, Charlotte "had been as a matter of course provided with clean sheets, orthodontia, lamb chops, living grandparents, attentive godparents, one brother named Dickie, ballet lessons, and casual timely information about menstruation and the care of flat silver. . . . She was immaculate of history, innocent of politics. . . . During the two years she spent at Berkeley . . . she had entered the main library once, during a traveling exhibition of glass flowers from Harvard. She recalled having liked the glass flowers."

Charlotte is an attractive woman in her early 40's who is married to an attractive and very successful San Francisco lawyer involved, in ways not directly explored, with the international sale of weapons. She insists that she is not "political"—and it is, ironically, her refusal to see that she is political that brings about her death; she knows that something is always going on in the world but "believed that it would turn out all right." On a blank map of the world she would have difficulty matching names with countries.

So it is appropriate that Charlotte Douglas, cut adrift and searching for her daughter, comes to Boca Grande, a Central American country that is as close to a blank as a country can be. It is devoid of history: no one is certain who its first settler was. Governments are unstable, but after "colorful" revolutions nothing much is changed. The cathedral is not Spanish Colonial but corrugated aluminum. Principal exports are copra, parrots, anaconda skins and macramé shawls. Planes between Los Angeles and Bogota, or New York and Quito, may stop in Boca Grande to refuel, but otherwise Boca Grande is not connected with the rest of the world. Rather like the Southern California Didion has explored so relentlessly in *Slouching Towards Bethlehem* and her second novel, *Play It As It Lays*, Boca Grande admits of no past. As the sun sets, each day appears to vanish from local memory, never to be recalled. In a state of shock, Charlotte Douglas arrives in this nullity of a country and, after a series of comic and grotesque misadventures with its leading citizens, she dies abruptly and senselessly—shot in the back during one of the colorful revolutions.

Joan Didion has never been easy on her heroines. Suicide always threatens them. In *Run River* the heroine drowns herself; in *Play It As It Lays* the heroine shares a bed with a man who happens to be committing suicide—after a breakdown she manages to survive, barely, minimally. In *A Book of Common Prayer* Charlotte Douglas suffers not only the loss of her daughter (whom she never sees again after the airplane hijacking), but the loss of her former husband (with whom she has desperately eloped, or reeloped) and the loss of an infant born prematurely, after an unwise pregnancy. Having sought to free herself from the burdens of personal history, she is ultimately forced to confront the ugly fact that her parents died lonely and pointless deaths. Her entire life is lived "underwater," as her husband shrewdly notes, and it cannot even be said of Charlotte that she chooses her death: it simply happens, more or less accidentally. Like her life.

Joan Didion is not, of course, alone in her passionate investigation of the atomization of contemporary society. But she is one of the very few writers of our time who approaches her terrible subject with absolute seriousness, with fear and humility and awe. Her powerful irony is often sorrowful rather than clever; the language of *A Book of Common Prayer*, like that of *Play It As It Lays*, is spare, sardonic, elliptical, understated. Melodrama is the nature of Didion's world, but very little emotion is expressed, perhaps because emotion itself has become atrophied.

Like Maria Wyeth of *Play It As It Lays*, Charlotte Douglas "dreams" her life. Traumatized by events, she is able to fix her attention only upon stray, fortuitous details. Sexual experience for both women is a blank, as is "love." As is marriage. Maria seeks custody of her retarded daughter and Charlotte withdraws to a remote Central American country because "in a certain dim way she believed that she had located herself at the very cervix of the world, the place through which a child lost to history must eventually pass." Womanhood and even personhood have little validity to Maria and Charlotte, but motherhood is very real and consequently very damaging. Because Charlotte loves her daughter unwisely, quixotically, and because that love is not reciprocated, she drifts into a permanent state of near madness and finally into death.

While *Play It As It Lays* was filtered through Maria's consciousness and was limited by her numbed state of mind, *A Book of Common Prayer* is narrated by a detached and highly critical observer whose intelligence we trust. Mrs. Grace Strasser-Mendana is a 60-year-old American woman who is dying slowly of cancer, a former anthropologist from Denver, who retired to marry a wealthy Boca Grande planter whom she has outlived by several years. She thinks of herself as a "witness" to Charlotte Douglas's experience (as Charlotte herself is not). But unlike Charlotte, she maintains her detachment and her sanity, and she is a survivor, of sorts, at the novel's conclusion. Bemused, disdainful and quite frequently moved by Charlotte's plight, Mrs. Strasser-Mendana allows Joan Didion a free play of her own speculative intelligence that would have been impossible had the story been told by Charlotte. The device of an uninvolved narrator is a tricky one, since a number of very private details must be presented as if they were within the range of the narrator's experience. But it is a measure of Didion's skill as a novelist that one never questions Mrs. Strasser-Mendana's near omniscience in recalling Charlotte's story. Nor do the parallels between the two American women become too aggressively pointed.

Some of the best parts of *A Book of Common Prayer* are incidental to the plot, but typically Didion: an asinine conversation between Charlotte, her former husband and an FBI man who questions them about their daughter; a brilliant description of the Boca Grande airport and of the queer opaque light of Central America. The doomed elopement of Charlotte and her alcoholic former husband involves a dizzying succession of scenes in cities in the South—Birmingham, New Orleans, Greenville—which unfold in a surreal, diffracted manner.

Has the novel any significant flaws? I would have wished it longer, fuller: I would have liked to know more about the daughter, for instance. But Joan Didion's art has always been one of understatement and indirection, of emotion withheld. Like her narrator, she has been an articulate witness to the most stubborn and intractable truths of our time, a memorable voice, partly eulogistic, partly despairing; always in control.

Joan Didion & Her Characters
John Romano

◆──

TWO PARADOXES CHARACTERIZE Joan Didion's writing. The first concerns her subject matter. She is drawn to the timely-verging-on-fashionable-verging-on-chic, to film stars and wealthy indolence and the sexuality of power. But unlike most writers who earn a living on the public's hunger for the glamorous, she brings a moral consciousness to bear on these subjects: she is acutely judgmental, vulnerable, and can be shocked. This paradox has prompted some reviewers, in discussing her novel about Hollywood, *Play It As It Lays*, to compare her to Nathanael West. But where West was scolding, Joan Didion is merely grouchy. She gives the impression, particularly in the essays collected in *Slouching Towards Bethlehem*, of having come to judge the *Zeitgeist* but of finding it actually beneath judgment; she is too disgusted even to preach.

The other paradox concerns her way of writing. It balances an objective-seeming precision of language and observed detail against the feeling that a particular person is speaking to us, an intelligent, likable, and utterly subjective, even prejudiced person; and, as it happens, someone who lives in or near a condition of unhysterical despair. In this balance there is an explanation for something that is often said about Joan Didion—that her essays are excellent, whereas her fiction is only just good. In *Run River* and *Play It As It Lays*, personal idiosyncrasies overrun the writing, and drench it in desperation; in the essays, with their necessary burden of fact and information, the balance is better kept.

The twin extremes of hopelessness and precision come together in Grace Strasser-Mendana, the narrator of Miss Didion's newest novel, *A Book of Common Prayer*. Grace began as a cultural anthropologist, then married into the leading family of a small country in Central America called Boca Grande. Her in-laws are a debauched and violent crew, jostling each other in and out of political office in bloody but phony revolutions. All of this Grace ignores to the extent that she can, intent instead on the study of biochemistry, which she has taken up in preference to anthropology. Having wearied of the ambiguities of human behavior, she has chosen "a discipline in which demonstrable answers are commonplace and 'personality' absent." The objects of her research are, first of all, cancer, of which she is dying, but also the chemistry of feeling, of character. What happens in *A Book of Common Prayer*, on one level, is that someone named Charlotte Douglas arrives in Boca Grande; that Charlotte turns out to be a person of heartbreaking emotional complexity; and that what is complex and touching and profound about her excites and ultimately overwhelms Grace Strasser-Mendana's will to know, as well as her capacity for knowing.

Charlotte Douglas grew up in the West, "immaculate of history, innocent of politics." As a child she prayed to "a small wooden angel, carved in Austria . . . that 'it' turn out all right, 'it' being unspecified and all-inclusive, and she had been an adult for some years before the possibility occurred to her that 'it' might not." By that time she has married Warren Bogart, who had been her teacher at Berkeley. Warren Bogart is obnoxious, viciously articulate, and a drunkard. He is made up of big, bottomless needs and a powerful sexual charm whose claims on Charlotte seem absolute. After a few years she leaves him, taking with her their daughter Marin. She never frees herself from Warren's enchantment, but she gets married again, in her blank and unperceiving optimism, this time to Leonard Douglas, a San Francisco lawyer internationally famous not only for his representation of left-wing radicals and rock stars in civil-liberties cases, but also as a legal agent in large international arms deals; the contradiction in this double career is almost unnoticeable in the book's dark thicket of cultural-political satire.

With Leonard, Charlotte leads, as Warren puts it, not a life but a "life-style," getting high on marijuana cigarettes that are kept near the bed in a silver box that plays "Puff the Magic Dragon" when the lid is opened. For a while we are in one of those queer, stylish crevices of the 60's counterculture upon which Joan Didion focused such piercing attention in some of the essays in *Slouching Towards Bethlehem*. But later, when Grace is piecing together the shards of Charlotte's past life, the years while Marin is growing up can hardly be accounted for, so impenetrable is the haze in which Charlotte was then living. "For days at a time her answers to Marin's questions would . . . strike the child as weird and unsettling, cheerful but not quite responsive. 'Do you think I'll get braces in fourth grade?' Marin would ask. 'You're going to love fourth grade,' Charlotte would answer."

But so much is background. Because the events with which the book is properly concerned begin on the morning when FBI agents come to Charlotte with the news that Marin, presumed to be away at school, took part in the bombing of the Transamerica building, hijacked a plane to Utah, and is presently in hiding from the law. Joan Didion does not dwell long on the atmosphere of a media circus that surrounds the search for Marin Bogart. What she does give us is apt and telling:

A man who described himself as a disillusioned Scientologist called Charlotte to say that Marin was under the influence of a Clear in Shasta Lake. A masseuse at Elizabeth Arden called Charlotte to say that she had received definitive word from Edgar Cayce via Mass Mind that Marin was with the Hunzas in the Himalayas. The partially decomposed body of a young woman was found in a shallow grave on the Bonneville Salt Flats but the young woman's dental work differed conclusively from Marin's.

When, after some weeks, Marin has not shown up, Charlotte leaves Leonard; returns to Warren; shares with him an aimless and dissolute journey through the South; eventually leaves Warren; finally arrives, in flight from a severe complication of personal and social and historical demons, in the airport at Boca Grande. She is forty. "There was the extreme and volatile thinness of the woman. There was the pale red hair which curled in the damp heat and stood out around her face and seemed almost more weight than she could bear."

As this summary suggests, *A Book of Common Prayer* is oddly sprawling and out of sequence. Only some of its important action takes place in Boca Grande, while most of it concerns Charlotte's life in the United States which Grace reports secondhand. Although the novel is "about" Charlotte Douglas, it's important to see why Miss Didion has established the history and circumstances of her narrator in such detail. Grace's own story is an allegory of the progress of the liberal, humanistic intelligence in the last twenty years. Out of a background informed by the fashionable cultural relativism of the 50's, through a disillusioning alliance with political power in the 60's, Grace emerges in the flat morning light of the present decade with a grim allegiance to secure, empirical systems of information, a will to plot the vagaries of the human individual on a graph of "significant" social and behavioral factors. This is the meaning of Grace's obsession with understanding Charlotte Douglas: "Give me the molecular structure of the protein that defines Charlotte Douglas," she writes. But the punch line is that Grace fails. The individual is at once bigger and more mysterious than the mechanistic models that are meant to comprehend her: that is the moral lesson at the center of this book, and at the center, too, of the humanistic sensibility, with its lingering residue of religious faith.

As for Charlotte, the portrait of her that is painted by Grace is of a woman who exists almost completely in the isolation of her own consciousness, and whose experience of others, of what the novel keeps calling "history," only drives her in deeper. "I think I have never known anyone who led quite so unexamined a life," writes Grace, which is surely right; but it is also true that we never hear the interior noises of Charlotte's own mind. It is of special, rather poignant, interest that Joan Didion, whose writing continually reflects a penchant for self-consciousness and introspection, should present so sympathetic a portrait of an "unexamined life." Through Grace, Miss Didion seems to be working against the grain of her own strongest predilections to signify Charlotte's dilemma: a woman locked in unconsciousness, lacking even the appropriate vocabulary for cursing God and dying.

It is this taking on of a subject matter not easily assimilable to her own broader tones which makes this novel a better book than *Play It As It Lays*. Maria, the central figure in that horrific earlier landscape, was in the grip of the monster nothingness, knew it from the beginning, and only got to know it better as the book progressed. It was a novel that could hardly be more anguished, but one curiously complacent, too, about the anguish it depicted; it seemed to deck itself out too gladly in the clichés of the contemporary novel of neurosis: the Hollywood setting, the drug scene, the mental hospital, the hip sexual self-destruction. *A Book of Common Prayer*, by contrast, provides a suffering heroine for whom we feel more compassion than she is capable of feeling for herself—she embodies Kierkegaard's unnerving paradox that a person can be in despair and not know it—and the result is that her character is not, like Maria's, swamped by the novel's emotional flow. By virtue of this, *A Book of Common Prayer* separates itself, as *Play It As It Lays* did not, from that unfortunate genre, the lyrical-precious novel of female desperation.

The mention of *Play It As It Lays* brings us back to an aspect of Joan Didion's work which I have already mentioned, the fascination with the glamorous. It is present in the new novel to a certain degree. The "beautiful people" hover in the wings of the story, cropping up in the scenes of Charlotte's life with Leonard, associated with Gerardo, Grace's profligate son, and with Warren's wide-ranging acquaintance. Some of the minor portraits seem vaguely *à clef*. There is one scene at least in which these glamorous trimmings pay off. Grieving furiously over her loss of Marin "to history," the one loss her consciousness cannot evade, Charlotte attends a party organized to raise funds for some ambiguous cause. While Leonard dances the limbo on a stage constructed over a pool in Beverly Hills, "an actress who had visited Hanoi" speaks to Charlotte of "the superior health and beauty of the children there":

> "It's because they aren't raised by their mothers," the actress said. "They don't have any of that bourgeois personal crap laid on them."
> Charlotte studied her wine glass and tried to think of something neutral to say to the actress. She wanted to get up but her chair was blocked by three men who seemed to be discussing the financing of a motion picture, or a war.
> "No mama-papa-baby-nuclear-family bullshit," the actress said. "It's beautiful."

War and show business turn into each other in a surreal dance before the eyes of Charlotte, still the child "immaculate" of history and politics. But politics of a theatrical order has also claimed her personally, has taken her child from her—and she herself, in Boca Grande, becomes entangled in a revolution performed, as it were, by marionettes with real guns.

Politics, however, is not what is memorable about this novel; Charlotte Douglas is. Indeed, she is better and larger than the novel she inhabits, and the finest creation in Joan Didion's fiction so far.

Passion and Delusion
in *A Book of Common Prayer*
Victor Strandberg

◆─────────────────────────────────────

IN HER PREFACE to *Slouching Towards Bethlehem* (which begins by quoting all of "The Second Coming"), Joan Didion wrote that for several years certain of Yeats's images—"the widening gyre, the falcon which does not hear the falconer, the gaze blank and pitiless as the sun"—comprised "the only images against which much of what I was seeing and hearing and thinking seemed to make any pattern." Above all, Yeats's image of the dissolving center— "Things fall apart; the centre cannot hold"—has proved to be Didion's master metaphor not only for society at large but for the individual personalities in her writings. Of her sojourn among the Haight-Ashbury dropouts that led to her title essay, "Slouching Towards Bethlehem," she writes, "It was the first time I had dealt directly and flatly with the evidence of atomization, the proof that things fall apart." Not surprisingly, her subsequent novel *Play It As It Lays* portrays the effect of the missing center in the suicidal vacuity of her two leading characters, whose final "Why?" and "Why not?" mark a barely distinguishable to be or not to be.

In *A Book of Common Prayer*, the problem of the missing center shows up not only in her fictional Haight-Ashbury type, the dropout-revolutionary Marin Bogart, but in all of her major characters. Discussing her novel with an interviewer from *The New York Times*, Didion responds to her interviewer's observation that Charlotte Douglas "doesn't seem to have a center, something in herself for which she's living," with this extension of the Yeatsian metaphor: "I don't know too many people who have what you could call clearly functioning centers. . . . It is a problem for all of us to find something at the center. . . . I think most of us build elaborate structures to fend off spending much time in our own center."[1] For lack of anything better in this post-Christian era, Didion observes that the center is likely to be filled with "certain contemporary demons"—Yeats's rough beast in the cradle—of which she specifies two: "flash politics, sexual adventurism."

Didion's disdain for flash politics is evident throughout her book, blatantly rendered in her juxtaposition of Latin American political violence against the playschool revolution of Marin's terrorist group, more subtly rendered in Leonard Douglas' radical chic activities, which include flying off to address a Day of Rage memorial fully aware that while he speaks another man is undertaking to run off with his wife. Sexual adventurism is the deeper issue, taking us into Didion's extended treatment of female identity that comprises the book's most original, profound, and brilliant achievement. In the end, what she has achieved is a female counterpart of *The Great Gatsby*—a book she favors in her essays[2]—redeploying in her own gender Fitzgerald's basic gambit of assigning a detective-narrator to search out the inner truth about a mysterious newcomer ("an outsider of romantic sensibility") who has set the neighborhood abuzz with reports of inexplicable behavior.

Like Nick Carraway, who begins by saying Gatsby "represented everything for which I have an unaffected scorn," Grace Strasser-Mendana opens her narrative with a negative judgment: "Charlotte would call her story one of passion. I believe I would call it one of delusion." But in the end, it is the sophisticated observer, and not the inalterably naive main character, who is transformed by a correction of vision. As Grace comes to see it, "I am more like Charlotte than I thought I was." "I am less and less certain that this story has been one of delusion. Unless the delusion was mine." Indeed, this alteration in the witness—from distaste and incredulity to affinity and admiration—gives both *The Great Gatsby* and *A Book of Common Prayer* their fundamental design, enabling Fitzgerald and Didion to defend America's traditional middle-class ideals, which is what Gatsby's "heightened sensitivity to the promises of life" and Charlotte's "delusions" turn out to encompass.

Among the passions and delusions that Grace discovers in Charlotte's center, sexual passion—or "adventurism"—comprises the most ambiguous and the most typical of modern life. Whereas Gatsby had to settle for a single ecstatic kiss, approached "at an inconceivable pitch of intensity," Charlotte Douglas practices free sexuality with a series of lovers. Grace's earliest impression of Charlotte as a sexual adventuress, with a large emerald having displaced her wedding ring and with "clothes that seemed to betray in their just perceptible disrepair . . . some equivalent disrepair of the morale, some vulnerability, or abandon," is later borne out by the "sexual freight" of Charlotte's gestures, her "reflexively seductive" manner.

Underscoring the emergence of sexual adventurism as a final bastion of meaning in modern life is its concurrence with the holiest festivals of the Christian calendar: two of Charlotte's most casual encounters, with Victor and with Pete Wright, take place on Christmas Eve and on Easter Sunday morning, respectively. By the time she meets Gerardo, her final lover, her sexual volatility is so obvious that his successful proposition comprises "the third thing Gerardo ever said to Charlotte Douglas." It is this volatility, and not the disappearance of his daughter—whom Warren Bogart dismisses with two words: "Fuck Marin"—that brings Warren across the continent in his effort to fill his own center with meaning before his time runs out. "You like it too much," Warren says, apropos of arranging a *ménage à trois*; "You like it more than anybody I ever knew." But he likes it too; Charlotte's passion is exactly what makes her his type of woman: "We could have been doing this all our lives. We should be doing this all our lives. We should have done this all our lives."

Unfortunately, Charlotte's liberated mores do not suffice to define her sex life as merely harmless fun. Even apart from Grace's rather old-fashioned tone of disapproval, Charlotte's sexual passions lead inescapably to a messy, emotionally chaotic life, surrounded by embattled males. The pleasant thrill of being fought over by strong men implies a female archetype as old as Helen; Daisy Fay filled her vacant center similarly for a time watching her husband and Gatsby locked in that primeval battle. When the males are Latin *macho* types, however, the game may quickly become dangerously unpleasant. Charlotte's eventual murder seems ordained within hours of her first night with Victor, in a chapter that leads off with Grace's image of two mating flies and concludes with a sample of Antonio's pistol-packing violence and psychopathic sexual spite: " 'Maybe I'll go get your *norteamericana* to sit on my face,' Antonio said to Victor."

Long before Antonio settles his account with Charlotte and Victor, however, her sexual freedom produces more emotional anarchy than fulfillment in her center of being. There is the delightful scene with the corkscrew, for example, which is worth citing in detail:

> she was . . . incapable of walking normally across a room in the presence of two men with whom she had slept. Her legs seemed to lock unnaturally into her pelvic bones. Her body went stiff, as if convulsed by the question of who had access to it and who did not. Whenever I saw her with both Victor and Gerardo it struck me that her every movement was freighted with this question. Who had prior claim. Whose call on her was most insistent. To whom did she owe what. . . . If she needed a bottle of wine opened . . . she could never just hand the corkscrew to Gerardo. Nor could she hand the corkscrew to Victor. Instead she would evade the question by opening the wine herself, usually breaking the cork.

And, much later, Grace complains that the "sexual current" in Charlotte threatens to "reverse the entire neutron field on my lawn." Certainly it does appear to be "disturbing and altering not only the mood but possibly the cell structure" of her three male spectators:

> Gerardo watched her as she ran across the lawn.
> Victor watched her as she ran across the lawn.

Antonio crouched on the lawn. . . ,
"*Norteamericana* cunt," Antonio said. . . .

In dealing with this motif of sexual current, Joan Didion has performed a
badly needed service for American literature. John Updike—no novice at
writing about sex in his own right—has observed that American literature is
notoriously thin in its portrayal of women. For one thing, a number of our
finest women writers have been less than typical of the gender—spinsters and
recluses like Emily Dickinson or lesbians like Gertrude Stein and Willa Cather.
For another, even our most sensitive male writers have displayed sharp limitations in their imagination of what it means to be a woman. Not Hawthorne
or Henry James or Faulkner ever rendered woman's sexual energy (and Grace's
response to it) with Didion's sureness of touch; nor did any of them ever
reach far enough into the female psyche so as to come up with Didion's twin
"commonplaces of the female obsessional life"—"sexual surrender and infant
death. . . . We all have the same dreams."

So far as sexual surrender is concerned, Charlotte's "passion" involves one
perfectly standard element of female psychology: the determination to entice
and to capture the most superior—that is, successful—male in the surrounding
herd. Thus it is not surprising that she chooses as bed partners the dictator
of Boca Grande and the playboy-scion of the island's wealthiest family, and
as husbands a prominent lawyer and her college English teacher (a superior
male from her coed's-eye-view, at least).

As a revelation of female sexual psychology, this latter relationship is the
most complex and fascinating in the book. On the face of it, Warren Bogart's
victory over Leonard in their battle for sexual possession of Charlotte appears
to be a mystery. Unlike Leonard, Warren is crude, obnoxious, totally selfish,
impecunious, professionally unsuccessful, and sexually unfaithful. But offset-
ting all those damaging characteristics are the intelligence and virility that
give Warren "the look of a man who could drive a woman like Charlotte right
off her head." That virility, beginning in the bedroom ("We should have been
doing this all our lives"), focuses upon Charlotte with a flattering and exciting
intensity. He has come these three thousand miles, Warren says, neither to
save Marin nor to bring Charlotte home with him (her surmise) but simply
because "I just wanted to fuck you again"—which had also been Leonard's
suspicion. A coarse approach, to be sure, but one which renders sincere tribute
to the woman's beauty. This biological nexus between female beauty and
male potency has evoked a memorable and relevant meditation by Isaac
Bashevis Singer: "The sexual organs are the most sensitive organs of the
human being. . . . An eye will not stop seeing if it doesn't like what it sees,

but the penis will stop functioning if he doesn't like what he sees. I would say that the sexual organs express the human soul more than any other limb of the body. . . . They tell the truth ruthlessly."[3]

Warren Bogart also tells the truth ruthlessly outside the bedroom. What perhaps most drives a woman like Charlotte off her head is the social virility and intelligence of the man, that total reliance on his own psychic resources which enables him to stand in clear definition against the spongy liberal chic of the times. Even his ethnic slurs—against Jews, Arabs, Armenians—are offered mainly as a liberal-baiting exercise (Charlotte had been to the Democratic National Convention in 1964, a year when Joan Didion voted for Barry Goldwater[4]); in any event, Warren evens the balance politically with his deft and total destruction of "Irving" the FBI man. For all his repulsive qualities, Warren Bogart exhibits a sexual magnetism that could be instructive to even our finest male writers.

So far as "passion" is concerned, in sum, Charlotte has been a sexually active, adventurous, liberated modern woman. But her sexual freedom has not filled her emotional center, as she makes clear in her parting remark to her last bed partner, Gerardo, when he begs her to flee with him on Day Eight: "I wasn't connected to you actually." In the old-fashioned preliberation style, she has continued to focus her deepest passion upon Warren, her first lover and the only male able to dominate her psychologically. Not even her ploy of conceiving a baby with Leonard could succeed in stifling that innermost flame from flaring out of control in Warren's presence. The reason Charlotte runs off with Warren, leaving Leonard, is no more mysterious in the end than the primitive rite on the Orinoco "where female children were ritually cut on the inner thigh by their first sexual partners, the point being to scar the female with the male's totem"; and though Warren's cut "doesn't show" on Charlotte, he asserts that totemic power the moment he greets her: "Get somebody to wash and iron that, Charlotte. . . . The suit just needs pressing."

If Charlotte turns out to be, under her avant-garde veneer, an old-fashioned, middle-class, one-man woman, the book's other characters cannot claim any superior success in more genuinely espousing the new freedom of sexuality. Apart from Warren, whose zeal appears heightened by his race against terminal illness, the sexual encounter does little for anyone's emotional center: Victor is bored by his noontime manicurist; the "intimations of sexual perfidy" that abound at Morgan Fayard's home lead to an evening of strident disharmony; the OAS man makes an ugly scene when Charlotte (who had saved his life with an emergency tracheotomy) refuses to fellate him on the hotel terrace; the two lesbians from Miss Porter's School virtually break up when the younger one makes a pass at Charlotte ("The older one wept"); and Bebe

Chicago's life as an aging gay seems pathetic: " 'Spare me any more of Bebe Chicago's calls.' Victor [having wiretapped them] mimicked a whispery falsetto. 'Ricardo? . . . *C'est moi, chéri.* Bebe.' " It all adds up to what Faulkner called "the vain evanescence of the fleshly encounter." Regrettably, sexual passion appears even less viable within marriage than in these joyless fornications and adulteries. As though confirming Updike's thesis (via Denis de Rougemont) about the incompatibility of marriage and passion,[5] Didion portrays both Charlotte's marriage to Leonard and the marriage of Dickie and Linda as having become sexless, while Grace's marriage to Edgar had never pretended to be anything more than an economic arrangement. Perhaps Grace's aunt was right "to locate the marriage bed as the true tropic of fever and disquiet."

If "passion"—sexual passion, at any rate—clearly fails to fill Charlotte's center of being, especially after she has left Warren, that leaves the other wing of Grace's theme statement to consider: "I would call it [her story] one of delusion." It is this motif of delusion which, modulating into the book's master theme, most closely identifies Charlotte Douglas as a female counterpart to Gatsby, for her "delusions" originate, like Gatsby's, in her upbringing as the archetypal all-American girl dedicated to the quintessential middle-class ideal of self-improvement ("improving one's world and one's self simultaneously" is how Didion's essay "Good Citizens" puts it [*WA*]). Thus Gatsby's regimen of self-improvement as a boy in North Dakota—"Dumbbell exercise," "Practice elocution," "Work," "Read one improving book or magazine per week," "Save $5.00 [crossed out] $3.00 per week," "Be better to parents"— finds its analogue in Charlotte's girlhood in Hollister, California: "As a child of the western United States she had been provided . . . with faith in the . . . virtues of cleared and irrigated land, . . . of thrift, industry and the judicial system, of progress and education, and in the generally upward spiral of history. She was a *norteamericana.*" To this portrait are added actions that bespeak the "diffusion of competence" that Eric Hoffer has pronounced a distinguishing characteristic of North American society. She kills a chicken with a bare-handed gesture; she field-strips her cigarettes; she performs a successful emergency tracheotomy; she dispenses cholera vaccine for thirty-four straight hours—actions that leave the Boca Grandeans "staring" and "speechless" and lead to Victor's violent revulsion: "Disgusting. . . . Filthy. Crude. The thought of it makes me retch . . . the kind of woman who would kill a chicken with her bare hands."

This reaction reveals as delusory another crucial component of the North American ethos: "She believed the world to be peopled with others like herself." Loss of innocence concerning this delusion has been a prevalent theme in American literature—one thinks of Melville's Captain Delano, of James's Isabel Archer or Christopher Newman, and, again, of Nick Carraway, who had to find out for himself, through witnessing Gatsby's ruin, the truth of his father's warning that "a sense of the fundamental decencies is parcelled out unequally at birth." In all these instances, passage from innocence to awareness involves a juxtaposition of cultures. Just as Scott Fitzgerald summoned Gatsby/Nick from their native midwest so as to limn their "fundamental decencies" against the corruptions of the Eastern elite, Joan Didion brings Charlotte/Grace to Boca Grande to establish in the highlight of contrast the superiority of their original *norteamericana* ethos. The quintessence of the North American ethic, outlined in Himalayan relief against the code of the jungle in Boca Grande, is summed up in four words: take care of somebody. "It doesn't matter whether you take care of somebody or somebody takes care of you," Warren says—"It's the same thing in the end." It's all the same, too, whether this moral stance is efficacious and reciprocal, or hopeless (taking care of the hydrocephalic baby) and without recompense (taking care of Marin). All that matters in the end is that this act of emotional investment fills Charlotte's center with an immensely vitalizing psychic energy and purpose, in the same way that Gatsby's impassioned devotion to Daisy fills his.

Having lost both of her husbands and both of her children, Charlotte finds in Boca Grande only one outlet for her *norteamericana* "delusions": she "takes care of" Boca Grande. Her work ethic, expanding in North American fashion from self-improvement to improvement of the surrounding environment, fastens upon three of the island's most dreadful needs: for cultural nourishment, she plans a film festival and boutique; for the public health, she dispenses cholera vaccine thirty-four hours without stopping; for limiting of population— Latin America's most desperate need—she works in a birth-control clinic. In thus taking care of her South American environment, the *norteamericana* is as ineffectual as she was in her earlier attempts to take care of her husbands and children. Her film festival and boutique never get past the laughter stage, she loses control over the supply of vaccine, and in the birth-control clinic she plumps witlessly for diaphragms, not discerning that the native women can use only the IUD effectively.

No question about it, in Boca Grande Charlotte's North American ideals are delusions. But these delusions are vindicated in the end by an insight perhaps best described by Joseph Conrad—a writer whom both Didion and Fitzgerald have acknowledged as a guiding influence.[6] Conrad was speaking, in *Heart of Darkness*, of the concept of empire, which "is not a pretty thing when you look into it too much. What redeems it is the idea only. An idea . . . and an unselfish belief in the idea—something you can set up, and bow down before, and offer a sacrifice to. . . ." The mistake does not consist in having the delusion; it lies in examining that vitalizing idea too closely, "not a pretty thing when you look into it too much." As Robert Penn Warren put it, speaking of Conrad, "the last wisdom is for man to realize that though his values are illusions, the illusion is necessary, is infinitely precious, is the mark of his human achievement, and is, in the end, his only truth."[7]

Both Gatsby and Charlotte become victims of delusion most of all by centering their passion upon love objects that are palpably unworthy of such devotion, creatures who in fact no longer resemble the sweetheart or daughter being lovingly remembered. In doing so, both characters exhibit arrested emotional development: "Can't repeat the past? . . . Why of course you can" (*Great Gatsby*) is as much Charlotte's delusion as Gatsby's, despite the warning from Grace's aunt—"*Remember Lot's Wife, avoid the backward glance.*" But in drawing this parallel between Charlotte and Gatsby, it is important to discern as well the differences between them grounded in gender identity. As a suitor who lost his woman to a superior male—superior by birth and wealth— Gatsby can repair his damage to his sense of worth, that "Platonic conception of himself" which Daisy subserves, only by making that woman admit she was mistaken; and this effort to make her admit "You never loved him" is exactly the point at which his five-year dream shatters ("Oh, you want too much! . . . I can't help what's past").

Charlotte, woman-wise (as Didion would have it), grounds her identity in her "occupation *Madre*"; her need is to repair the damage to that self-image caused by her daughter's repudiation. By waiting for Marin to fly to Boca Grande, much as Gatsby waits at the end for Daisy's phone call—and both wait faithful unto death—Charlotte illustrates a theme that was, again, of paramount importance to Joseph Conrad: "Those who read me know my conviction that the world, the temporal world, rests on a few very simple ideas. . . . It rests notably . . . on the idea of Fidelity."[8] For Joan Didion, who describes herself as "committed mainly to the exploration of moral distinctions and ambiguities," fidelity translates into "our loyalties to those we love" (*STB*), especially within the context of "the basic notion that keeping promises matters" (*WA*). Inasmuch as Didion couches these precepts—the only absolutes in an age of moral chaos—in terms of woman's psychology, perhaps her truest analogue traces back beyond Gatsby and Conrad to Henry James's Isabel Archer in *The Portrait of a Lady* (a work cited in Didion's essay "The Women's Movement" [*WA*]).[9] Especially in the image of "Charlotte's body . . . found, where it was thrown, on the lawn of the American embassy," do we see the elevation of the "*norteamericana* cunt" to Portrait of a Lady status, both parts of Antonio's vulgar phrase being transfigured by Charlotte's martyrdom into her highest encomium. In James's novel, the distinctive American ideology—"Take hold of something"—begins with "the sense that life was vacant without some private duty that might gather one's energies to a point" and develops into an attitude perfectly descriptive of Charlotte in Boca Grande: "[Isabel] had said to herself that we must take our duty where we find it, and that we must look for it as much as possible." In the end, "Take hold of something" for James, as for Didion, means "take care of somebody," portrayed in Isabel's self-martyring care of Pansy.

Not even the imaginative empathy of James, however, can measure up to Joan Didion's rendering of the female psyche, especially as portrayed in her novel's prevailing Mother-Child imagery. The two supremely moving scenes in the book raise that imagery virtually to Madonna and Child magnitude. One of those scenes is that in which Grace reclaims Marin by the power of a single word ("'Tivoli,' I said,"), on behalf of Charlotte's memory. The other episode shows Charlotte, with her doomed baby, demonstrating exactly what it means to take care of somebody:

> Mérida was where she had taken the baby to die of complications, her baby, Leonard's baby, . . . the baby born prematurely, hydrocephalic, and devoid of viable liver function in the Ochsner Clinic in New Orleans. . . . The doctors had said the baby would die in the hospital but it did not. . . . Toward the beginning of the two weeks she waited for the baby to die she moistened its lips with tap water and told it about the places they would see together. . . .
>
> The night in Mérida when the diarrhea finally came Charlotte held the small warm dehydrating creature in her arms all night. . . . she had not wanted the baby to die without her. . . . She walked with the baby on the dark asphalt. She sang to the baby out on the edge of the asphalt . . . walked there with the baby in her arms, trusting at last, its vomit spent. The doctor . . . marked the death certificate in English: *death by complications*.

Further heightening the maternal consciousness that pervades this book are numerous additional allusions to births, babies, and child-rearing. Boca Grande itself—the name "Big Mouth" could be a sexual pun—is a place of "amniotic stillness" to which Charlotte came in hopes that here her child would be reborn to her: "in a certain dim way Charlotte believed that she had located herself at the very cervix of the world, the place through which a child lost to history must eventually pass." (In so far as Marin is in danger of arrest anywhere in the United States, Charlotte's move to Boca Grande is far from scatterbrained; it also shows yet a further dimension of her maternal self-sacrifice.) The references to child-rearing, in addition to the book's central focus on Charlotte's rearing of Marin, range from the anthropologically primitive

(Grace's "extensive and well-regarded studies on the rearing of female children in the Mato Grosso") to the radically modern:

> ...at Charlotte's table, an actress who had visited Hanoi spoke of the superior health and beauty of the children there.
> "It's because they aren't raised by their mothers," the actress said. "They don't have any of the bourgeois personal crap laid on them."
> Charlotte studied her wine glass....
> "No mama-papa-baby-nuclear-family bullshit," the actress said. "It's beautiful."...
> "I know why you're crying," the actress said after a while.

Implicit in some of Didion's baby imagery is her critique of an adult world that has lapsed backward toward infantile behavior. "More and more we have been hearing the wishful voices of . . . perpetual adolescents," she writes in her critique "The Women's Movement" (*WA*); "how much cleaner to stay forever children." Thus, in her novel, the political conspiracy in Boca Grande is led by a man named Bebe Chicago, while Marin's political aberration is strewn with reminders of her unformed adolescent condition: the orthodontal retainer that identifies her to the FBI; the impacted logic of the tape message; the fact that Marin's root motive appears to be her failure to get admitted (like her friend Lisa) to Stanford ("Marin cried when the letter came from Stanford"). And the book's theme of immature sexual conduct relates to the baby motif in Warren's outcry over oncoming impotence: "'I can't get it up,' Warren said when she tried to wake him. 'Baby, baby, I can't get it up.'" Culturally, the "most offensive of the poets" at Charlotte's "evenings" exhibits a different kind of lapse from adult propriety in his "sequence of Mother-and-Child sonnets to present to the people of Cuba." Finally, there is Charlotte's own reversion to childhood behavior as a reaction to Marin's disappearance: lying all day on Marin's bed and developing the persona that initially impresses Grace as comparable to a seven-year-old's.

But beyond these disparaging nuances in the baby motif lies a larger and opposite meaning: that dependence of every human creature, child and adult alike, on the care and fidelity of others, which makes their communal life a Book of Common Prayer. With respect to this theme, it is the relationship between Grace and Charlotte that proves, for Grace, radically transforming. At the beginning, Grace's persona evinces two paramount and—she comes to discover—related characteristics: (1) absolute independence, financially, politically, and, above all, emotionally (she has no delusions); and (2) a hollow-woman condition (she has no center). Like Charlotte, she has "lost" her child, Gerardo, and has lost her husband, Edgar; but she has long since ceased to grieve over these losses—if she ever did grieve ("The morning Edgar died I called Victor, signed the papers, walked out to the Progreso as usual and ate lunch on the sea wall.") But this dead-soul state, perhaps indicative of too long a stay in Boca Grande, gives way in the end to Grace's *norteamericana* mores, dormant for decades but now revitalized through her relationship to Charlotte. "For better or worse," Didion says in "On Morality," "we are what we learned as children." Both Nick Carraway and Grace, by rediscovering the values of their respective Midwestern and *norteamericana* upbringing, earn narrow escapes from the corruptions of a dangerously subversive alien society, Nick fleeing back West from "the rotten crowd" (though he had come "East, permanently, I thought"), Grace filling her center by taking care of Charlotte.

The gradual rekindling of maternal care in Grace is related to an increasing use of child imagery to portray Charlotte in the book's closing chapters. Merely childish in her earlier encounters with Grace—using words "as a seven-year-old might" at the Christmas party and wearing a "bébé dress" the night she seduces Gerardo—Charlotte becomes appealingly childlike as the nature of her "delusions" becomes clarified. Her work with the cholera vaccine, when exposed as a delusion, evokes in Grace a powerful surge of parental feeling:

> I think I loved Charlotte in that moment as a parent loves the child who has just fallen from a bicycle, met a pervert, lost a prize, come up in any way against the hardness of the world.
> I think I was also angry at her, again like a parent, furious that she hadn't known better. . . .

It is Charlotte's fatal delusion, however—her refusal to flee Boca Grande—that brings this rendering of the mother-child motif to its highest expression. The episode opens with Grace's vain efforts at persuasion—" 'Charlotte.' I felt as if I were talking to a child. 'I've told you before, there is trouble here. There is going to be more trouble. . . . ' " It continues with the scene of Charlotte's farewell to Grace at the airport: "The last time I saw Charlotte alive . . . she pinned her gardenia on my dress . . . [and] dabbed her Grés perfume on my wrists. Like a child helping her mother dress for a party." And it concludes, following Charlotte's overnight detention at the Escuela de los Ninos Perdidos (School for Lost Children), with Grace's rites for Charlotte's body—reminiscent of Nick's last fidelity to Gatsby—which conjoin the *norteamericana* motif with that of the child in the image of "a child's T-shirt . . . printed like an American flag" on Charlotte's coffin.

As the title implies, *A Book of Common Prayer* weaves its various motifs together—birth imagery, the mother-and-child motif, taking care of somebody—through reference to the central "delusion" of the Western world, the Christian faith. Though no longer an orthodox believer, Didion, who calls herself "quite religious in a certain way" (she was raised an Episcopalian[10]) renders her final meaning by touching deeply into our Western religious consciousness, most notably in her greatly original and powerful manipulation of Christian symbolism. In the end, Charlotte's martyrdom evinces a Christlike effect, such that the passion of Charlotte Douglas, sexually considered, gives way to the Passion of Charlotte Douglas, a sacrificial scapegoat and testament to grace who (as Didion put it in an interview) "finds her life by leaving it."[11]

Our first indication of Charlotte's assignment to this Christlike role is the happenstance that she first appears before Grace at a Christmas party, celebrating a holiday whose Spanish name—"*Feliz Navidad*," Victor tells Grace—adds a double meaning to the book's birth imagery. Not only was this occasion the "birth" of her "child" Charlotte into Grace's life, it also presaged the Happy Birth (or rebirth) of Grace's own psyche, eventually rescued from its dead-soul condition by the advent of this stranger on Christmas Eve. Among later echoes of the Gospel story, perhaps none is more poignant than the book's Communion symbolism, used in connection with those who are closest to Charlotte and betray her. Her brother Dickie, for example, fails to remember the burnt biscuits they had shared as children—this when Charlotte is deeply in need of this communal bond. And her betrayal by Marin evokes not only the eucharistic "body and blood" but also a touch of the *lama sabachthani*: "she [had] believed that when she walked through the valley of the shadow, she would be sustained by the taste of Marin's salt tears, her body and blood. The night Charlotte was interrogated . . . she cried not for God but for Marin." And perhaps even her menstrual issue when the bomb goes off is a kind of female stigmata ("She remembers she bled"); her immolation, after all, relates directly to her being female, a "*norteamericana* cunt."

Apropos of her name, Grace's own role is couched at last in terms of the Gospels. In an interview, Ms. Didion says "the whole thing was a prayer. You could say that this was Grace's prayer for Charlotte's soul."[12] Reinforcing that effect are not only the book's title and its paratactic, repetitive style, like that of the Bible or an Anglican litany, but also its use of the Gospel term, "witness." Between the novel's opening statement, "I will be her witness," and its terminal line, "I have not been the witness I wanted to be," there transpires the change in Grace's personality—a religious conversion, in effect—that measures the efficacy of Charlotte's life and martyrdom. And perhaps the most crucial index of the change in Grace is something that her role as witness, chanting a prayer for Charlotte's soul, implies: her new attitude toward memory.

"This do ye . . . in remembrance of me." These words in I Corinthians 11:25 clearly aim at preserving the Savior's sacrifice perpetually in human memory, which is just what the Christian Communion ritual has achieved for two millennia now. But as a Waste Land figure (before her "conversion"), Grace knows well the meaning of T. S. Eliot's warnings, in "Rhapsody on a Windy Night," for example, or at the outset of *The Waste Land*: "April is the cruellest month . . . mixing/Memory and desire." She, too, prefers the "Winter kept us warm" attitude—"covering/Earth in forgetful snow, feeding/A little life with dried tubers." Confirming Eliot's wisdom is the advice from Grace's aunt: "*Dwelling on the past leads to unsoundness and dementia. . . . Remember Lot's Wife, avoid the backward glance.*" And, in less elegant phrasing, there is the corresponding advice of brother Dickie, just before the conversation about burnt biscuits:

> "Listen," Charlotte said finally. . . . "Dickie, I've been remembering some things since Marin left."
> "That's no good for you, Char, remembering. Remembering is shit. Forget her."

But in the end Grace devotes both her life—as in the "Tivoli" episode with Marin—and her narrative to the remembrance of Charlotte. In so doing, she finds the answer to two problems of our age that, for lack of a "converted" or religious sensibility of some kind, appear nigh insuperable in twentieth-century literature. The first of these is alienation, the condition that leads her to describe herself as " '*de afuera*,' an outsider. I am *de afuera*. I have been *de afuera* all my life." Even Warren Bogart, for all his social presumption, shares this malady: "He belonged to nothing. He was an outsider. . . . We were both *de afuera*, Warren Bogart and I. At the time I met him we were also both dying of cancer, Warren Bogart and I, which perhaps made us even more *de afuera* than usual. . . ." And Charlotte, despite her delusion that "Marin and I are inseparable," is so "afflicted by what she called the 'separateness' " that she telephones the California Highway Patrol just to hear (taped) voices. With sex proving a weak and evanescent bond at best, Charlotte's answer to this problem is Conradian—a total immersion in her work in Boca Grande that, though a delusion, evokes some of Conrad's finest sentences: "From the hard work of men [is] born the sympathetic consciousness of a common destiny. . . . For the great mass of mankind the only saving grace that is needed is steady fidelity to what is nearest at hand and heart in the short moment of each human effort."[13] For Grace, the answer to the *de afuera* state is finally her life of Common Prayer, her sense of her bond or communion that makes her "more like Charlotte than I thought I was."

The other great problem of our age—like alienation, it was once called an existential problem—is that of coping with mortality. Initially, Grace and Charlotte represent polar opposites of experience and innocence with respect to the Burial of the Dead. Grace, who lost her mother at age eight and her father at age ten, attained her freedom from delusion as a result of the latter bereavement ("I have been for fifty of my sixty years a student of delusion"). Without delusions, she has used her emotional independence as a stay against death, avoiding the backward glance as she does when her husband dies: "Unlike Charlotte, I learned early to keep death in my line of sight, keep it under surveillance, keep it on cleared ground and away from any brush where it might coil unnoticed. The morning Edgar died I . . . walked out to the Progreso as usual and ate lunch on the sea wall." Charlotte, by contrast, follows the *norteamericana* pattern of denial or suppression concerning awareness of mortality. She refuses to submit to Leonard's and Grace's assertions that Warren is dying ("*He is not dying*"), and she evades other intimations of mortality—including reminders of her parents' deaths—until the moment her lawyer recommends "declaring your daughter legally dead," whereupon Charlotte tears up the stock certificates that would thus have become cashworthy. Now at last Charlotte realizes that "People did die . . . and she had been too busy to notice," an acknowledgment that prompts a momentary feeling of superiority in Charlotte's witness: "When I think of Charlotte Douglas apprehending death at the age of thirty-nine in the safe-deposit vault of a bank of San Francisco it occurs to me that there was some advantage in having a mother who died when I was eight, a father who died when I was ten, before I was busy."

But here Grace herself is wrong. Though aware of mortality, she has not found a meaningful way of coping with it, as is evident in her inability to deal with fear of the dark. "Fear of the dark exists irrelative to patterns of child-rearing in the Mato Grosso or Denver, Colorado," she observes, referring to her own North American habitat in childhood—an admission that, combined with her extravagant love for the light in Boca Grande ("I continue to live here only because I love the light") indicates an *angst* beyond assuagement by her usual practice of emotional detachment. Because it is beyond assuagement, Grace commits her nearest approximation of self-delusion at this point, knowing very well the irrelevance (however clinically correct it may be) of her biochemical analysis: "Fear of the dark is an arrangement of fifteen amino acids. Fear of the dark is a protein." Once again, by way of effecting the "conversion" of Grace to a new sensibility, it is Warren Bogart who formulates the truth to live by (he had done similar duty for "take care of somebody"), and it is Charlotte Douglas who verifies the truth in act and deed.

As the pioneering figure for the theme of mortality—the first main character to die—Warren proclaims the subject at Morgan Fayard's party with his typical truth-teller's forcefulness: " 'You're all dying. You're dying, your wife and sister are dying, your little children are dying, Chrissie here is dying, even Miss Tabor there is dying. . . . But not one of you is dying as fast as I'm dying.' Warren Bogart smiled." To cope with this fact, Warren turns not to Grace's biochemical science but to passion (his sexual odyssey) and poetry. Although used in a partly satiric context, the poetry Warren selects is greatly moving and relevant in light of his own terminal illness: Tennyson's "Crossing the Bar," Bryant's "Thanatopsis," Pope's "that long disease, my life," W. H. Auden's "Time and fevers/Burn away/And the grave proves the child ephemeral." In the end, Grace proves the efficacy of Warren's example by abandoning her protein molecule in favor of poetry: "*Sand-strewn caverns cool and deep/ Where the winds are all asleep.* . . . I will sit in the dark reciting Matthew Arnold as usual." And, reversing her earlier judgment that "Also, for the record, Charlotte was afraid of the dark," Grace concludes her narrative with the image of Charlotte striding briskly through the dark the night she died: "All I know now is that when I think of Charlotte Douglas walking in the hot night wind toward the lights at the Capilla del Mar, I am less and less certain that this story has been one of delusion. Unless the delusion was mine."

Grace's discovery that "I have not been the witness I wanted to be" recalls the conversion motif affecting previous witnesses in American literature such as Jack Burden, Nick Carraway, and Lambert Strether. But Joan Didion's use of that tradition gains extra power from its apocalyptic setting, her analogue to Yeats's line, "Mere anarchy is loosed upon the world." The anarchy in *A Book of Common Prayer* ranges from the political (the *guerrilleros* in Boca Grande, terrorism in the United States) to the moral (Charlotte's *norteamericana* ideals are delusions) to—perhaps most important—the religious (the night Charlotte died, she cried not for God but for Marin). And for Didion the anarchy seems ubiquitous and final: unlike Eliot, she poses no Anglican sanctuary from chaos; unlike Pound, she eschews the State as a conceivable refuge; unlike Fitzgerald, she has no friendly, stable Middle West waiting back there to receive the lost child who has learned his lesson. (That lesson, Nick's discovery that "They're a rotten crowd," has its analogue in Charlotte's "*Goddamn you all.*")

But Yeats, who posed the issue of the collapsing center, also went furthest to resolve it. In "Two Songs from a Play," Yeats acknowledges the mutability

of all centers—including civilization-sustaining centers like Christ and
Dionysus—but as against this "darkening thought" he ascribes to mankind
an eternal flame of spiritual creativity: "Whatever flames upon the night/Man's
own resinous heart has fed." That Yeatsian flame is exactly what Grace comes
to see in Charlotte Douglas. She sees, moreover, that, delusory or not, it
sheds the only light men have ever had, comprising their "perilous triumph
of being over nothingness" (*STB*), their taking up arms against "that dread
of the meaningless which was man's fate" (*WA*).

In portraying this theme, Joan Didion thereby subjects "The Second Coming"
to a significant correction. Although it may be true that in her book "the worst
are full of passionate intensity," the novel belies Yeats's assertion that "The
best lack all conviction." Isolated from her text, Joan Didion's central convictions—"take care of somebody," "keeping promises matters," "Loyalties to
those we love"—may seem hackneyed or banal, but in context they are no
more so than Henry James's "Take hold of something," Conrad's "idea of
Fidelity," or Fitzgerald's "there is literally no standard in life other than a
sense of duty."[14] Further, although written in a mood of elegy, like Updike's
tribute to "the Protestant kind of goodness going down with all the guns
firing," Didion's novel captures something of Updike's hope—"Only goodness
lives. But it does live"—in her motif of the witness transmitting the flame or
the memory into a morally darkening era.[15]

In writing from these deep-seated convictions, Joan Didion clearly links
herself to a major tradition in American fiction. But to say that she displays
important affinities with these other artists is not at all to say that Didion is
merely imitative or derivative. In fact, her fiction maintains T. S. Eliot's
classic balance between tradition and individual talent. With respect to the
artistic rendering of her moral vision, her mastery of fictional elements like
style, mood, characterization, narrative design, setting, and imagery, Didion
is very much her own person, an original talent. "I think . . . a novel is nothing
if it is not the expression of an individual voice, of a single view of experience,"
she says, "—and how many good or even interesting novels, of the thousands
published, appear each year?" (*STB*). At the time this analysis is being completed, *A Book of Common Prayer* has lived barely two years within the
public domain, hardly time enough to acquire a substantial readership, let
alone ascend to permanent glory. Nonetheless, on the basis of its significant
moral vision, its enviable artistic power, and—behind all else—its penetrating
intelligence, *A Book of Common Prayer* easily transcends Joan Didion's "good
or even interesting" category and approaches the category of a great reading
experience. It may, and I believe should, become one of the landmark novels
of the decade.

NOTES

[1]Sara Davidson, "A Visit with Joan Didion," *The New York Times Book Review*, 3 April 1977, p. 38.

[2]In *The White Album*, Didion compares Bishop Pike to Gatsby and Tom Buchanan in "James Pike, American"—a devastating critique of the eminent churchman. Additional references to Fitzgerald occur in *WA* essays "In Hollywood" and "Sojourns," as well as the *STB* essays "On Keeping a Notebook," "On Self-Respect," and "I Can't Get that Monster Out of My Mind."

[3]Richard Burgin, "Isaac Bashevis Singer Talks...About Everything," *The New York Times Magazine*, 26 November 1978, p.26.

[4]Joan Didion's vote for Barry Goldwater in 1964 is disclosed in Michiko Kakutani's essay, "Joan Didion: Staking Out California," *The New York Times Magazine*, 10 June 1979, p. 38. Professor Mark Winchell's forthcoming book on Joan Didion astutely discusses the ideological theme in *A Book of Common Prayer*.

[5]John Updike's "Foreword" to *Assorted Prose* (New York: Fawcett Crest, 1966), p. ix.

[6]Didion expresses her debt to Conrad's *Heart of Darkness* in Davidson, p. 38 and in the *WA* essay, "On the Morning After the Sixties." (See also "Sojourns" [*WA*] for her debt to *Victory*.) Andrew Turnbull's edition of Fitzgerald's *Letters* (*The Letters of F. Scott Fitzgerald* [New York: Charles Scribner's Sons, 1963]) includes seventeen references to Conrad, e.g. "God! I've learned a lot from him" (p. 482).

[7]Robert Penn Warren, *Selected Essays* (New York: Vintage Books, 1966), p. 45.

[8]Joseph Conrad, "A Familiar Preface," excerpted in the Norton Critical Edition of *Heart of Darkness* (New York, 1971), p. 140.

[9]For further evidence of Didion's debt to Henry James, see Davidson, p. 38; "Where the Kissing Never Stops" and "The Seacoast of Despair" in *STB*; and "Sojourns" in *WA*.

[10]Davidson, p. 37.

[11]*Ibid.*, p. 38.

[12]*Ibid.*, p. 37.

[13]Joseph Conrad, "Tradition" and "Well Done," excerpted in Norton, pp. 141, 142.

[14]See *The Letters of F. Scott Fitzgerald*, p. 530.

[15]Updike's comment about "Protestant goodness" occurs in *Time* magazine, 26 April 1968, p. 74. His assertion that "Only goodness lives" comes at the end of *The Centaur*.

Against Interpretation: Narrative Strategy in *A Book of Common Prayer*
John Hollowell

◆

> "We interpret what we see, select the most workable of the multiple choices. We live entirely, especially if we are writers, by the imposition of a narrative line upon disparate images, by the 'ideas' with which we have learned to freeze the shifting phantasmagoria which is our actual experience. . . . Or at least we do for a while."
>
> —Joan Didion, "The White Album"

> "Ideally, it is possible to elude the interpreters in another way, by making works of art whose surface is so unified and clean, . . . whose address is so direct that the work can be . . . just what it is."
>
> —Susan Sontag, *Against Interpretation*

JOAN DIDION'S NOVELS and works of nonfiction are about people, usually women, whose lives are tangled and troubled. The books may be set in Haight-Ashbury, in Hollywood, or in an imaginary Central American republic. The women view their lives as a series of jump cuts, the variable sequence of juxtaposed images torn from personal experience in no coherent pattern. Didion has learned the technique from movies. Didion's novels, however, are only superficially about the women or about the trouble; on a deeper level, they are about the making of meaning, and the writer's inability or unwillingness to do just that. For Didion is preoccupied, stylistically and thematically, with the concerns about interpretation and evaluation that Susan Sontag raises in *Against Interpretation*.[1] Like Sontag, Didion wants to promote a fiction with an illusive surface without a final meaning that is imposed by narrator or author.

In all her work, Didion is obsessively fascinated with the interpretation of facts, events, the motives of people. Over and over, in different ways, she must ask: What does it mean? What do all the disparate events add up to? Quite frequently, however, the act of interpretation breaks down, or the storyteller becomes frustrated with the act of constructing meaningful patterns. Instead, the narrator reverts to recording a series of disconnected snapshots.

In the title essay from *The White Album*, Didion discusses everyone's need to find meaning in experience:

> We tell ourselves stories in order to live. The princess is caged in the consulate. The man with the candy will lead the children into the sea. The naked woman on the ledge outside the window on the sixteenth floor . . . is about to commit a mortal sin or is about to register a political protest. . . . We look for the sermon in this suicide, for the social or moral lesson in the murder of five. We interpret what we see. . . .

As an antidote to the perpetual need to interpret and evaluate, several of Didion's heroines attempt to live entirely in the present. They cut themselves off from the past, and they do not attempt to forecast the future. Their minds may become a blank, as does Maria's mind in *Play It As It Lays*:

> She thought about nothing. Her mind was a blank tape, imprinted daily with snatches of things overheard, fragments of dealers' patter, the beginnings of jokes and odd lines of song lyrics. When she finally lay down nights in the purple room she would play back the day's tape, a girl singing into a microphone and a fat man dropping a glass, cards fanned on a table and a dealer's rake in closeup and a woman in slacks crying and the opaque blue eyes of the guard at some baccarat table. A child in the harsh light of a crosswalk on the Strip. A sign on Fremont Street. A light blinking.

Maria attempts to avoid the pain of her life, since the old humanistic ideas by which she constructs *meaning* in life have become invalid or at least, as she herself says, *not applicable*.

This anti-interpretive stance, found throughout Didion's work, indicates that causality no longer operates very well as a way of satisfactorily explaining the fragmented aspects of the daily lives of her heroines. *Play It As It Lays* first shows Maria in a neuropsychiatric hospital, where she is given a series of diagnostic tests, but even there the phenomena of nature cannot be explained rationally. "Why should a coral snake need two glands of neurotoxic poison to survive," Maria wonders, "while a king snake, *so similarly marked*, needs none. . . . Unless you are prepared to take the long view, there is no satisfactory 'answer' to such questions. . . . To look for 'reasons' is beside the point."

If life is not, as Maria suspects, experienced in a series of connected, explainable units, then it may lead toward a cataclysmic abyss. Seen in this light, life is no longer a coherent whole, but "flash pictures in variable sequence, images with no 'meaning' beyond their temporary arrangement, not a movie but a cutting room experience."

Didion's three novels and two works of nonfiction are permeated by what we might refer to as a language of meaning. Obsessively she uses and reuses a certain lexicon at crucial points throughout her narratives. *Reasons, answers* are sought; there is a passionate desire to make *sense*, or to imbue with *meaning*; *to explain* is an important infinitive for Didion. Her third novel, *A Book of Common Prayer*, employs the quintessential pattern for this lexicon of meaning. The narrative strategy she evolves reinforces the importance that the making of meaning takes on at every juncture of the text. An exploration of the narrative strategy of *A Book of Common Prayer* will demonstrate how this concern operates in Didion's work both as theme and technique. Two women form the core of the book: Grace Strasser-Mendana, the narrator and would-be interpreter; and Charlotte Douglas, the mysterious text which Grace sets out to interpret posthumously.

Among other things, *A Book of Common Prayer* is about two women's lives disrupted and entangled by the social dislocations of the last two decades. Grace, the novel's central intelligence, is a member of the wealthy family that runs Boca Grande, the imaginary Central American country in which the novel is set. Charlotte Douglas, a woman adrift in the world, briefly lives in and chooses to die in Boca Grande. Grace assumes for herself the role of Charlotte's "witness." She would bear witness to the life of Charlotte Douglas in an attempt to find reasons, to explain motives, to establish connections, in short, to interpret the enigmatic and distinct strands of Charlotte's life. Grace's ways of knowing at the outset of the novel represent the fundamentally privileged ones in Western culture: the rational, the empirical, the causal. Trained in anthropology at Berkeley under Kroeber, and later in the field by Lévi-Strauss, Grace wants to establish at the outset of *A Book of Common Prayer* the credibility of her own voice. Her mind is analytical and rational; Charlotte Douglas, on the other hand, knows about things sensually and personally. "Charlotte would call her story one of passion. I believe I would call it one of delusion." Charlotte's mode of knowledge is intuitive, the product of subsidiary awareness, in the sense that Michael Polanyi discusses in *Personal Knowledge*.[2] In terms of the current research on the human brain, Grace is left-hemisphere dominant; Charlotte's mind is governed by the intuitive right hemisphere. Grace is seemingly unbiased; Charlotte openly redesigns reality according to her own past and present circumstances.

In fact, a good deal of the language that Grace uses to describe her subject encourages a "textual" view of Charlotte Douglas's life. Early on, Grace says that "she used to think that the only event in Charlotte Douglas's life to resist her revisions and erasures was Marin's disappearance." Later, in discussing Charlotte's repression of her parents' deaths, Grace reports that "she had erased other things too. She had been too busy." In another reference, Grace compares her own early days in Boca Grande with Charlotte's. She had made some mistaken judgments herself, Grace admits, "but I revised my impressions to coincide with reality. Charlotte did the reverse." In her "Letters," Charlotte clearly wants to revise the sterility of Boca Grande into the "economic fulcrum of the Americas" and, more importantly, she wants to erase the revolutionary in her daughter, Marin, and convert her into a little girl in a flowered Easter dress.

Importantly, Grace begins her tale with the sentence: "I will be her witness." Forming an implicit contract with the reader, Grace leads us to believe that what follows will be an accurate account of the circumstances of Charlotte's sojourn in Boca Grande and her eventual death:

> I tell you these things about myself only to legitimize my voice. We are uneasy about a story until we know who is telling it. In no other sense does it matter who "I" am: "the narrator" plays no motive role in this narrative, nor would I want to. . . . I will die (and rather soon, of pancreatic cancer) neither hopeful nor its opposite. I am interested in Charlotte Douglas only insofar as she passed through Boca Grande, only insofar as the *meaning* of that sojourn continues to elude me. [Italics mine.]

The narrative contract implies that we will learn the mystery, the enigma of Charlotte's life, or at least the meaning of her stay in Boca Grande. But what kind of a narrator have we here? What are her biases? Why must she tell and retell the story of Charlotte Douglas so obsessively? What might she hope to learn for herself? Is she really as without a motive as she claims? What might *we* learn? In order to seek answers to these questions, we must first explore how Didion's narrator is established early in the novel, and then turn to a comparison of *A Book of Common Prayer* and *The Great Gatsby*. Finally, we shall return to Grace's role as narrator to explore the gradual revelations she experiences about Charlotte Douglas's life and her own.

Several things about Grace's introduction of herself strike us as immediately interesting: 1) that she is to die soon, 2) that she claims to be unbiased or disinterested, and 3) that the search for the answer to a question, a search for meaning, propels her narrative account of Charlotte's stay in Boca Grande. These aspects of Grace's narrative stance are not only interesting, they form the basis for any interpretation of *A Book of Common Prayer*, since they permit an exploration of the major theme and technique of the novel. We must examine the ebb and flow of Grace's remarks about herself, her comparisons of her own life to Charlotte's, and indeed, the eventual undercutting of her narrative authority.

First, it is important that Grace is old (over sixty) and that she is dying. As Frank Kermode explains in *The Sense of an Ending*, it is a fundamental feature of human consciousness to shape fictions, to construct reality, with an awareness of death as the end of the fiction: "In 'making sense' of the world we still feel a need, harder than ever to satisfy because of an accumulated scepticism, to experience that concordance of beginning, middle, and end which is the essence of our explanatory fictions. . . . "[3] Charlotte's enigmatic behavior and attitudes present to Grace an alternative role against which she may measure her own life. Charlotte represents an individual case that cannot be subsumed into some total system, a specimen that does not fit readily or conveniently into the cognitive categories by which she has organized her version of reality. In order to "make sense" of Charlotte, Grace must construct a theory, a version of the truth, that will incorporate Charlotte's various attitudes, opinions, and actions. Or, at least, she must for a while.

The underlying narrative strategy offers little surprise, since it follows a pattern found in such familiar novels as *The Great Gatsby* and *Lord Jim*, in which the interaction between a central character and a narrator who reconstructs the story is crucial to the novel's meaning. As readers, we become a third party in a contract of narrator, character, and reader. As Edward Said has shown in *Beginnings*, the main character in a novel often embodies an alternative life that is added to or subtracted from incrementally as we proceed through a text.[4] The attitudes and behavior of a central character (Gatsby, Jim, Charlotte) are unfolded by an involved narrator (Carraway, Marlow, Grace) who is sometimes unreliable.

Aspects of the narrative strategy of *The Great Gatsby* in particular are worth comparing to those of *A Book of Common Prayer*. Just as Grace begins her narrative by trying to distinguish herself sharply from a subject that obsesses her, so Nick Carraway makes an unqualified yet baffling statement about Gatsby. Even though he admires Gatsby's "romantic readiness," his "heightened sensitivity to the promises of life," Nick says that Gatsby "represented everything for which I have an unaffected scorn." Charlotte Douglas is similar to Gatsby, too, in the wild rumors that surround her in the opening passages of the novel. Because her name appears on a State Department list requiring "special treatment," the leaders of Boca Grande are determined to discover her motives. Similarly, Gatsby is surrounded by an aura of speculation when Nick first hears of him: "Well, they say he's a nephew or cousin of Kaiser Wilhelm's"; "He was a German spy during the war"; "Somebody told me that they thought he killed a man once." The narrators of both novels also reconstruct their stories retrospectively after the death (murder?) of their major subjects, Gatsby and Charlotte. And, as Grace judges that Charlotte "dreamed her life," so Nick tells us that Gatsby "sprang from his Platonic conception of himself."

Most importantly, just as Grace's response to her subject shifts, so Nick Carraway's reaction to Gatsby vacillates subtly and gradually during his narrative account. When Gatsby, for example, produces a medal from "little Montenegro" that validates his account of his war experiences, a wide-eyed Nick concludes, "Then it was all true." And in the showdown scene at the Plaza Hotel, when Tom Buchanan badgers Gatsby about the phoniness of his background, Nick can still say, "I wanted to get up and slap [Gatsby] on the back. I had one of those renewals of complete faith in him that I had experienced before." But later, after the car accident that kills Myrtle Wilson, Carraway says, "I disliked [Gatsby] so much by this time that I didn't find it necessary to tell him he was wrong [that the police knew whose car it was]." Yet immediately after this statement, when Gatsby says that he will take the responsibility for the accident, freeing Daisy from blame, Nick changes his mind about Gatsby again. His new opinion is confirmed when he discovers that Daisy and Tom are seated at the table "conspiring together." The last time Nick sees Gatsby alive, he again reveals his ambivalence toward Gatsby's personality: "They're a rotten crowd. . . . You're worth the whole damn bunch put together," Nick shouts to Gatsby from across the lawn; then Nick tells the reader, "I've always been glad I said that. It was the only compliment I ever gave him, because I disapproved of him from beginning to end."

Unlike Nick Carraway, who looks back on his experience with the superior knowledge of hindsight, Grace's confusion about Charlotte Douglas builds progressively throughout the text. Yet Grace tries to present herself as an objective narrator, a scientist with a working hypothesis about Charlotte's life: that she dreamed her life, that she made too few distinctions, that she was an incurable romantic. Grace is a coy enough narrator to begin with a crude summary of the whole story:

> Here is what happened: she left one man, she left a second man, she traveled again with the first; she let him die alone. She lost one child to "history" and another to "complications" . . . she imagined herself capable of shedding that baggage and came to Boca Grande, a tourist.
>
> . . . .
>
> Of course the story had extenuating circumstances, weather, cracked sidewalks and paregorina, but only for the living.

We sense, however, in the cheap summary a starting place for the narrative account, and we know that the novel will be mainly about the "complications" and about "the extenuating circumstances."

Although Grace views Charlotte's motives in coming to Boca Grande as principally romantic and escapist, she begins almost immediately to cast doubt upon her early reliability as a narrator. As she proceeds with her account, she reports to us a question that guides her inquiry into the life and death of Charlotte: "It did not occur to me that day I would ever have reason to consider Charlotte Douglas as an outsider of romantic sensibility. In any case I am no longer sure that she was. Possibly this is the question I am trying to answer." For reasons that become apparent as the novel progresses, Grace's view of her own life is bound to her responses to Charlotte. But she begins by insisting upon a scientific method of analyzing the data; she prefers a mechanistic view of human behavior. In the early pages, Grace explains that she has retired from her primary field of anthropology to take up the amateur study of biochemistry, "a discipline in which demonstrable answers are commonplace and 'personality' absent. . . . I am interested for example in learning that such a 'personality' trait as fear of the dark . . . can be synthesized in the laboratory. Fear of the dark is an arrangement of fifteen amino acids."

Similarly, Grace prefers a mechanistic, unsentimental view of human sexuality. When she describes the instinctual attraction of Charlotte and her son Gerardo, she wants to describe it in scientific terms. She is tired of the romantic imagery; instead, she suggests that sex is electrical:

> Sexual current.
> The retreat into pastoral imagery to suggest this current has always seemed to me curious and decadent.
> The dissolve through the goldenrod.
> . . .
> As usual I favor a mechanical view.
> What Charlotte and Gerardo did that afternoon was reverse the entire neutron field of my lawn, exhausting and disturbing and altering not only the mood but possibly the cell structure (I am interested in this possibility) of everyone there.

Like Fitzgerald, Joan Didion has created a novel in which the narrator encounters a series of revelations about the central character. Yet in the process of reading, we are confronted with often contradictory opinions and conclusions. Didion, even more so than Fitzgerald, wants to give the impression that her narrator comes to her final conclusions in the process of writing a narrative account, but as we shall see the hope of a final interpretation remains illusory.

We come to see, in the final pages of the novel, that the narrative authority which Grace has carefully established for herself in the beginning is seriously undermined. And Grace's opening remarks about her account are crucial to our reading of the novel's final pages. When she says, "I will be her witness" and "Call this my own letter from Boca Grande," we are promised that the delusions and romantic sensibility that becloud Charlotte's version of things will be swept away by a more objective and scientific narrator. As we have seen, Grace clearly wants to establish her own vantage point as superior to Charlotte's. She will, as the biblical tradition of bearing witness implies, redeem Charlotte's life from anonymity. It promises to become, somehow, an exemplary life. Didion's narrator implies that she will explain the ambiguities, analyze the complexities, and resolve the "complications" mentioned on the novel's first page.

By the end of the novel, however, Grace has succeeded only in creating a version of Charlotte Douglas that remains a multivalent sign, an infinitely interpretable text whose *meaning* is never final or totalized. Grace is aware, of course, that one of her problems is the constitutive nature of language itself. In that solipsistic world of language (as opposed to the "real" world), the act of rendering on the page also retracts. Every sallying forth with possible meaning, every attempt to fix the character of Charlotte Douglas upon the page, implies a violation of those very assertions. Didion obviously recognizes this when she uses the weather of Boca Grande as a metaphor that could apply equally to Grace's account of Charlotte:

> Termites eat the presidential palace, rust eats my Oldsmobile.
> Twice a year the sun is exactly vertical, and nothing casts a shadow.
> The bite of one fly deposits an egg which in its pupal stage causes human flesh to suppurate.
> The bite of another deposits a larval worm which three years later surfaces on and roams the human eyeball.
> Everything here changes and nothing appears to. There is no perceptible wheeling of the stars in their courses, no seasonal wane in the length of days or the temperature of air or earth or water, only the amniotic stillness in which transformations are constant. As elsewhere, certain phases in these transformations are called by certain names ("Oldsmobile," say, and "rust"), but the emotional field of such names tends to weaken as one leaves the temperate zones. At the equator the names are noticeably arbitrary. A banana palm is no more or less "alive" than its rot.
> Is it.

Like the attempts to arrest the transformation of tropical flora and fauna with language, Grace's attempts to locate Charlotte Douglas in words are doomed

to failure. Like a tropical landscape, Charlotte Douglas keeps changing, transforming from one phase to another, before Grace can freeze her in words.

This is one aspect of the nature of fiction, fiction's inferiority to the superior
text of reality, that Edward Said has described as the interaction between
narrative authority and molestation. Said develops these concepts as the process
of ebb and flow in prose fiction, and they prove useful to describe the changes
that Grace undergoes during the course of the novel:

> . . . these meanings [of authority] are all grounded in the following notions:
> (1) that of the power of an individual to initiate, institute, establish—in
> short, to begin; (2) that this power and its product are an increase over what
> had been there previously; (3) that the individual wielding this power controls
> its issue and what is derived therefrom; (4) that authority maintains the
> continuity of its course. . . . Molestation . . . is a consciousness of one's du-
> plicity, one's confinement to a fictive, scriptive realm, whether one is a
> character or a novelist. And molestation occurs when novelists and critics
> traditionally remind themselves of how the novel is always subject to a
> comparison with reality and thereby found to be illusion. Or again, moles-
> tation is central to a character's experience of disillusionment during the
> course of a novel.[5]

As we read Grace's obsessive attempts to come to grips with the illusive
nature of Charlotte's *character* in the final chapters of the novel, we witness
the disintegration of Grace's carefully constructed system of knowledge. Our
narrator, who has portrayed herself as scientific and objective, learns that her
life too is caught in a web of self-delusions; the impenetrability of Charlotte
Douglas teaches her this. She decides that life cannot be explained in the
laboratory, as she might hope: "I know how to make models of life itself,
DNA, RNA, helices double and single and squared, but I try to make a model
of Charlotte Douglas's 'character' and I see only a shimmer."

Thus progressively in the course of her writing it occurs to Grace that
throughout her life she has nurtured her own illusions, and it occurs to the
reader that Grace's demystification of her own life is the major revelation of
her account of Charlotte Douglas's life. Grace realizes gradually that she is
more like Charlotte Douglas than she would like to admit. For example, when
she describes the "sexual current" that Gerardo and Charlotte generate at her
lawn party, she concludes, "It occurred to me that my attempt to grow roses
and a lawn at the equator was a delusion worthy of Charlotte Douglas."

Toward the end of the novel, Grace reports a conversation she has had with
Charlotte's daughter, Marin, whom she visits in a boarding house in Buffalo.
After Grace fails to explain satisfactorily to the daughter what the mother had

"done" in Boca Grande, Marin concludes that her mother "had died on the wrong side of a 'people's revolution.' " Confronted with the futility of further explanation to a young woman who cannot understand, Grace again undercuts her attempts to constitute meaning and responds, instead, personally and nostalgically. "She had Charlotte's eyes. Maybe there is no motive role in this narrative. Maybe it is just something that happened. Then why is it in my mind when nothing else is." Grace's response is at first intellectual, in her sense of frustration with her own narrative, and later emotional, in that she notices how much Marin resembles Charlotte.

In the final chapters of the novel, Grace confirms what her life shares with that of Charlotte Douglas. She begins to accept her own delusions, her own revisions of reality. When Leonard Douglas informs her that her husband, Edgar, had been involved in the revolutionary politics of Colombia, this new knowledge strikes her with the force of a revelation:

> "You didn't know about Bogota, did you."
> "No."
> "I shouldn't have told you. It upset you."
> "I should have known."

To accept that she "had never heard or seen that Edgar played the same [revolutionary] games Gerardo played," Grace must also acknowledge that her view of her husband as a forthright and honorable leader of Boca Grande had been an illusion. She also recognizes that all memory is selective and personal; she consequently must validate Charlotte's way of seeing the world:

> We all remember what we need to remember.
> Marin remembered Charlotte in a tennis dress and Charlotte remembered Marin in a straw hat for Easter. I remembered Edgar, I did not remember Edgar as the man who financed the Tupamaros. Charlotte remembered she bled. I remembered the light in Boca Grande.
> . . . .
> Another place I have no business being.
> It seems to me now.

In an earlier version of this same passage in manuscript form, the final line reads, "I am more like Charlotte Douglas than I thought."[6] Perhaps Didion deleted the line because it made too explicit what she merely wanted to imply, but we see on its evidence the gradual process by which Grace accepts Charlotte's way of constructing the world.

On the final page of *A Book of Common Prayer*, Didion's narrator comes to renege finally on all of her earlier narrative promises; the undercutting of narrative authority becomes complete. The final line of the novel reads: "I have not been the witness I wanted to be." Grace distrusts the empirical evidence about the life of Charlotte Douglas, and she realizes that what remains are the second-hand information and the worn formulas of indirect speech: "I am told," "So she said," "I heard later," "According to her passport."

Although Grace struggles in vain for some final, coherent version of reality, Didion's narrative strategy deliberately underscores the difficulties in our era of writing fiction at all. In Grace's attempt to pin Charlotte down, the subject has been transformed before the narrator's eyes. Grace must then acknowledge that she will never get Charlotte's life to yield the final "secret" that will unify her character, since she "also recognize[s] the equivocal nature of even the most empirical evidence." The strands of the story are all present, but just as Grace picks up one, the others slip through her fingers.[7]

Recent criticism in France has elucidated the difference between writing in the classical period of the novel's beginnings and the more radical situation of the writer today who inherits the worn conventions of the genre's earlier periods. One of the effects of this legacy, Roland Barthes argues, has been the unusual self-consciousness of today's writers. In "The Death of the Author," Barthes points out several differences between classical novelists and contemporary writers. He emphasizes the slippery nature of reality's superior text and the inevitability of fiction's secondary and reconstructive aspects:

> In the multiplicity of writing, everything is to be *disentangled* nothing *deciphered*; the structure can be followed, 'run' (like the thread of a stocking) at every point and at every level, but there is nothing beneath: the space of writing is to be ranged over, not pierced; writing ceaselessly posits meaning to ceaselessly evaporate it, carrying out a systematic exemption of meaning. In precisely this way literature (it would be better from now on to say *writing*) by refusing to assign a 'secret,' an ultimate meaning to the text (and to the world as text), liberates what may be called an anti-theological activity, an activity that is truly revolutionary since to refuse to fix meaning is, in the end, to refuse God and his hypostases—reason, science, law.[8]

Such a self-conscious narrator as Grace approaches the character of Charlotte Douglas, but the closer approach comes to a final interpretation, the more it recedes away from the center, away from any finally fixed meaning. Grace has described Charlotte's character as a "shimmer," an interesting point in light of what Didion has said elsewhere about these "shimmers." In an autobiographical essay entitled "Why I Write," she explains that the beginning impulses for her novels often come from images. Certainly the description here employs many of the metaphors Grace uses in depicting Charlotte:

> When I talk about pictures in my mind I am talking, quite specifically, about images that shimmer around the edges. There used to be an illustration in every elementary psychology book showing a cat drawn by a patient in varying stages of schizophrenia. This cat had a shimmer around it. You could see the molecular structure breaking down at the very edges of the cat: the cat became the background and the background became the cat, everything interacting, exchanging ions. People on hallucinogens describe the same perception of objects. I'm not schizophrenic, nor do I take hallucinogens, but certain images do shimmer for me. Look hard enough, and you can't miss the shimmer. It's there. You can't think too much about these pictures that shimmer. You just lie low and let them develop. You stay quiet. You don't talk to many people and you try to locate the cat in the shimmer, the grammar in the picture.[9]

So, just as Grace struggles with the shimmer to attain some coherent version of reality, Didion seems to emphasize with her narrative strategy the very difficulties of writing fiction at all. The old stories, the old humanistic values and ideas that provide for life a coherence, do not apply in her fiction nor, she would argue, in contemporary life. Seen in this light, as Didion recognizes implicitly in *The White Album*, all narrative becomes sentimental. Grace's retelling of Charlotte Douglas's story then becomes a loving, nostalgic attempt to understand—even to revive—her lost friend. For Didion this stance seems to be a radical lesson born of the disruptive social history of the 1960's and 1970's: there is no *message* in the suicide; there is no *sermon* to be heard in the multiple murder; the ultimate logic dissolves.

In the title essay in *The White Album*, Didion recounts a number of incongruities that passed through her own life in the late sixties, typified by interviews with Black Panther Huey Newton and Manson groupie Linda Kasabian, observations on singer Jim Morrison of "The Doors," and her own frequent fears of violent death. Near the end of that essay, Didion notes with characteristic irony that one of the killers of silent film star Ramon Novarro, now serving a life term in prison, received a P.E.N. writing award. "Writing had helped him," Didion tells us, to "reflect on experience and see what it means." Unlike Novarro's killer, Didion and the narrator of *A Book of Common Prayer* can find no final determination. As Grace says in the end, "Maybe there was no motive role in this narrative. Maybe it is just something that happened." In the last paragraph of "The White Album," Didion tries unsuccessfully to tie together the various strange events and discontinuities that she has recorded in the essay. That essay's final sentence reads: "Quite often I reflect on the big house in Hollywood, on 'Midnight Confessions' [a violent motorcycle film] and on Ramon Novarro and on the fact that Roman Polanski and I are godparents to the same child, but writing has not yet helped me to see what it means."

NOTES

[1]Susan Sontag, *Against Interpretation and Other Essays* (New York: Farrar, Straus & Giroux, 1965), pp. 3–14.

[2]Michael Polanyi, *Personal Knowledge: Towards a Post-Critical Philosophy* (Chicago: University of Chicago Press, 1958).

[3]Frank Kermode, *The Sense of an Ending: Studies in the Theory of Fiction* (New York: Oxford University Press, 1967), pp. 35–36.

[4]Edward Said, *Beginnings: Intention and Method* (New York: Basic Books, 1975), pp. 81–188, *passim.*

[5]*Ibid.*, pp. 83–84.

[6]The manuscript page with its additions, insertions, and deletions appears in "The Art of Fiction," *Paris Review*, 74 (Fall–Winter, 1978), facing p. 138.

[7]Didion has recognized the illusiveness of the novel as a major part of her narrative intention. In an interview, when asked whether she had had a "technical intention" for *A Book of Common Prayer*, Didion replied: "Yes, I wrote it down on the map of Central America. 'Surface like rainbow slick, shifting, fall, thrown away, iridescent.' I wanted to do a deceptive surface that appeared to be one thing and turned color as you looked through it." Sara Davidson, "A Visit with Joan Didion," *The New York Times Book Review*, 3 April 1977, p. 36.

[8]Roland Barthes, "The Death of the Author," in *Image - Music - Text*, ed. and trans., Stephen Heath (New York: Hill and Wang, 1977), p. 147.

[9]Joan Didion, "Why I Write," in *The Writer on Her Work*, ed. Janet Sternburg (New York: W. W. Norton & Co., 1980), p. 20.

The Album of Anxiety
Irving Malin

IN THE BRILLIANT title essay of *The White Album* Joan Didion writes that "we tell ourselves stories in order to live." The statement is direct, risky, and odd because it assumes that we learn to *live* by listening and that we survive purely (or impurely) by deliberate acts of attention. There is the hint of danger, the suggestion that life is always on edge. Didion clarifies the opening sentence. She mentions the "caged princess," the mysterious seduction of children, the "suicide." We look for meanings in these stories of violence, the "sermon in the suicide." We seek order, the "imposition of a narrative line upon disparate images." Thus there is deception in story-telling and conjunctive meanings—we play with (or prey upon) shifting images—"our actual experiences"—hoping that we can contain shifts of power, tone, and topic in our daily lives. We make an album, if you will, out of divisive snapshots (pun intended).

Didion, however, alerts us soon to her discovery—life and art are at war. She begins in 1966 to recognize that her daily routines—civic and private—lack cohesion; even her name seems to be apart from her existence. The script of her life is said to be a series of "flashes in variable sequence. . . ." Didion longs for old ways, comfortable narrative, intelligent beginnings and endings—for "ethics," not "electricity." If we take these two long paragraphs and join them (as she does), we see magical, great conflict—the style is pure, controlled, and tight, but it attempts to shape energetic reversals of fortune.

In the last part of the first section we are shocked to listen to a scientific "story" of a patient—it is Didion herself as narrated by an outsider who controls her life (and presumably his own—by using "scientific" language filled with jargon-words of "poorly comprehended" insight). The various story lines—Didion's, the "psychiatric report," the traditional narrative—fight one another and, by doing so, fight our sense of order—essays are not meant to be "messy" (even deliberately)!

The second part of the essay is filled with violent images. We have a "senseless" neighborhood, a transcript of the murderers of Ramon Novarro, reports of the Manson family, some police clippings. Such images (and gossip) suggest once more that "reality" is always threatening to overturn our interpretations (or vice versa). If we take, for example, the story about Novarro, we are misled. His murder is bizarre; his acting—this occupation is, after all, very important in his life—is bizarre. Is there any relation between two *performances*? Does life follow art? Does art follow life? And, furthermore, as Didion implies, does asking such questions help to put life/art in perspective?

Part three begins suddenly with another flash—story. Didion watches the Doors perform; they are "missionaries of apocalyptic sex" in their "*break on through*" lyrics to "Light My Fire." Jim Morrison, the leader, regards himself as an "erotic politician." Morrison is, therefore, a symbolist, who hopes not only to capture his audience but to kill it with his sexy force. But this description is one of a recording session; it is true to life because of its *erratic, terrifying exchanges*. It is highly charged, variable, chancy, although Morrison himself (and Didion) want desperately to connect things, to *control* the flow, recognizing that by doing so—an impossibility!—they will deaden things—they will, in effect, *put out the fire*.

Part four plays (pun again intended) with rock music. Such "music people" as Joplin hope to find salvation in their art, but they cannot slow down and concentrate; they keep moving; they inherit the Romantic myth. They drink to escape life—or to *waste* it—in much the same way this writer *hides* to write these very words. Didion has, of course, never retreated from her main concerns in the essay; her detours—even her surrogates or doubles—are inevitably chosen to suggest that *she* controls the characters and events described. She also recognizes, as her psychiatrist would, that the detours are *her story, her choices in life. Or are they*? Does *she tell* stories or, more to the point, do the *stories tell her*? We have, underneath the glitter of California, a religious, traditional narrative of the world, the flesh, and the spirit.

Part five gives us another kind of performance. The Black Panthers, like the Doors, claim to offer salvation (by revolution), to *recreate* the closed social system (an old Western "story"). They use language to outwit the white man's "game," but they cannot communicate except in all-too-common language. Their testimony is the old script—after all, we have heard it before every revolution. And when in a short part six, Didion speaks to Eldridge Cleaver, she recognizes that they share all writers' concerns—even offering secrets about royalties and sales.

What can follow these various clashes in one life? In the next two sections Didion travels—the whole essay is one of "moving on" spiritually—to Hollywood and San Francisco. She makes lists, hoping that by using these, she can shape her destiny. The lists, however, like the records heard on the speeding car-radio, are *not enough*: they are short; they avoid the confrontation between the pat standard "story" and the chaotic, charged life. The lists try to "erase words"—Didion's words—and in a real sense, they are attempts to kill more serious thought. And Didion, ironically, understands her motives.

In sections nine and ten Didion uses another variation on the "communication gaps." She recognizes that student revolution, personal injury, even murder are media jargon. Her own psychiatric case-history (not mentioned at this point) is more jargon. The jargon is quiet misinformation; words, in effect, are in themselves misinformation because they mean different things to each listener and teller. Words are perverse enemies. They are, however, the only device she or Morrison or Cleaver can ever use. The dilemma which slowly haunts (hunts) her is simply this: if we write and express "clearly" our daily lives—as "crazy" or "sane" as they are—we cannot *surprise* ourselves or, indeed, reflect our history (another "story"). Should we remain silent and, if we do, is silence itself a kind of secret language?

The bizarre division of words and events is clear in section eleven. A murderer, one of Charlie Manson's angels, dreams of "opening a combination restaurant-boutique and pet shop." Linda is a "good" person—she wants to feed others and to take care of animals. She also kills. Didion calls the experience of the interview "eerie and unsettling." Somehow the dreams of the future make *her* own notebook a "*litany* of little ironies." I underline the word "litany." Linda is presumably human; she commits inhuman acts. Didion is human; she uses ironic knives. Both, however, have prayers of wholeness despite their different travails, litanies, trials. Writing is, to use Didion's words, "eerie and unsettling," because it freezes, even in this *apparently* disjointed essay, organic growth; it "murders" as it "creates." It is sinful because it condemns humanity (as well as celebrating the condemnation). It is, if you will, *the* white album containing all colors and yet merely empty.

In part twelve Didion continues her lists, counterpointing her events with the death of Kennedy or one dress with another worn by Linda Kasabian. The deep connections are not made—they are listed—but they lead to one basic question I have asked many times—a "koan" (asked in part thirteen) by a Mormon motel-manager: "*If you can't believe you're going to heaven in your own body and on a first-name basis with the members of your family, then what's the point of dying?*" If you can't write as someone else—and no one can!—then why write at all? If you can't believe in writing about Sharon Tate or Linda Kasabian or Joan Didion—and seeing their lives as somehow one life—then why write at all? And how do you devise a *pattern* which revolutionizes the *essay* so that it becomes *your story*?

Part fourteen begins with Didion's body. The body is seen as another test case; various word-patterns are used to describe it. Finally the words are "multiple sclerosis" but the words, we are told, are an "exclusionary diagnosis and meant nothing." These perverse phrases are the culmination of the old, "spacey" conditions met before; Didion is told *simply* that life must be led *simply*. (We don't know *what* helps.) Her body is "another story without a narrative." By connecting private disease with public disorder, Didion offers another clue to the essay—there is a mysterious plan—at least that's my "story"—to all the mixed events of the ten years she has described.

In the final section we get endings, deaths, exits of one kind or another: Morrison dies; Linda Kasabian, by turning state's evidence, flees "in search of the pastoral"; Cleaver goes to Algeria; Didion ends by not believing that we live better lives because of stories. But she lies (and knows it). She deliberately writes this essay to *affirm* (after all the empty spots) that her experiences, which she claims have no significant meaning, *do have a meaning*. I think the meaning is quite clear in spite of the various lies and games and detours: there is a pattern that we make (criticism often does); if the pattern is not "correct"—whatever such a word may mean—we should not care because criticism reflects our larger cares and it helps us to live better days. We write criticism—which is, after all, a "story" about a "story"—to demonstrate that we can *bring it home*, "that we can light private fires." Maybe such fire is finally enlightening.

Beyond Words: Narrative Art in Joan Didion's *Salvador*

Frederick Kiley

CONCLUDING THE DESCRIPTION of her arrival at the comparatively new El Salvador International Airport, Joan Didion writes that the surreal landscape presages a "plunge into a state in which no ground is solid, no depth of field reliable, no perception so definite that it might not dissolve into its reverse." The nearby massive Pacific resort, projected by previous regimes to be served by the airport, lies abandoned. San Salvador, the capitol, is forty dangerous miles away at the end of a highway that cuts through hilly jungle and on which cruise the reinforced, bulletproofed Cherokee-Chief pickup trucks that have been featured in so many disappearances and murders. Eye contact at customs is risky. Documents are gravely inspected upside down. The threatening ubiquity of automatic weapons enforces an uneasy docility. The year is 1982.

Reflecting themes implicit in this introduction, the rest of the brief account of Didion's visit to Salvador skillfully portrays a deadly Central American dilemma that engages us as a nation politically, economically, militarily and morally. She presents a staggering collage of carefully arranged metaphors and images that enable the reader to experience a nightmare, horrifying and mad, that mangles rational explanations and descriptions. She attempts figuratively to probe the dark heart of a real situation, where logical reasons somehow only complicate the puzzle, where even one's sense of outrage is frustrated by contradictions, collective illusions and maniacal compromises with conscience, expediency and other people's lives. And the result, without quite encroaching upon the perimeters of fiction, is much more than good journalism. Somehow, Didion has created a literary counterpart to Picasso's *Guernica*. Depending on the cumulative effect of macabre details, similar to the design of the bitter, 1937 black-and-white masterpiece, she arranges images, metaphors, sketches and impressions in a dense texture that steadily expands into the shape of the abomination that is Salvador.

Didion foreshadows the grim narrative to come in the epigraph, the passage in Joseph Conrad's *Heart of Darkness* where Charles Marlow rhapsodizes Kurtz's treatise on the "solution" of the African problem, commissioned by the International Society for the Suppression of Savage Customs. After quoting Kurtz's recommendation that, "By the simple exercise of our will we can exert a power for good practically unbounded," Marlow tells how at the "end of that moving appeal to every altruistic sentiment," he finds the exhausted scrawl, "Exterminate all the brutes."

But just who are the brutes? It is the ambiguity of identity in Kurtz's after-thought that the rest of Didion's book addresses with ambiguities of its own, ironies that question our sanity, imagery that offends our sense of decency and paradoxes that herald the tragi-comic hopelessness of our apparent humanitarianism.

United States efforts to keep Salvadorans from killing each other daily, Didion writes, are labeled imperialist blackmail. Americans, on the other hand, continue doggedly to encourage and aid a mentality they righteously prosecuted and condemned at Nuremberg. Appearances and illusion become more tangible than verifiable reality. Even statistics vary with the time of day, issued only because someone needs to hear the unspeakable expressed in numbers. *Solucións* quickly evolve into desperate problems and yet are still energetically pursued as solutions. Situations arise where even those in author-ity dare not ask questions that demand definite answers because a refusal to reply could easily bring about arrest and possible death.

"So I don't ask," President Magaña says, shrugging.

The most vital news of El Salvador comes from the United States, even to those professionals who have been sent there to report conditions and events. Confused by the strange acceptance of daily terror and death, Didion can find little of substance to record.

Then she meets the grandson of General Maximiliano Hernández Martínez, notorious Salvadoran dictator between 1931 and 1944, murdered while exiled in Honduras. Martínez had, in 1932, massacred many thousands of citizens as a lesson. A man of deranged habits, he held séances, acted on eccentric insights, recommended that the children go barefoot, dispensed bottles of colored water as cures for serious diseases, resorted to magic for political decisions and once attempted to halt a smallpox epidemic by stringing colored lights around the city.

The grandson, Victor Barriere, who attended school with the sons of men Martínez had executed, has a deep respect and appreciation of his grandfather's intellectual influence. He maintains an uncomplicated and enthusiastic ap-proval of present political conditions in Salvador and feels that Americans come and then leave without properly understanding his country. He considers former ambassador, Robert White, "A real jerk." He compares murdered Archbishop Oscar Arnulfo Romero to Adolph Hitler and calls him "A real bigot." Very strong men like his grandfather, he claims, were sometimes misunderstood.

His companion, an eighteen-year-old man from Chalatenango, unable to speak English, depends upon Barriere for his survival. Barriere explains:

> If he were cutting cane in Chalatenango, he'd be taken by the Army and killed. If he were out on the street here he'd be killed. So. He comes every day to my studio, he learns to be a primitive painter, and I keep him from getting killed.
> It's better for him, don't you agree?

Stunned by Barriere's facile juggling of the contradiction between his political sympathies and the real situation he acknowledges, Didion says, ". . . this was the first time in my life that I had been in the presence of obvious 'material' and felt no professional exhilaration, only personal dread."

Body dumps, another on the growing list of twentieth-century atrocities, become visitor attractions. In a passage reminiscent of Marlow's musing about hair continuing to grow after death in his description of Kurtz, Didion observes "that a skull surrounded by a perfect corona of hair is not an uncommon sight in these places." Corpses are viciously mutilated beyond recognition. Informal snapshots of the dead are collected in albums and kept by the Human Rights Commission for the living to identify relatives and friends. Death squads of *desconocidos* (unknown men) execute even those only suspected of opposition to the present government, including their families. Being known as a friend of or related to a victim can often be a death sentence.

The entire village of Mozote was massacred methodically in December, 1981. The sole survivor, Rufina Amaya, described how the men were shot in the town's center. The women were taken to the hills, raped and later killed and burned. Rufina, in her hiding place, heard the soldiers discuss choking the children. In a while she heard children crying for help, but no shots.

Even rain excites sporadic automatic weapons fire at night on the streets of San Salvador. Holocaust conditions are described and defended in the language of advertising. *La verdad*, the truth, has been degraded to a bumper-sticker status and takes its meaning from whoever happens to be in charge.

Nothing is definite. Didion finds that the more one tries to narrow definitions and make concrete sense, the more elusive and vague and contradictory the situation becomes. The grisly details build toward a balance that precariously sustains an intolerable, unspoken agreement, a silent communion of madness. Didion explains that improving the human rights situation by contriving ways to make it look better, trying to have the Salvadoran government "appear" to be doing what the United States needed done to make it "appear" that the aid was justified, is the general shape of this grotesque riddle. To compound the horror, present United States policy prevents the administration from even acknowledging that political persecution exists in El Salvador. Aid, she says, was the card we used to get Salvador to do it our way; appearing to do it was the card by which Salvador secured the aid. Anti-communism, even when the enforcement is more barbaric than the threat, offers the bait Americans cannot resist.

And if these ironies are not bewildering enough, Didion claims that the absence of United States influence would worsen conditions. Eerily, our conscience prevents us from abandoning a murderous state of affairs that our presence only encourages.

In battle-torn Gotera, waiting for Colonel Salvador Beltrán Luna's permission to get nearer to the fighting, Didion and her party wait in the heat and dust of the town.

> Any event at all—the arrival of an armored personnel carrier, say, or a funeral procession outside the church—tended to metamorphose into an opera, with all the players onstage: the Soldiers of the Garrison, the Young Ladies of the Town, the Vendors, the Priests, the Mourners, and, since we were onstage as well, a dissonant and provocative element, the *norteamericanos*, in *norteamericano* costume, old Abercrombie khakis here, Adidas sneakers there, a Lone Star Beer cap.

The details fuse the Salvadoran street scene and the ever-present Americans into a scale metaphor that, even in its quaintness, reflects Didion's vision of the larger gloom of a country in mortal turmoil encumbered by a powerful, dispassionate, outside presence from an entirely different world. This kind of pressure, as modern history reminds us so often, can result in a very dangerous self-consciousness.

Colonel Luna, the man for whom they wait, has already been killed in a helicopter crash either near the Honduran border or in Honduras. No one seems certain of any detail, and reports grow more contradictory and "vaporous" as the investigation proceeds. Uncertainty becomes a necessary attitude toward the incident.

Later in the day, sitting on a courtyard porch nearby, drinking Pilsener beer with two nuns and some Franciscan priests, Didion wonders rhetorically if this might be civilization's last stand. Instead of discussing parish matters, they talk quietly of how fewer bodies have appeared in the neighborhood since the elections. Then someone recalls a *guardia* who had been killed last Wednesday.

"Thursday," he is reminded.
"Was it Thursday then, Jerry?"
"A sniper."
"That's what I thought. A sniper."

In a few weeks she learns that even this small oasis has been eliminated. Under pressure from the military at Gotera the priests and nuns abandon the parish house.

In an earlier passage Didion describes the Metrocenter, a shopping mall across from the Camino Real, her hotel in San Salvador. The muzak plays American pop tunes while a guard checks customers for weapons. Middle-class Salvadorans, wearing tight Sergio Valente jeans, buy beach towels printed with maps of Manhattan, merchandise usually featured at Bloomingdale's. Within shouting distance people are being "disappeared" and having their throats cut as they sleep in bed.

"This was a shopping center," she writes, "for which Salvador was presumably being saved."

With similar irony Didion describes lunch with Deane Hinton at the American Embassy. Ambassador Hinton, she finds, believes in the possible and has an enthusiastic faith in the present United States policy in Salvador. Didion drinks wine from crystal glasses, eats fish from porcelain plates bearing the imprint of the official American eagle. Hinton's English sheep dog bounds across the lawn, startled by the sound of shots, "rifle practice at the *Escuela Militar* beyond the wall and down the hill," making a sinister comment on the Ambassador's statements about doing what he can to facilitate American policy in this strange land.

Normally, it is the function of the reporter to make sense of an event and to present it as clearly and as objectively as he can. Didion quickly realizes the futility of this procedure in portraying Salvador's infectious asylum temperament. The incidents and conditions she witnesses present themselves as untranslatable. She attempts to solve this by shaping her observations as metaphors, communicating in each the conflict, the paradoxes, the irony that she sees as characteristic of the larger puzzle. These accumulate as the book progresses, reinforcing each other thematically and structurally, until at the end the collective effect renders the massive depth and terror of her experience of Salvador.

One of the more effective examples of this technique occurs in Didion's description of her visit to a craft festival in Nahuizalco, the sixth annual Feria Artesanal de Nahuizalco, sponsored by the Casa de la Cultura program of the Ministry of Education to encourage indigenous cultures. By noon the celebrants have arranged themselves in two separate groups. The *ladinos* sit in the shade of the village schoolyard. The Indians squat outside under a punishing sun. The Queen of the fair, wearing a wicker crown, sits with local *guardia*, who carry automatic weapons, sidearms and bayonets. A Suprema Beer sound truck, parked in the plaza, blares, "Roll out the Barrel," "La Cucaracha," and "Everybody Salsa."

The Indian dances and crafts seem hardly genuine, in part because of recent history. In 1932, Nahuizalco Indians were "tied by their thumbs and shot against church walls, shot on the road and left for the dogs, shot and bayoneted into the mass graves they themselves had dug."

The survivors sensibly abandoned native customs and no longer dared speak their language in public. In order to survive in a society that is ready at any moment and for any excuse to annihilate those it despises they denied their heritage and tried to assimilate. Uncomfortable in their native costumes, they dance, Didion says, a listless shuffle, something "derived not from local culture but from a learned idea of local culture." They try desperately in their dances and crafts to present themselves as imposters.

This is a clear example of an intention turning into its opposite. The sponsored fair expects the participants to display with pride and skill the various cultures indigenous to the area. But historical and present hatreds make any genuine indulgence in native practices too hazardous. The heavily armed *guardia* next to the Queen with European features should be enough to make even those with the poorest memories cautious. These Indians have been methodically terrorized out of their identities.

"In many ways," Didion concludes, "race remains the ineffable element at the heart of this particular darkness."

In the church across the plaza she attends a mass baptism of thirty or forty babies. The altar is decorated with asters in condensed milk cans. Mothers pacify fretting babies with Fritos. Only four men are present among several hundred women.

"The reason for this may have been cultural," Didion writes, "or may have had something to do with the time and the place, and the G-3s [assault rifles] in the schoolyard."

In a cinematic transition she moves from this village church to a description of the neglected Metropolitan Cathedral in San Salvador, site of Archbishop Romero's assassination. "Rain sluiced down its corrugated plastic windows," Didion observes, "and water puddled around the supports of the Sony and Phillips billboards near the steps." Rusting structural steel rods protrude from raw concrete. Wiring is exposed. Warped plywood backs the high altar. The altar cross is shaped by bare incandescent bulbs, none of which is lit. The globe of the world is not lighted, nor the dove above it. Finding a somber kinship between her earlier observations and this pathetic tableau, Didion writes: "In this vast brutalist space that was the cathedral, the unlit altar seemed to offer a single ineluctable message: at this time and in this place the light of the world could be construed as out, extinguished."

The United States Embassy in San Salvador had been built in 1965 to remain fluid under stress in order to withstand earthquake displacements. But in the past few years, as Didion notes, since "shelling the embassy came to be a favorite way of expressing dissatisfaction on all sides," the building had been reinforced with steel exterior walls, sandbags and a bomb shelter dug underneath, rendering it an unyielding fortress. As a consequence, during the earthquake that measures 7.0 on the Richter scale, reported 6.8 another day and then back to 7 the next, the embassy sustains serious damage. Ceilings fall, pipes burst, the elevator is disabled, the commissary shattered.

The hotel Camino Real, which appears to have been thrown together in the carefree tradition of most tropical construction, pitches and rocks but suffers no damage. Not even the glasses behind the bar are broken. By the time Didion is able to get downstairs, the discothèque off the lobby has resumed its entertainment as patrons dance to Jerry Lee Lewis's "Great Balls of Fire."

The passage bristles with the kind of irony that characterizes the imagery throughout the book. ". . . no ground is solid, no depth of field reliable, no perception so definite that it might not dissolve into its reverse." The rigid embassy, fortified against the assaults of men, is the building the earthquake punishes most. The hotel revelers continue their celebration practically uninterrupted in a structure that casually surrenders to the violence of the earth. As always, the tropics have a way of erasing their mistakes, politically and botanically.

Although Didion finds the texture of life in this political climate impossible to express in a conventional manner, she later sees with momentary clarity the helpless dread one can easily find himself experiencing daily with no warning and in the most casual circumstances. She visits the San Salvador morgue in search of news with another American reporter and her husband. The morning entries list seven male corpses. All had been shot. Since only seven unidentified murder victims in Salvador are not important enough to warrant a story worth investigating, they leave.

When they arrive at their car, they find it surrounded by three men in uniform. Two stand on the sidewalk. A third sits on a motorcycle in front of the car. A second motorcycle soldier arrives and parks directly behind. The men in uniform do not move. They avoid eye contact. They remain expressionless. The reporter asks in Spanish for one of the motorcycles to be moved. The young man in front stares directly ahead and plays with the flash suppressor on his automatic weapon. The others do not respond to the request.

Didion, her husband and the reporter find themselves in a deadly impasse, not unlike Marlow's confrontation with the group of armed natives in his path as he bears Kurtz on a stretcher to the steamer, prompting the Russian to mutter, "Now, if he does not say the right thing we are all done for."

There is no one to whom Didion can appeal. These four armed brutes are answerable to no one. They do not even seem to know what they are trying to provoke. Finally, in a breathholding maneuver, the reporter inches the car around them and drives off. Didion writes:

> Nothing more happened, but what did happen had been a common enough kind of incident in El Salvador, a pointless confrontation with aimless authority, but I have heard of no *solución* that precisely addresses this local vocation for terror.

The book ends with Didion's return flight to Miami. The plane stops at Belize, where a team of student missionaries from Georgia and Alabama board. She engages one of the young men in a conversation and learns that he has eagerly renewed his commitment to take the good news of Jesus as personal savior to New Zealand, Iceland, Finland, Colorado and El Salvador, which in Spanish means Savior. One wonders if this might be another mission sponsored by the International Society for the Suppression of Savage Customs. One wonders how many more saviors these sad people can endure before they have been totally dehumanized.

Didion's Salvador is a terrifying enigma that frustrates each new promising effort to solve it, ironically merging solution and problem into a new dilemma. Men of good intention who attempt to stop the slaughter eventually join in lunatic political games and make bizarre compromises that turn initial humanitarian impulses into their reverse. Terror and violent death remain "the given of the place," like hunger during a famine, thirst during a drought. Thugs with government approbation roam free to kill and kill again. Didion sees the modern guise of evil in this hideous landscape and, with imagery and metaphor shaping her observations, she presents it as a mirror that reflects us all in a collective conspiracy to nurture it, revealing the awful capacities that lie dormant in the human heart of darkness. And the result is, in spite of her frequent protests of the ineffability of the place, a remarkably successful literary approach to a dismal truth that lies far beyond words.

CONTRIBUTORS

JENNIFER BRADY teaches English at Marianopolis College in Montreal and has published articles on Ben Jonson and Samuel Richardson.

C. BARRY CHABOT chairs the Department of Literature at The American University and is author of *Freud on Schreber: Psychoanalytic Theory and the Critical Act* (University of Massachusetts, 1982); his essay on Joan Didion is part of a work-in-progress on American fiction and thought since WWI.

SARA DAVIDSON is the author of *Loose Change: Three Women of the Sixties* (Doubleday, 1977) and *Real Property* (Doubleday, 1980).

ELLEN G. FRIEDMAN is the author of *Joyce Carol Oates* (Ungar, 1980), a critical study; and essays and reviews in *English Literature in Transition*, *Studies in American Fiction*, and elsewhere. She directs the writing program at Trenton State College.

DAVID J. GEHERIN, Professor of English at Eastern Michigan University, has published two books on mystery fiction: *Sons of Sam Spade* (1980) and *John D. MacDonald* (1982).

KATHERINE U. HENDERSON, editor of the soon-to-be released *Half Human Kind: Writings from the Controversy About Women in Renaissance England*, is Professor of English at the College of New Rochelle. She has published the critical study *Joan Didion* (Ungar, 1981).

JOHN HOLLOWELL is the author of *Fact and Fiction: The New Journalism and the Non-Fiction Novel* (University of North Carolina, 1977). Director of the writing program at the University of California at Irvine, he is currently working on an essay concerning Didion's nostalgia.

MICHIKO KAKUTANI is on the staff of *The New York Times*.

FREDERICK KILEY, author of stories, essays and reviews that have appeared in *Epoch*, *The English Journal*, *College English* and *Eire-Ireland*, is currently an associate professor of English at Trenton State College in New Jersey.

IRVING MALIN, who teaches at City College of New York, has written books on Bellow, West, Singer, and Faulkner.

THOMAS MALLON's articles and reviews have appeared in *Biography, Contemporary Literature, Harvard English Studies,* as well as *National Review.* A Professor of English at Vassar, he has published a critical study of the English poet Edmund Blunden (G. K. Hall, 1983) and is currently finishing a study of diarists; the working title is *A Book of One's Own.*

JOYCE CAROL OATES is the author most recently of *The Profane Art: Essays and Reviews* and *Mysteries of Winterthurn,* a novel. She is currently on the faculty at Princeton University.

JOHN ROMANO, a Mellon Fellow at the Center for the Humanities at Columbia University, has authored *Dickens and Reality,* as well as several screenplays.

SUSAN STAMBERG hosts "Every Night at Five," a segment of National Public Radio's *All Things Considered.* Her interviews have been collected in *Every Night at Five: Susan Stamberg's All Things Considered Book* (Pantheon, 1982).

VICTOR STRANDBERG is a professor of English at Duke University whose most recent books are *The Poetic Vision of Robert Penn Warren, Religious Psychology in American Literature: A Study in the Relevance of William James,* and *A Faulkner Overview: Six Perspectives.*

LEONARD WILCOX received his Ph.D. from the University of California at Irvine. He currently teaches in the American Studies Programme at the University of Canterbury in New Zealand.

CYNTHIA GRIFFIN WOLFF, Professor of English at M.I.T., is the author of *A Feast of Words: The Triumph of Edith Wharton* (Oxford, 1977).